Modern R

Modern Religious Rebels

Presented to John Kent

edited by
Stuart Mews

EPWORTH PRESS

The Editor and Publisher gratefully acknowledge the award of a grant by the Twenty-Seven Foundation Historical Awards, c/o The Institute of Historical Research, University of London, which has made the publication of this volume possible.

0 7162 0488 6

First published 1993
by Epworth Press
1 Central Buildings,
Westminster, London SW1H 9NR

Typeset by Regent Typesetting, London
Printed in Great Britain by
Mackays of Chatham, Kent

Contents

Preface

It is entirely fitting that a commemorative volume of essays should be presented to John Kent in honour of his seventieth birthday and retirement from the University of Bristol. Also that it should be concerned with religious rebels. The subject is of considerable interest and importance in itself and John Kent would be the last to deny that he himself has been, if not a religious rebel, at least one of the religious world's stormy petrels. Whatever comes up, whether in university business or in his scholarly work, his immediate instinct is to ask: Who is up to what? Fellow historians and university colleagues sometimes feel that he overdoes the conspiracy theory, but even if so, the question he asks is the right one for the historian to ask, and it is a good thing for both university and historical establishments to have it asked relentlessly by someone who is too shrewd to be turned aside with a soft answer.

It is a sadness to me that an essay I prepared for the book on the early mediaeval theological rebel Gottschalk of Orbais turned out to be too disparate from the other contributions to be included;* it was prepared as a warm tribute to a colleague with whom I worked happily in Bristol for some seven years. It would be idle to pretend that John is always an easy colleague, but I quickly learned that he was one whose judgment was not to be undervalued or lightly neglected, and his constant support and friendship were very welcome and warmly reciprocated. I know I speak for all the contributors to this book and for all John's other friends and admirers in thanking him for what he has done and wishing him and Deborah a long, happy and fulfilling retirement.

Dennis Nineham, Oxford

* It has been published in the *Journal of Ecclesiastical History* vol. 40 (1989) pp. 1–18.

Introduction

Modern religious rebels come in all shapes and sizes. As the essays contained in this book demonstrate, they are as much a phenomenon of the Catholic wing of Christianity as the Protestant. Some were restless spirits forever seeking some deeper truth, others only abandoned the old landmarks with the utmost reluctance. Some found it painful to be out of step with fellow members of the household of faith, others exulted in being counted members of God's awkward squad. Rebellion was sometimes directed against what had come to be seen as an oppressive inheritance, especially when it was found to entail an interpretation of the world which no longer squared with experience. Family, class, church and nation were perhaps the most common targets for iconoclasts, as well as anguished souls. Some were better at casting down than raising up. Rebellion might be manifested in the clash of superiors with subordinates, priests with bishops, those with national responsibilities and those trying to cope with local situations, machine-minders versus intellectual adventurers. Sometimes a preacher might be led by his congregation into more radical rhetoric than was perhaps intended. The expectations of congregations differ. Some denominations have prided themselves on their intellectual diversity, others have not hesitated to crack the whip.

There have been conservative rebels, who saw themselves as heroes of the resistance, standing out against what they saw as the dangerous lunacy of the current fashion or fad. There have been rebels who have tried to compensate for divergence in one area of belief or behaviour by a display of rigid conventionality in another. Few have displayed a consistent spirit of rebellion. And some of those who have claimed the greatest liberties for themselves have been unsympathetic to the refusal of others to toe the line. There have been occasions when a rebel against social norms has been in opposition to someone whose rebellion was intellectual.

This volume invites reflection on what it is which makes some people with strong religious convictions stand out and expose themselves to censure and public obloquy. They may even run the risk of losing their livelihood. Is there a prophetic tradition in Christianity which values and encourages the quality of nonconformity? Or is the more important question, why has Christianity not produced more rebels? Is it in any case all a matter of temperament?

The essays in this collection present evidence from four continents of men and women who were regarded as in some sense rebellious. If most of them are men, this probably only means that women had fewer opportunities to rebel publicly, and ever so much more to lose. Some of those who were described by detached observers as rebels would have resented the title, others took the rebel's mantle as a form of self-advertisement, but were in reality not as valiant for truth as they liked to think.

These essays were all written in honour of Professor John Kent, a scholar who has never accepted the conventional assessments of religious notables. The contributors do not accept all John's judgments, and would be amazed if he was not critical of their efforts. Nevertheless it is our earnest hope that if we have not launched an 'arsenal of rockets', to use Richard Hanson's description of one of John's most provocative essays,[1] we might at least have shed some light on a few dark corners.

I would like to thank the contributors for their co-operation, Cyril Rodd of the Epworth Press for his patience and helpfulness, and Janice Parkes, whose secretarial skills and diplomacy have been invaluable.

Stuart Mews

Note

1. R.P.C. Hanson, 'Introduction', Jean Daniélou, A.H. Couratin, John Kent, *Historical Theology*, Penguin 1969 p.21.

1

Kent in Context: Some Personal Reflections

H. J. HANHAM

I first met John Kent in the early fifties. He is linked in my memory with the village of Linton outside Cambridge. I didn't get to know him well, however, until we both moved to Manchester, he to Hartley Victoria College, I to the university. There we talked, rather noisily I fear, about history, chiefly church history. Though I had once thought of writing about the Reformation, I was profoundly ignorant of the literature of church history; under John's influence I repaired some of my deficiencies. When I became a professor of history at Harvard in 1968 I found that John's crash course enabled me to pinch-hit as an examiner in the Divinity school. For John was and is a voracious reader, constantly chewing through new books and spitting out the many passages that he rejected as injurious to his health.

Quite why John had consented to become a Methodist minister I never quite found out. My own family background (a mixture of Unitarians, Roman Catholics, Anglicans and atheists) had left me more respect for religion than for churches. My Cambridge friend Maurice Cowling and I were attracted to the revival of a sort of Actonian national church which transcended ecclesiastical divisions. But the construct was to be an intellectual not an ecclesiastical one. In those days Herbert Butterfield's *Christianity and History* seemed to be a natural extension of his *Whig Interpretation of History*. Where John Kent, Maurice Cowling and I met on common ground was in the rejection of the facile secular optimism of G.M. Trevelyan, still to be seen strolling in the Fellow's garden at Trinity College, Cambridge, and basking in the popular success of his *English Social History*. It was not that we had anything personal against Trevelyan, whom I remember as benignly humble about the fact that many of his historical postures had been handed down to him by his father, the nephew and biographer of Macaulay. It was rather that the Whig tradition, moribund since the beginning of the century, still seemed to provide the framework of historical orthodoxy at a time when the world badly needed something new to replace it.

So much of what we had been taught seemed a sham; that politics was the special preserve of the high-minded, the great and the good (those were the days of the deification of Churchill); that the nation was Christian; that the Commonwealth was a transcendent Empire; that John Stuart Mill knew more about human nature than Hobbes. Maurice Cowling and I wanted to uncover the reality of politics, not at the theoretical level of Michael Oakeshott's *Experience and its Modes*, but at the operational level. John Kent's target was the churches, viewed not as ecclesiastical corporations but as political systems. There was respectable Methodist ancestry here, evidenced by E. R. Taylor's *Methodism and Politics*; there was also the current influence of Butterfield, himself a Methodist. There was also a salutory Wesleyan tradition of savage ministerial conflict about contentious issues going back to the eighteenth century that needed to be preserved in an age of namby-pamby ecumenism. One side of John Kent seemed to belong to the controversial world of the *Fly Sheets* when Wesleyan gloves were off.

In retrospect it is easy to see that we were all three wrestling with a single problem. The last glow of Victorian triumphalism was fading. The British empire that had encircled the globe for a century was being wound down, like a derelict public company. Butskellism, then in the ascendant in politics, was merely a device for postponing serious thought about the future. To come to terms with the future, however, one must first come to terms with the past. Why had Britain, like Spain, Portugal and Holland before it, first risen to wealth and empire and then sunk into decline? Was there still a way of rescuing something from the wreckage of empire?

The wreckage was most visible in the Christian churches. There had been no persecution, no secularization of church property, nothing more than indifference, but the churches (apart from the Roman Catholics and the Jews) had collapsed. The English had never been enthusiastic churchgoers, but now they had begun to eschew churchgoing altogether. The membership of the Nonconformist churches, once the mainstay of Victorian Liberalism, had declined particularly precipitously, even more precipitously than the number of Liberal voters. The same thing had happened in the eighteenth century; why had it happened again in the twentieth century? Nineteenth-century Liberal Nonconformists, nudged by Thomas Carlyle, had sometimes thought of the nineteenth-century Nonconformist revival as Cromwell's belated revenge on the Restoration of 1660 (a late nineteenth-century Unitarian member of my family erected a statue of Oliver Cromwell shaking his sword at Manchester cathedral). What had to be explained might be the religious equivalent of trade cycles, or either the building up or the decline of popular religious enthusiasm. There was also the mystery of church leadership. Are church leaders made by their churches or are they themselves the makers of churches? Is the cause of religion best served by a multitude of churches capable of drawing on different styles of leadership? Did it matter that in the 1950s the declining churches were clearly not drawing the best talent into the ministry?

In the background lay the soggy issue of the establishment of religion by the state. The coronation in 1953 was a reminder that there were in Britain two established churches – one in England, the other in Scotland – and that the English Free Churches now hovered on the fringes of establishment. As a member of Selwyn College, still a Church of England college with an exceptionally high proportion of ordinands, I was aware of tugs in many directions. The dead hand of the state was a fact of everyday life. It provided the mechanism of a parochial system, but failed to breathe life into the system. The Revised Prayer Book, rejected by parliament in 1928, but in common use, like the English Missal and its variants, reflected a profound ambiguity about the relation of the state to worship. I rather liked the schoolmasterly way in which Geoffrey Fisher, then Archbishop of Canterbury, talked as though parish priests and their curates were like army or school chaplains sent out by the bishops to ensure that every Englishman might enjoy the ministrations of the church, even if it was only at weddings and funerals. But on the ground the parochial system was flagging, starved of money and lacking a sense of mission. The Church of England that lived was a church of essentially non-parochial ministries that brought together the like minded, be they High Church or Evangelical, plus a church of the respectable suburbs, where the traditions of regular churchgoing survived. In this it followed far closer the pattern of Roman Catholic worship than we were inclined to admit. There was little awareness that in the United States the separation of church and state had actually worked to the advantage of the churches, giving a freedom to experiment and regroup that had helped to keep them lively at a time when too many English religious congregations had become decayed relics of their Victorian past.

The truth is that we were all very anglo-centric in the early 1950s. We were preoccupied with the national past and the need to build a national future. As I became an increasingly convinced 'European' at the end of the decade I was conscious that I was making a significant break with the culture of my student days. My own work had led me to talk to German church leaders and realize that in creating the mixed Catholic-Protestant Christian Democratic party Konrad Adenauer had moved the discussion of the future of the churches on to a new plane. There were bitter Protestant complaints, but Adenauer single-mindedly created a federal civil service that was equally recruited from Catholics and Protestants, in sharp contradistinction to the old German civil service, which was self-consciously Prussian and Protestant. In West Germany, indeed, the state provided theological facilities for all recognized churches, including the Old Catholic faculty at the University of Bonn, whose professors staffed the Bonn churches I occasionally attended.

Reading through John Kent's works published over thirty-five years I am very struck by their Englishness. His roots are in the England of Kitson Clark's book *The English Inheritance* (SCM Press 1950; not a book that he greatly admired). There is warmth and empathy for old-style Methodists who cared for their people in the round. Norman Sykes also gets brownie points for persisting in presenting a national rather than sectional view of the Church of England. When John Kent writes about foreigners, they are usually held at arms length, often castigated. He has little sympathy for American evangelists (I remember his feeling of repugnance after attending a Billy Graham rally in Manchester), he denounces American missionaries in China as misguided, and he can't bear American politicians. The Scots he barely mentions at all. Foreign missionary activities in general he deplores as a distraction from national realities, and the world-wide ecumenical movement is for him merely an aberration born of John R. Mott's early twentieth-century American student missionary movement. The real work of intellectual and religious reconstruction must be done at home in England. It can't be left to foreigners.

Every English Methodist must come to terms with the fact that Methodism in North America has been much more successful than in England. American Methodism may be dismissed in England as unsophisticated, but it has just as long a pedigree as English Methodism and much more diversity; it also has bishops. Since the days when English and American Methodists disputed control of the Canadian missionary field, American Methodists have also felt very ambivalent about English Methodism. One of the reasons why Methodist historians have devoted so many of their energies to the study of John Wesley and the publication of his works is that it is easier to write about the great progenitor of Methodism than to come to terms with his divided heritage. English Methodists have been driven to emphasize their Englishness, American Methodists their Americanism.

For John Kent, Methodism exists in a world in which John Wesley has become an icon rather than a fallible religious leader. Like Isaiah, in his lifetime Wesley had been a prophetic figure, interesting in his own right, but far removed from the everyday life of Methodist Christians. From the day of his death the fight had been on for a share of Wesley's mantle. John Kent is most interested in those figures who become obsessed with their own fragment of that mantle; Jabez Bunting who spoke as though he still had the whole mantle wrapped about him, the craggy country Methodists who clung obsessively to the belief that

Wesley's message was to the countryside, and even Sir Robert Perks, who sometimes seemed to think that John Wesley had been in the chapel construction business. There is little sympathy for those who engineered ecclesiastical mergers or who quietly dissolved the circuit system that had been at the heart of Methodist expansion. The wily ecclesiastic is not a figure who appeals to him.

English religion in the early nineteenth century appears in John Kent's work as a many-headed hydra. When the churches and the sects felt the winds in their sails, and convinced themselves that it was the breath of God rather than the winds of change that was blowing them forward, their reactions were very diverse. There was no such thing as a single Evangelical movement, as many historians have assumed. Rather, there was a diversity of responses to a changed situation. For a time it seemed possible for anyone to claim to speak with divine inspiration, whether it be a Joanna Southcott, an E.B. Pusey or a Nicholas Wiseman. Kent is antagonistic to the Oxford movement, whose pseudo-mediaevalism he regards as an anachronism, and is rather alarmed by post Tridentine Roman Catholicism, but he cherishes the diversity. He understands that it was not possible at such a time for a single body, Wesleyan Methodism, to contain all those who welcomed the Methodist message, and he occasionally speaks warmly of the Primitive Methodists and the Bible Christian, though he is warier of other branches of nineteenth-century Methodism.

Notoriously, however, the wind bloweth where it listeth. The sails fell slack and the churches began to decay. At first English church leaders thought that it was but a passing phase (as it was in America) and strove by new initiatives to prepare for the day when the wind would begin to blow again. But by the 1920s England had finally followed France into secularism. As a young man John Kent was inclined to blame the church leaders and the 'nonconformist conscience' of the late nineteenth century for much of what had happened. These days he is more charitable; he no longer expects them to have foreseen a change that is even to him inexplicable.

The question remains, why did the churches collapse so easily and so quickly? Momentum had already begun to wane at the beginning of the twentieth century, as the statistics showed, but it would have been a rash person to prophesy the near-disappearance of English nonconformity, apparently entering its golden age after the Liberal victory of 1906. No single explanation will do. For one thing, as John Kent concedes, the Roman Catholic Church was exempted from decay for another couple of generations.

At the heart of the question is what church members expected of their churches. The Roman Catholic Church alone attempted to supply everything: community, intellectual leadership, schools, marriage-partners, distinctive reading-matter. Its separateness gave it the strength of ethnic groups in North America, where religion and community were fused. The other churches had no such stout bulwarks to defend them against the secular. In the United States the churches existed before the state and were in a position to take it over. (The separation of church and state had the paradoxical effect of giving the churches a stronger sense of self-identity than the state.) In England the state ante-dated the established church, which was a state creation, from which all the other Protestant churches were descended. Primacy thus lay with the state and that primacy could be exerted at the will of the state. In competition with the state the churches could be expected to lose because they were internally divided. Thus the state was able effectively to strip the Protestant churches of the power of self-taxation, of the right to control education, and even of the power to determine their own doctrines (as the Free Church of Scotland found to its dismay in 1903). The Protestant churches never succeeded as did their American counterparts in shaping the ideology of the state so that it became an organ of Protestant missionary expansionism.

The great British population explosion of the nineteenth century with its fast flow of internal migrants created in Britain conditions that were recognizably similar to those of the American frontier; new hamlets, new towns, new suburbs housing the uprooted – all turned to the churches in search of a sense of community. In the newly-established Nonconformist, Anglican and Roman Catholic chapels in particular they often found it. In a few places, notably in the Welsh valleys, the chapels very early became the be-all and end-all of community life, but whole sections of the population were left untouched by the movement, either perennially churchless or committed to the old-established parish churches. Nonetheless for a time the future seemed clearly on the side of the chapels.

What the English Nonconformist churches notably failed to do was to establish an effective lay leadership. There were no English equivalents of the American church colleges, whose alumni provided the leadership for the American state universities. There were no lay 'missionary statesmen' like John R. Mott, and there was no equivalent of Woodrow Wilson, drawn from the presidency of an American Presbyterian college into the presidency of the United States. The largest English Protestant church, the Church of England, did not even have a tradition of lay congregational support for church maintenance. Most active laymen and laywomen thus turned to lay causes as a source of satisfaction: to politics, to philanthropy (especially in the building of hospitals and in work for the poor), to friendly societies and masonic lodges, to working-men's clubs and to trade unions. The transition to politics was particularly easy, for the political parties had since the seventeenth century been linked – at arms length – with the churches; the Tories with the mainstream of the Church of England, the Whigs with the erastian wing of the Church of England and the Nonconformists. When the political parties began to seek mass support, notably in the 1870s and 1880s, they were thus in a position to draw lay support away from the churches and into politics. Even those churches with a strong tradition of lay leadership, like the Primitive Methodists, experienced the same phenomenon as more and more of their leaders were drawn into secular careers, ending in a good many notable cases with membership of the House of Commons.

The clerical leadership of the churches welcomed these developments, because they professed to believe that commitment to the church was a precondition for success in secular affairs. They may well also have felt relieved that some of the pressure was off them. It is in the 1880s that one first becomes aware of a sense that the churches were failing to adapt. Significant articles appeared in the reviews deploring the decline of the pulpit. New magazines and newspapers were started, most notably the *British Weekly*, which aimed to by-pass the clergy and appeal directly to the man and woman in the pew. There was not (nor has there been to this day) an effective replacement for Charles Spurgeon, whose works are still in print in the 1990s, all volumes of them. Increasingly the public mind was dominated by a newly self-confident newspaper press, headed by the *Daily Telegraph*, the *Manchester Guardian* and the *Daily Mail*. This press often used the language of conventional Protestant piety, but its aims were frankly secular.

What the churches needed was an internally-sponsored revival, which would give them a new sense of mission and draw back into them the lay leadership they were losing to the secular world. Attempts at revival were in fact made, most notably through campaigns by the great American evangelists Moody and Sankey and through the city mission and foreign mission movements. But these did not address the central problem of the day. This was that the Church of England and the Methodists were suffering dramatic losses in the countryside. The great depression of English agriculture that began in the 1870s drained away men and money from the grain growing areas. Because the incomes of substantial numbers of Church of England clergymen were determined by corn prices and these had fallen dramatically, the large proportion of English country clergymen who had never been even comfortably off found themselves impoverished. All the churches were confronted with the need for a redirection of clerical labour and resources from the country to the towns and an almost complete lack of machinery for bringing it about.

The problem of the churches in the countryside would not have mattered had they been able to preserve the outward signs of success in the towns, as the Roman Catholics and Jews were so significantly able to do. A series of unofficial religious censuses revealed not merely the diversity of English religious life, which was very much to the good, but also the failure of the churches to keep up with the growth and movement of the population, which was alarming. Charles Booth's great *Life and Labour of the People in London*, the beginning of serious English religious sociology, is in effect a lament that the English were ceasing to be a nation of churchgoers. This might not have mattered so much had the politicians not turned out to be more effective than the preachers in capturing the mind of the nation. The politicians had none of the churches' ambivalence about advertising and mass rallies. And they, unlike the churches, had national heroes to lead them. The churches had no counterpart of Gladstone, who though a devout High Churchman, became the greatest of all Nonconformist heroes.

In this situation the Nonconformist churches were peculiarly vulnerable. They had a long tradition of campaigning for 'religious equality', which had deeply emeshed them in politics. When they temporarily enjoyed a stranglehold on the weakened Liberal Party of the 1890s they unwisely drove it into adopting a party programme that included the disestablishment of the Church of England and 'local option' as a first step towards prohibition. Neither issue was of sufficiently central concern to the nation to be capable of providing a rallying cry for the Liberal Party, which had quietly to abandon them. In the run-up to the general election of 1906 Nonconformist influence again led the Liberal Party to adopt policies designed to secure the Nonconformist vote, particularly in connection with education. But when the Liberal leadership failed once again to deliver on its promises, it was not abandoned by its increasingly secularized Nonconformist supporters. The Nonconformist leaders were once again shown to be paper tigers, by now entirely captured by the Liberal leadership. Lloyd George, who had begun his career as a Nonconformist radical whose power base was rural Welsh nonconformity, was by 1911 talking of an all-party secular coalition that would free him of the remaining constraints of his Nonconformist origins.

John Kent has been rather savage about the Nonconformist leaders who were blind enough to put sectarian interests like disestablishment and secular concerns such as temperance before the need to preserve the religious vitality of their churches. He sees them as falling into the snare of believing that the city of man can be turned into the city of God, the snare that had trapped their seventeenth-century predecessors. He cannot forgive them for their confused response to the outbreak of war in 1914, which led them to put the interests of the state before those of the churches. He underestimates, I think, the extraordinary effect of the First World War on English Nonconformity. Historians, being writers, have paid too much attention to what was written at the time about war and peace, and about war aims. They have paid too little attention to who was conscripted and what happened to them. A liturgical church like the Church of England, though weakened by the absence of clergy, can survive without clergy. A non-liturgical church, like the English Nonconformist churches, is built on a symbiosis between pew and public. Remove the minister and it can survive for a time, though only for a brief one. Remove the male leadership from the pews and the young men destined to be leaders, and the fire goes out of its belly. When soldiers returned from the army in 1918 they found chapels full of old women, both male and female, both in the pews and in the pulpit. Something had been lost which could never be regained. The sense of alienation was increased by the bewilderment with which conscript soldiers had viewed the antics of Liberal politicians during the war. The party of Nonconformity had proved itself impotent in time of crisis. In the 1918 election it was erased as a serious force in English politics.

A significant part of the problem of war-time nonconformity was its pre-war neglect of the army. Even the Wesleyans, once most active of all the churches in recruiting high-quality army chaplains, had turned back on their traditions and virtually abandoned its chaplaincy services. The wartime armies formed in 1914 therefore almost entirely lacked a Nonconformist religious tradition, though there had been plenty of Nonconformists in the pre-war regular army. Lloyd George's belated attempts to create a Nonconformist chaplaincy service did something to restore the situation. But for most Nonconformists in the armed forces the war meant an abrupt exclusion from the forms of religious worship in which they had grown up. This was not the fault of the army chaplains, adequate or inadequate as they might be as individuals, but of a sudden change of life-style. For four years, unless a soldier was in a distinctly Nonconformist Welsh regiment, the patterns of a lifetime were broken. The strong returned from the war to pick up the threads of their old religious life; the remainder, already uprooted, were permanently alienated, becoming passive pew holders or drifting away altogether.

The embittering thing about the First World War was that after the war there was no enemy left to fight. After the French Revolution there was a reaction; the Roman Catholic church on the continent, and especially in France and the lands occupied by the French, was forced to rebuild from the ground up. There was despondency but there was also hope. Monasticism, once virtually eliminated, returned, revived and strengthened, to Solesmes and Beuron. The Jesuits, not so long since disbanded by the Pope, began their work of education anew. The parish system was painfully reconstructed. The mass of the people was still untouched but the life of the church had a new leanness and vigour. In a situation just as revolutionary in secular terms, though without martyrdoms or physical destruction, the English Protestant churches simply wilted. There was no pain; just nostalgia and amnesia. The tired men who emerged from the war continued to occupy their pulpits, but they had lost their voice and their audience.

The exceptions were commoner among the established churches than among the (newly-designated) Free Churches. Brave war-time soldiers made good parish priests and dons; I remember many of them with respect and affection. But George Macleod's Iona Community, however gallant a try, was no Solesmes. But at least some did try. As in France after the Revolution, whole stretches of urban life had to be conceded to paganism, but the true activists among the laity were regrouped in defensible strongholds. The parish system, the network of Nonconformist churches, was tacitly abandoned to the slumberers and the traditionists. The community church (an American church) with its family communion began to take hold.

What has all this to do with John Kent? Like Maurice Cowling among Anglicans, he was left high and dry in academia. The secular university, paradoxically, had proved to be another bastion against the damp revolution of the English. The young, long interested in movements of protest, have come to recognize in him a protector of protestors. He has now had his say about church historians. It is time that he should put aside all those other projects that he has always had in such abundance and celebrate his retirement by writing, if not about himself, then about his vision of the world.

2

Johann Christian Edelmann: A Rebel's Pilgrimage

W. R. WARD

There were few options available in the religious world of the early eighteenth-century Habsbury Empire against which Johann Christian Edelmann did not rebel, yet the circumstances of his birth in 1698 had seemed to predestine him to conformity. His father Gottlob Edelmann was a musician and tutor to the pages at the tiny Albertine court of Sachsen-Weissenfels. On the musical side Gottlob entered a rich tradition. A generation before Heinrich Schütz had completed his great Passion compositions here; in 1694 Handel had made his début at the age of nine on the organ of the Court chapel. On the tutorial side he had to sustain the Saxon obsession with the Unaltered Augsburg Confession and the Formula of Concord. The young Edelmann owed his baptismal names to the Duke Johann Georg and his younger brother Duke Christian who stood as his (absentee) godparents.

At school at Sangerhausen he was drilled in the great textbook of Saxon Orthodoxy, Leonhard Hutter's *Compendium Locorum Theologicorum*. Yet Gottlob Edelmann did not follow the local requirement of sending his son from Sangerhausen to the gymnasium at Weissenfels, but sent him on to one uncle at Lauban, and then to another at Altenburg. It was here that a strain in Edelmann's heritage began to show which put him in touch with an alternative to Lutheran Orthodoxy. For both his mother[1] and his father[2] had forbears in Silesia where there had long been traditions of tender piety,[3] traditions which had now begun to issue in religious revival; and among the first areas of Saxony to be affected by them was Lusatia, Saxony's most recently acquired and restless province. It was here that Edelmann was to continue his schooling, earning an honest copper meanwhile by tutoring the sons of Silesian nobility.[4]

There was a similar ambivalence about the next stage in his education at Jena under Buddeus (1667–1729). Johnn Franz Buddeus had been appointed to Jena from Halle to restore its reputation as an Orthodox school of merit. The appointment was a very successful one, but Buddeus was never a polemical hard-liner. He extended a sheltering hand to Pietists, and his time in Jena was marked not only by traditional student hooliganism, but by a series of religious revivals which heralded a new age in Lutheranism.[5] Buddeus retained Edelmann's affection and respect life-long,[6] and his teaching introduced the young man in an intellectual way to two of the newer options in religion, Pietism and Wolffianism. At Halle Buddeus had taught Spener's son, and, like Spener himself, sought to get back to a Luther who had got rid of scholasticism, to the traditions of Johann Arndt and (in the hallowed Puritan phrase) of the practice of piety. Buddeus also separated dogmatics from polemics,[7] and began the process of putting both into a historical context. Buddeus's guide in matters historical was Christoph Matthäus Pfaff (1686–1760), a boy professor and later Chancellor at Tübingen, deeply involved in his youth in schemes of church union, who set church history in a political context; listing Quakers, Fanatics, Weigelians, Behmenists, Rosicrucians and Socinians as heretics, he classified Pietism, Jansenism and Molinism, with a generosity foreign to the hard-line Orthodox, as 'Memorabilia'.[8]

There is no doubt that all this made a great impression on Edelmann. He began his pilgrimage from an Orthodox standpoint but with sympathies for Pietism. Even more striking, as a loyal disciple of Buddeus, he followed the master in a wholesale rejection of Wolff whose work might have fortified his own mature position. For Christian Wolff (1679–1754), a protégé of Leibniz, attempted to apply the Leibnizian logic to every corner of the world of intellect, and, in so doing, became both the uncrowned king of the early German Enlightenment, and the hated bugbear of the Halle Pietists.[9] Edelmann admitted that he was turned against Wolff by his respect for Buddeus, and was soon involved in a disputation with him.[10] But even in 1740 he was still declaiming against Wolffians, claiming that they prattled about reason as the Moravians did about the Saviour; the best that could be said about Wolff was that he helped to open Edelmann's eyes.[11] In all this the influence of Buddeus was reinforced by Edelmann's life-experience; as a controversialist who received more brickbats than he gave, he was not attracted by the Leibnizian theodicy, or arguments that this world was the best of all possible worlds;[12] and his mind proved to be not of a mathematical bent.

The expenses of graduation at Jena were sufficient to deter Edelmann from formally concluding his course there, and he turned for employment to a quarter where lack of paper qualifications was actually an advantage, to Protestant Austria. The years 1723 to 1731 yield some of the most entertaining passages in his *Selbstbiographie*,[13] a combination of travel, culture-shock, and services with the protestant aristocratic Kornfeil and Auersperg families and with the mercantile Mühls of Vienna. The great days of the Protestant aristocracy in Upper Austria were long past. Faced with the choice of abandoning the characteristic public functions of their order or emigration, the bulk had chosen the latter, as the Kornfeils were to do during this time in Austria.[14] Forbidden to maintain a protestant chaplain, the Kornfeils had taken an unqualified theologian as tutor to their children. The harshest times for the Austrian protestants when Maria Theresia seriously set about the business of restoring religious uniformity were still to come, however, and it is clear that Edelmann knew nothing of the convulsive history of Protestant peasant revolt in Bohemia and Moravia. He was impressed, if also vexed, by the immense wealth and culture of Melk and other great monasteries, impressed with the urbanity shown by the members of religious orders towards himself and his employers, vexed with his own attempts to get the better of local clergy by serving up gobbets of Saxon polemical theology.[15] Above all he began for the first time to see the religion in which he had been raised from the standpoint of an oppressed minority.

The immense journeys at communion season, which were to become so prominent in the history of the American frontier, were already an annual feature of the lives of Protestants in Silesia and the Habsburg family lands. The Kornfeils went off to the Protestant embassy chapels in Vienna, or to the German-speaking Lutheran communities at Ödenburg in Hungary. Hungary was fine, especially the wine and tobacco, but what case could there be for the gentry to take all the seats in the meeting-house, while peasants who had walked miles had to stand, and be treated to minatory three-hour sermons by the pastors?[16] Vienna, where Edelmann preached in embassy chapels and served with the Mühl family, had other disadvantages. Protestant merchant families there were sufficiently serviceable to the dynasty to be more secure than Protestants in the country, but the dominent influence was that of Pietism. Edelmann who had developed a taste not only for wine and tobacco, coffeehouses and chat, but also for dancing (of which even the great Buddeus had disapproved)[17] was irked by a narrowness unknown to his gentry patrons; still worse was the damage done to his employer Herr Mühl by the Hallensian diatribes of his previous chaplains. A man of good natural blend of 'sanguine, melancholic, and choleric temperaments' he had been irretrievably unbalanced in the direction of melancholia. Mindful of his own periods of depressive illness, Edelmann was shocked.[18] Unable to gush in prayer in the pietist manner, but ready enough in clerical small talk,[19] he concluded it was time to move back to his native land and pursue his career there. He denied later charges that he left Austria for better pay,[20] but one feeling of guilt remained; he had advised the Count of Kornfeil to sell his property at a loss and emigrate to Protestant territory for the sake of a faith he (Edelmann) came later to regard as an oppressive nonsense.[21]

Residence in Austria had changed Edelmann by enabling him to see Orthodoxy and Pietism from the outside, as Buddeus had enabled him to see Wolffianism from the outside, but it had not given him a new standpoint. He was still Orthodox, and had applied to Erdmann Neumeister (1671–1756), the ferocious Orthodox polemicist of Hamburg, for assistance with his clerical career.[22] In the Orthodox manner he was still addicted to polemics; he preached against Socinianism; he still believed in the infallibility of the Bible.[23] But Austria had shown how hard it was for the religious systems of the day to deliver the goods of which they claimed a monopoly. Edelmann was receptive to a new viewpoint should he encounter one; and the years 1731 to 1734 proved to be the decisive break in his life. The early 1730s were years of heightened religious expectation in South Germany as tens of thousands of Protestant exiles from Salzburg came streaming through. That this host had been able to survive and increase its numbers in the kingdom of Antichrist without any church at all was an affront to the principles of Orthodoxy, whose great spokesman, Valentin Ernst Löscher, admitted as much.[24] Outbreaks of religious revival began which led enthusiasts to believe that the whole structure of established religion was about to collapse.[25] Edelmann was tempted by this route, but was saved by a new course of reading which led to his discovery of a vocation for the first time. The temperature of the new mood was revealed in his reading 'day and night'; the substance of his study was provided by Baxter's *A Saint or a Brute* (1662) which made him wonder whether the brute creation was not better off than the most sanctified sinner, Marperger's commentary on the first Epistle of John which made him doubt whether he was among the regenerate,[26] and most especially Gottfried Arnold's *Unpartheyische Kirchen-und Ketzer-Historie* (1699–1700),[27] the most influential work of its kind and period.

From Arnold Edelmann acquired a great deal of information he had not previously possessed, and a whole new perspective. Though now a zealot in the means of grace, he had begun to suspect that Orthodox methods of Christianizing the people did not work, that baptism did not convey regeneration; now he learned that, almost from the beginning, the history of Christianity had been filled with the formation of religious bodies claiming to be orthodox and anathematizing their rivals, neither party having a monopoly of the truth.[28] Only too often were the true Christians among the persecuted. 'In this work' (noted Edelmann) 'written with the utmost frankness, I found recorded, to my great surprise, so many indecent and irresponsible acts of the clergy, which alone claim to possess the true Christian religion, that I became greatly disgusted with so-called Orthodoxy and began to lean towards the Pietists; in spite of their shortcomings they appeared at least to aspire to a godly life, whereas the Orthodox, who, for all the faith they pretended, neglected all good works, and preferred to remain righteous believers but poor sinners rather than to become right-living examples for their flock.'[29] Clearly the problem of regeneration and sanctification, of delivering the goods, was a good deal more complicated than he had supposed. He began to find sermons on appropriating the work of Christ 'so much wind', and to yearn for 'a Christian perfection according to the measure of Scripture in the community of worldly goods'.[30] In short, like Wesley a few years later, he began to ask himself whether Christian perfection existed in this world, and in particular whether it existed in the Moravian community at Herrnhut.

Edelmann already knew of Zinzendorf's enterprise by repute, and hoped not only 'to get to know this rare bird in his feathers', but also, in Arnoldian style, to find true Christians in Herrnhut 'because they were taken for fools by other so-called Christians'.[31] Zinzendorf issued an invitation and provided the travelling costs, and Edelmann arrived about Whitsuntide in 1734. Like Wesley's account of Herrnhut in 1738, Edelmann's cannot be checked in any detail against Moravian sources, though the latter agree with his own comment, that he left after a fortnight with regret;[32] unlike Wesley's narratives, those of Edelmann were written after the first flush of enthusiasm had been extinguished by violent revulsion, and, in the case of the autobiography, written long afterwards. He was met by Spangenberg (1704–92) whom he had known long before in Jena, and for whom he still possessed all the Orthodox distrust.[33] His distaste for Zinzendorf was less remarkable, for the major enigma of Zinzendorf's character was his capacity both to make an instant good impression, and, in the longer run, to alienate almost everyone of independent mind. In retrospect Edelmann deplored the hierarchical character of the Count's management of the community. He found the multiplication of devotions so much 'spiritual forced labour', could not bear the way faith displaced reason in Dober's religious prattle, and, despite the support which Zinzendorf still enjoyed among Württemberger scholars, felt preserved from Moravian enthusiasm by his residual Orthodox respect for the Bible.[34] In 1740 when, for once, the Wetterau separatists were giving a lead to the Orthodox in swinging attacks on Zinzendorf, Edelmann joined them in a rather bitter tract, *Christus und Belial*, in which he published much of his correspondence with Zinzendorf, and other material. He was then in a position to assail the Count for the expensive building-habits which in the end were almost to ruin his community,[35] maintaining that 'the true followers do not build themselves costly nests with other people's money', and that 'the living God does not dwell in temples made with hands'.[36] And these attacks were the more damaging as they appeared to illustrate his fundamental complaint that Zinzendorf differed from the Orthodox not a whit in offering 'the fashionable gospel of the imputation of the death of Christ from the outside'.[37] The grounds for this view had already been set out in a new religious journal Edelmann had commenced in 1735 and to this we must now turn.

The real reason why Edelmann rejected the Moravians to whom he had still thought himself likely to return when he left Herrnhut, was that he had at last found a vocation as religious journalist for which the earnest study and devotion of the early 1730s had prepared him, and was writing his *Unschuldige Wahrheiten* (1735–43) – *Innocent Truths* – with a vigour which more than compensated for the shapelessness of the publication as a whole. The last thing he wanted now was to be sent on a mission to the ends of the earth or to be selected by lot as a husband for one of the Plain Janes of Herrnhut. He had entered a rising market which extended from the Lutheran Orthodox theological heavyweight originally edited by Löscher from which he borrowed his title, the *Unschuldige Nachrichten* (*Innocent Reports* or *News*) to moral weeklies which spawned forth in emulation of Addison and Steele, and included on the way the *Teutsche Socrates*, elegantly produced by Zinzendorf in 1725–6. Within two years from the autumn of 1734 Edelmann had written the first dozen parts (which became 1366 printed pages) and added a further three later while he was writing his mature works. He aimed to be up-market rather than down, for although he eschewed the formidable theological digest of the *Unschuldige Nachrichten* to which he himself owed a good deal, he provided protracted theological argument livened principally by polemical tone and dialogue form. And, following Arnold, he sought a way through his difficulties with both Orthodoxy and the problem of religious vitality, by placing himself firmly in the tradition of what is called in German *Spiritualismus*, that stress upon the universal aspects of the work of the spirit of God and of the spirit of man which might be conveniently bracketed together in the Logos doctrine of the Fourth Gospel.

From the beginning 'innocence' was equated with unsectarianism. 'Do you take me for an indifferentist or atheist because I can find so few truths in the multiplicity of opinions among those self-described Christians, and yet live in one of them? Then must Christ and his apostles have been indifferentists and atheists, because they found so few or no truths among the manifold opinions of the various sects of Jews ... *Whoever lives in the Christian church, as Christ lived in the Jewish, in such a way as to bind himself to no particular party* ... is, in my view ... a true disciple of Christ'.[38] What the Orthodox called indifferentism was really 'God's *impartiality* and *non-respect of persons*', his willingness to save men of every sect and religion.[39] Baxter had been right to talk of the *True church in all sects*, '*none of the great visible sects of Christianity is the true church*' and what was required was not an artificial syncretism, but a willingness of every party 'to be led by the spirit of truth from opinions to truth'.[40] The new pietist background to Edelmann's pilgrimage came out not only in his repeated reference to 'our excellent theologians Arndt, Scriver, Spener, Francke, Arnold',[41] but in his appeal to religious experience.[42] If the Pietists' concern with spiritual vitality drove them to beat the drum of the New Birth, so did Edelmann's. The New Birth could not take place in baptism for the 'regenerate man is one who (NB) CAN not sin';[43] it was a 'bringing forth of faith' and it came *after* 'illumination, conversion, renewal, sanctification and justification', not before.[44]

Yet Edelmann was not at this stage a Pietist. The Logos principle meant 'that Christ is in all men even before the New Birth', though his mere presence did not imply regeneration, any more than life in the womb necessarily implied birth. Until the light which shines in darkness is accepted, the Spirit of God cannot 'dwell' in men, and it is this 'dwelling' which is regeneration.[45] The division of spirits was now only too clear. 'The servants and slaves called by Christ ... are those whom the clergy of the sects hunt from one town to another';[46] of course the Orthodox, appealing to an Augsburg Confession the very text of which was uncertain, 'constantly ... maintain that the sufficiency of Christ already took place through his suffering for all men 1700 years ago, and it was now simply a matter that men should appropriate his merits through faith'. The Orthodox directed men to institutionalized means of grace which were not known in primitive Christianity, and to which persons who could have no fellowship with Christ were now constantly admitted.[47]

In the midst of this work, Edelmann discovered the writings of Johann Konrad Dippel (1673–1734), a man who divided spirits as did no one else of that day, and discovered also his complete agreement with what he found.[48] Dippel's course of life indeed resembled that of Edelmann. He went up to Giessen at the age of sixteen at a point where a violent controversy between the Orthodox and the Pietist party favoured by the Hessian government had ended in the victory of the latter, and became a champion of Orthodoxy. Yet a marked tendency to see faults and virtues on both sides exposed Dippel dramatically to the influence of Gottfried Arnold, the more so as he had begun to discover for himself that Orthodox polemic had often very little basis in the doctrines it claimed to defend. Dippel did not become a dependent or follower of the great man – this Arnold himself would have approved – and he was influenced chiefly by his view of the church. For Dippel, disappointed of a career in the philosophical faculty, reacted equally independently against the growing influence of mechanistic theories of the universe, and became involved in alchemy and the search for the philosopher's stone. Driven from place to place, Dippel settled the last years of life in the tolerant territory of Wittgenstein, in active contact with the Inspired and the Moravians who also shaped Edelmann's career. For Dippel the breaking-point with Orthodoxy came in christology. Christ, he believed, had undergone a process of religious development and could not be regarded from the beginning as the perfect God-Man. If this was so then the Orthodox doctrine of justification, basing itself on the idea of satisfaction, would not do. Edelmann fastened increasingly on this point in the later parts of the *Unschuldige Wahrheiten*. Making no bones about his agreement with Dippel,[49] Edelmann pressed the issue upon the Orthodox that 'Christ must do enough [not *for* them but] *in them* for God his heavenly father for the total offering up of their brutish humanity'.[50] If the Orthodox maintained that justification was the issue by which the church stood or fell, and then got the doctrine wrong, their game was up.

The four years of Edelmann's life from 1736 to 1740 would be worth a small monograph. The publication of *Unschuldige Wahrheiten* attracted the notice of other religious radicals who wished to recruit his assistance. This meant in practice migration to the Wetterau, northeast of Frankfurt, where there was a group of tiny Reformed principalities, governed by penniless but pious Counts, who offered toleration as a matter of conviction and also (by raising toleration taxes) as a much-needed device for raising funds.[51] Edelmann's invitation came from Andreas Gross, a Frankfurter of means, who promoted separatist literature, and it was an invitation to assist Johann Friedrich Haug (1680–1753) with the production of the Berleburg Bible, one of the many productions of Philadelphian communities in the Wetterau. Beside Philadelphians, the Wetterau contained refugee Pietists, both Lutheran and Reformed, there were Moravians, New Baptists and the Inspired. The latter were a group mainly Lutheran Pietist in origin, who had been transformed early in the eighteenth century by contact with the French Prophets, but were now losing their gift of prophecy. Edelmann could revel temporarily in the comforts of Gross's home, and in the Wetterau, in the luxury of religious toleration. He could enjoy the stimulus of other religious seekers, make contact with the literature now in vogue there, especially Antoinette Bourignon and Pierre Poiret (whom he helped to translate). Johann Samuel Carl, the most important of a penumbra of doctors attracted to the Inspired by a professional interest in the interpretation of dreams, got him to edit the *Geistliche Fama*,[52] the fascinating house-journal of the awakened, sometimes believed to have been begun by Dippel himself. There is no question but that Edelmann enjoyed his Berleburg years, and produced his best work there.

Of course it was not all joy, and to a man of Edelmann's temperament the discomforts were more educative than the amenities. He disliked Haug from the beginning, and claimed never to have received a penny of the salary due to him.[53] He found some of the self-denials of the Inspired silly,[54] their Z-shaped posture for prayer (knees on ground, head on seat) absurd,[55] and, still worse, the content of their prayer miserable, tasteless and feeble.[56] Dippel had put his finger on the matter in 1731: 'The confessions are made up almost entirely of words from the scriptures. To deduce divine inspiration from the well-intended admonitions and continuously repeated phrases from scripture is a false conclusion. He whom the Holy Spirit moves directly and through whom he speaks does not have to steal his words from other prophets. He possesses in himself the same source as that from which all scriptures flow, and further I do not find that a Holy Scribe inspired by God has babbled others' words'[57] To Edelmann it was apparent that the preaching of the Inspired compared ill with that of the Old Testament prophets.[58] He was discovering on inspection that, just like the Orthodox, the Pietists and the Moravians, the Inspired failed to deliver the goods they themselves promised. He was in short getting ready for another clash with community discipline, and another leap forward in his own views. A fortunate flutter in the Erfurt Bible Lottery enabled him to get away from Haug, the financial support of a Berlin merchant called Pinell permitted an escape from the Inspired, congenial lodgings with a Socinian family showed the way his mind was moving.[59] And as Edelmann's pietist period had left him with a positive concern for the living God, his contact with the Inspired enhanced his emotional sensibilities and a responsiveness to nature which would ensure that if he became a sceptic he would be a sceptic of a Rousseau-ian rather than a Wolffian kind.[60]

The development of his views on the central issue was made clear in 1743 when he published *Die Göttlichkeit der Vernunft* (*The Divinity of Reason*), an amorphous collection of fragments written between September 1738 and February 1740, of whose appearance under a single title he was later a little shame-faced.[61] The work is partly a defence of Locke against John Edwards, partly an attempt to state a position of his own against the Inspired and to show that his identification of God, Logos, reason and conscience had a respectable Christian pedigree. This pedigree went back through the humanists and neoplatonists to Justin Martyr, Clement of Alexandria, Dionysius the Areopagite, and the writer of the Fourth Gospel, not to mention Plato and Pythagoras. The whole fall of man consisted in transforming the invisibility of God into visibility. Reason became flesh not only in Christ, but in the spirits of men who proceeded from the original light and were sent by him into the flesh. Edelmann recommended his readers to approach the light without fear, in the knowledge that it was those who loved darkness who crawled before the unknown God.[62] Despite a life of poverty Edelmann had now accumulated a library of three hundred books. The paradox of his venture into the history of thought was that it revealed how dependent he still remained on the slabs of undigested source material which formed half the substance of the Orthodox journal, the *Unschuldige Wahrheiten*. Nor was that dependence lessened when Edelmann received from his Berlin patron, Pinell, a copy of the great work of the 'chief of atheists',[63] Spinoza's *Tractatus Theologico-Politicus* (1670), the bombshell which blew away the final impediments to his maturity.[64]

The subterranean influence of Benedict Spinoza (1632–77), the excommunicated Jew who was never baptized a Christian, has been much studied lately.[65] He was attractive to scientists in pursuit of wholeness of vision, to Behmenists looking out for a new impulse. Though the effect of censorship was to some extent neutralized by the shoal of 160 rebuttals which Edelmann evoked, he cannot be said to have added much to Spinoza's long-term influence; on the other hand his *Moses mit Aufgedeckten Angesichte* (*Moses with uncovered Face*) dashed off within five months of receiving the *Tractatus*, and within six of the accession of Frederick the Great, was not only his livliest and most important work, it was celebrated by no less a connoisseur than Emanuel Hirsch as hitherto unparalleled in German, denying 'the whole faith of the Bible and also of Christian dogma from beginning to end, openly [confessing] Spinoza's doctrine of God and the World, and [demolishing] conventional ideas of providence miracle and prayer'. At the same time he remained 'morally and religiously much more suggestive than his master Spinoza'.[66] Though treated by the Orthodox as an arch-scoffer, Edelmann was indeed a *religious* rebel; and if Lessing later turned from literature to liberal theology, Edelmann turned radical theology into spritely prose.

A writer virtually resurrected in *Moses* was contemporary of Spinoza's, the atheist and materialist Matthias Knutzen (1646–74). Knutzen is known principally from a clash he had in 1674 with Johann Musaeus, Rector of the university of Jena, who quoted him extensively in his counter-attack. A precursor of Reimarus in radical biblical criticism, Knutzen was also a social and political critic. How the memory of such men could persist in spite of all the political difficulties in Germany is well illustrated in Edelmann's case; he first dropped across Knutzen in the hostile columns of the *Unschuldige Nachrichten*, and then discovered more from MS copies of his works circulating from hand to hand.[67] Armed with his own speculations about the Logos doctrine, Spinoza's doctrine of *deus sive natura*, and Knutzen's notion of conscience, Edelmann was now prepared to do battle against the Orthodox belief in the literal inspiration of scripture, against the intolerance of kings and established clergy, and against those who took a mechanical view of the universe (i.e. they separated the creator from his creation), all in the name of the living God. In particular the pursuit of the real Moses behind the veil was designed to put paid to the Orthodox notion that the Mosaic ceremonial and sacrifices were meant to point the way to Christ and his perfect sacrifice for the sins of men.[68] Nothing delighted Edelmann more than Spinoza's assertion that 'the people venerate the books of the Bible more than the word of God itself'.

Edelmann plunged straight in in swashbuckling style, claiming that the Luther Bible was the great Diana of the Lutheran Ephesians,[69] and that even those 'spiritual sleepwalkers, the so-called Herrnhuters' were causing rumblings in the Lutheran world.[70] The Spirit of the living God who spoke rationally in men's hearts did not wish to tie them to a dead letter, still less to the chronological contradictions of the books of Kings and

Chronicles.[71] Where, in any case, was the letter to which they could be tied? It was impossible to harmonize the scripture translations of the last fifty years, there were thousands of transcription errors in the text of the scriptures themselves, and the radical tradition in the church had demonstrated that little or nothing written by Moses himself remained.[72] Of course it was only the spirit of humbug in those deformed Jews known as Christians which could find the Spirit of God in a handful of the supposed faithful, bound to the letter of supposedly sacred texts. The Bible itself declared that the Spirit of God was to be found in all things, and hence in all men.[73] The Orthodox tried to defend an objective, i.e. ossified, notion of the word of God against the unfettered exegetes, Quakers, fanatics and enthusiasts, oblivious of the fact that the voice of the living God can be heard only in heart and mind, that in the unsullied times of the patriarchs there were no exegetes, and that Christ himself looked to the day when he would no longer speak in parables, but say openly what he received from the Father.[74] The witness of the Holy Spirit in scripture was confirmed by his witness in the heart, by that light of reason which lightens every man.[75] At this point Edelmann was bound to consider whether, in expanding the notion of conscience thus in Knutzen's style, he was not hunting authority out of the world altogether. Here he explicitly distanced himself from the seventeenth-century radical, and maintained in the Lutheran manner that authority was indispensable while men lived in their present brutish condition. Nevertheless authority should confine itself to punishing evil.[76] No man came to the Father except through Christ, of whom the Bible witnessed that 'in his true nature and essence he is nothing other than the Logos living in all men, or the reason which the Old Testament witnesses call wisdom'.[77] God (or nature) was indeed the essence of all things, and matter was his shadow. When Paul said in Acts 17.28 that we live in God, he knew that we lived in the world; but when man is said to be in the image of God it is implied that he is a small world as God (or nature) is the great world.[78] And as the living God was all the time (in matter) moving his shadows, so philosophy consisted 'not in words but in deeds and good examples'; it was a signpost to the freedom of which the brute creation was incapable, to the truth which Christ declared would make us free, and liberate us from slavery to earthly things.[79]

In *Moses* Edelmann said most of what he had to say. Whether in the end Spinoza's materialistic pantheism could be made to square with Edelmann's attachment to the idea of the living God was questionable. Edelmann's answer was partly political, that it was better to risk charges of atheism with Spinoza than be a fellow-traveller of the Orthodox,[80] and partly exemplified the eclecticism of the early Enlightenment; in his own copy of Pratje's hostile biography,[81] Edelmann noted that 'he neither approves of everything that Spinoza said, nor of everything Pythagoras taught'.[82] On the other hand, in taking up the idea of conscience from Knutzen and developing it,[83] Edelmann was engaging with what became one of the chief concerns of the great generation at the end of the eighteenth century, of Kant, Schiller and Goethe alike. But if there was not much new to come, he still had at least two notable works left in him, the *Confession of Faith* (*Glaubens-Bekenntnis* (1746) and the autobiography.

These works responded in different ways to political circumstances. Changes in the political temperature of Berleburg and the notoriety aroused by *Moses* caused Edelmann to take the road again, and, after two and a half years in Hackenburg (1741–4), he took refuge in Neuwied (1744–47) as did Zinzendorf after his breach with the counts of Ysenburg a few years later.[84] A year after his arrival in Neuwied, the consistory demanded that Edelmann produce a confession of faith. By the time this confession was printed, it had grown to a fat book, and the Count Alexander was (unsuccessfully) challenging his clergy to make a reply.[85] The circumstances in which the *Confession of Faith* came to be written almost invited Edelmann to produce an anti-clerical tirade, and he roundly declared that he would rather take his staff in hand than be required to submit to the drudgery again.[86] More than in any of his other works he sang the praises of the English critics and especially Toland; his lack of English made access to them difficult, but their being in print at all made them a beacon of liberty of conscience. He resumed his onslaught on biblical literalism and championed the voice of God in conscience.[87] The main contribution of the *Confession*, however, was to produce a new portrait of Jesus. He was endowed with outstanding gifts from God, and was justly entitled the Christ as the gifted and enlightened one.[88] When the disciples called him the 'Son of God', they meant simply to convey his pre-eminence among men, and when he called God 'Father', he did so in the sense that all men do; for God has neither one nor many sons.[89] Above all the aim of Jesus was to unite in love men separated many wicked opinions about God, and to get rid of religious bickering. He went to his death because the clergy thought he might turn the mob against them and reduce their incomes. The last judgment commences in anyone who arises from the sleep of his old errors, confesses himself to God and begins a rational life.[90] Thomasius had argued that the way to get people out of their ingrained prejudices was to tell them the whole story of clerical manipulation under heathens, Jews and Christians; this was also the way to peace, for fearful as the scourge of war was, it was not the work of the hateful devils conjured up by the clergy.[91] Alas! the reign of reason did not arise in time to save Edelmann. In 1750 the Imperial Book Commission solemnly burnt *Moses*, the *Confession of Faith* and the *First Epistle of St Harenberg* at Frankfurt, in 1747 Edelmann took to his staff again,[92] and eventually settled in tolerant Berlin. He denied altogether Pratje's charge that he was given asylum on the condition that for the future he held his peace;[93] but the effect was the same, he published no more.

He wrote, however, but he did not publish, the most entertaining of his books, the *Autobiography*, which was first published in 1849 by the Hamburg scholar Karl Rudolph Wilhelm Klose, who also published a good part of the *Defence* of Hermann Samuel Reimarus. The autobiography belongs to that numerous class which were written for defensive purposes,[94] in this case formally as well as really. Edelmann was replying to an anonymous pamphlet *Des berüchtigten Johann Christian Edelmanns, Leben und Schriften* (Frankfurt 1759) and at the beginning of each section quoted a passage whose errors he would controvert in detail. Thus a sheet of very little worth was allowed to provide the structure for a work of some significance in the history of autobiographical writing. It cannot be said that, like the great autobiographers of a later generation, and especially Goethe,

Edelmann ever developed a sense of history. Too many of the ills of mankind were ascribed to the interested machinations of priests to carry conviction, while the great struggle between Hohenzollern and Habsburg which provided a framework for the religious development of his generation gets never a mention. On the other hand, Edelmann contrived to give an account of his intellectual development as Wesley, in his *Journal*, did not, and on the way provided a rich pageant of life in small provincial courts, of the pecularities of small sects, and so forth, which is not unique, but is a valuable addition to a small body of sources. It was not to Edelmann's point nor within his capacity to plumb the depths of his psyche, but he conveys the development of his thought in a vocabulary of abuse so sparkling that one recent critic has thought it worth while to gather an anthology,[95] a vocabulary which illustrates how speedily he went over from defence to attack.

Notorious in 1750, Edelmann died unnoticed and virtually forgotten in 1767. The next generation of *Aufklärer* were much more cautious in the way they pressed their points,[96] and Edelmann had to wait till revolution was about in the 1840s before he was reprinted (or, in the case of the autobiography, published for the first time). He then had the distinction of being championed by men like Bruno Bauer[97] and Engels who put him in a pantheon with Voltaire, Danton and Hegel.[98] Meanwhile his professed aim 'to confess the truth to the best of his ability' had enabled Edelmann to press a radical critique of religion on a broader front than any other rebel of his day, and gave a standing warning to religious communities not to promise what they cannot deliver.

Notes

1. Edelmann's *Sämtliche Schriften in Einzelausgaben* (referred to below as *Works*) were edited and reprinted in 12 volumes at Stuttgart/Bad Canstatt 1968–79, by Walter Grossmann. Here see *Selbstbiographie*, *Works* 12. 6.
2. Ibid., *Works* 12. 9.
3. See e.g. Julius Mützell, *Geistliche Lieder der evangelischen Kirche ... von Dichtern aus Schlesien und dem umliegenden Landschaften ver-*

fasst (Braunschweig 1858; repr. Hildesheim 1975): H. Zimmermann, *Caspar Neumann und die Entstehung der Frühaufklärung. Ein Beitrag zur schlesischen Theologie-und Geistesgeschichte im Zeitalter Pietismus* (Witten 1969).

4. *Selbstbiographie*, *Works* 12. 20.
5. The importance of Jena to the Protestant world as a whole was that, being cheaper than Leipzig, it was the primary resort of prospective clergy from the protestant communities of Hungary and hard-pressed Slavonic peoples from elsewhere in the Habsburg domains. See e.g. Herbert Peukert, *Die Slaven der Donaumonarchie und die Universität Jena 1700–1848* ([East] Berlin 1958). Wesley wrote a natural theology in a work largely derived from Buddeus, *A survey of the wisdom of God in the Creation* (2nd edn Bristol 1770; a new edn is planned as vol. 17 of the *Bicentennial Edition of the Works of John Wesley*).
6. *Selbstbiographie*, *Works* 12. 138: *Unschuldige Wahrheiten*, *Works* 6. 426–7.
7. The substance of Buddeus's work in this field was presented by his son-in-law Johann Georg Walch, in two 5–volume treatises, *Historische und theologische Einleitung in die Religions-Streitigkeiten der Evangelisch-Lutherischen Kirche* (Jena 1733–39; repr. Stuttgart/Bad Canstatt 1972–85) and *Historische und theologische Einleitung in die Religions-Streitigkeiten ausser der Evangelisch-Lutherischen Kirche* (Jena 1733–36; repr. Stuttgart/Bad Canstatt 1972).
8. On Pfaff see H. Hermelink, *Geschichte der Evangelische Kirche in Württemberg von der Reformation bis zur Gegenwart* (Stuttgart/Tübingen 1949) p. 170: Emanuel Hirsch, *Geschichte der neuern evanglischen Theologie* (5th edn Gütersloh 1975) 2. 336–54: Hartmut Lehmann, *Pietismus und weltliche Ordnung in Württemberg von 17. bis zum 20. Jahrhundert* (Stuttgart 1969), pp. 90–1: Arnold F. Stolzenburg, *Die Theologie des Jo. Franc. Buddeus und des Chr. Matth. Pfaff. Ein Beitrag zur Geschichte der Aufklärung in Deutschland* (Berlin 1926; repr. Aalen 1979).
9. On Wolff see Hirsch, op. cit. 2. 49–91: C. Wolff, *Logic, or rational thoughts on the power of the human understanding ... to which is prefixed a life of the author* [by Johann Christoph Gottsched] (London 1770): *Christian Wolff als Philosoph der Aufklärung in Deutschland* ed. H.-M. Gerlach, G.Schenk and B. Thaler (Halle 1980).
10. *Selbstbiographie*, *Works* 12. 42–3.
11. *Moses mit aufgedeckten Angesichte*, *Works* 7, Anblick 3 pp. 109, 116, 118, 122, 126.
12. Ibid., *Works* 7 Anblick 2 p. 65.
13. The material in the *Selbsbiographie* is usefully filled out by Edelmann's modern biographer and editor, Walter Grossmann, in *Johann Christian*

Edelmann. From Orthodoxy to Enlightenment (The Hague 1976) pp. 23–41.

14. There is no question but that the history of religious revival in these years was closely linked with that of emigration; and many outside the revival camp, like Edelmann now, must have felt the force of exodus texts with new power. In this case the text was Genesis 12.1, 'Now the Lord had said unto Abram, Get thee out of thy country and from thy father's house, unto a land that I will shew thee' (*Selbstbiographie*, *Works* 12. 52).
15. Ibid., *Works* 12. 67, 81, 116–8, 75, 71.
16. Ibid., *Works* 12. 82–4.
17. Ibid., *Works* 12. 46, 100.
18. Ibid., *Works* 12. 91–2, 28–9.
19. Ibid., *Works* 12. 87, 95.
20. Grossmann, *Edelmann*, p. 40.
21. *Selbstbiographie*, *Works* 12. 108–9.
22. On Neumeister see C.G. Jöcher, *Allgemeines Gelehrten Lexicon* Ergänzungsband 5 (Bremen 1816; repr. Hildesheim 1961), p. 583.
23. *Selbstbiographie*, *Works* 12. 107, 126, 132, 128.
24. Valentin Ernst Löscher, *Drey Predigten von der Erkenntnis und Ehre des Sohnes Gottes ... also insonderheit der Salzburgischen Emigranten* (Dresden/Neustadt 1733), p. 26.
25. *Geistliche Fama* 23. 6–7.
26. *Selbstbiographie*, *Works* 12. 124–5.
27. Ibid., *Works* 12. 130.
28. For modern discussions of Arnold see e.g. Jürgen Büchsel, *Gottfried Arnold – Sein Verständnis von Kirche und Wiedergeburt* (Bielefeld 1970): Hermann Dörries, *Geist und Geschichte bei Gottfried Arnold* (Göttingen 1963): Klaus Wetzel, *Theologische Kirchengeschichtsschreibung im deutschen Protestantismus 1660–1760* (Giessen/Basel 1983), pp. 175–209.
29. Grossman's translation, *Edelmann* p. 47.
30. *Selbstbiographie*, *Works* 12. 139–40.
31. Ibid., *Works* 12. 141.
32. Grossmann, *Edelmann* p. 59.
33. *Selbstbiographie*, *Works* 12. 143.
34. Ibid., *Works* 12. 148, 152–3. It is fair to say that Zinzendorf's account of their breach which ascribes it to his refusing Edelmann a loan of 150 thalers, has an equally *ex post facto* ring about it. *Christus und Belial*, *Works* 11. 139.
35. On this see my paper 'Zinzendorf and Money', *Studies in Church History* vol. 24 (1987), pp. 283–305.
36. *Christus und Belial*, *Works* 11. 210, 235.

37. Ibid., *Works* 11. 38.
38. *Unschuldige Wahrheiten*, *Works* 1. 10–11.
39. Ibid., *Works* 1. 17, 24.
40. Ibid., *Works* 1. 63, 91, 66.
41. Ibid., *Works* 2. 375: 6. 680.
42. Ibid., *Works* 2. 376.
43. Ibid., *Works* 2. 429–432.
44. Ibid., *Works* 2. 433–437, 465.
45. Ibid., *Works* 2. 549–568.
46. Ibid., *Works* 2. 352.
47. Ibid., *Works* 2. 504–5; 3. 714, 769; 4.1022.
48. On Dippel see Karl-Ludwig Voss, *Christianus Democritus. Das Menschenbild bei Johann Conrad Dippel* (Leiden 1970): Rüdiger Mack, *Pietismus und Frühaufklärung an der Universität Giessen und in Hessen-Darmstadt* (Giessen 1984): Martin Schmidt, *Pietismus* (Stuttgart 1972), pp.134–5.
49. *Unschuldige Wahrheiten*, *Works* 3. 639, 633, 639.
50. Ibid., *Works* 3. 713, 692–5, 702.
51. On this subject see Max Goebel, *Geschichte des christlichen Lebens in der rheinischwestphälischen Kirche* (3 vols, Coblenz 1840–60): Max Goebel, 'Geschichte der wahren Inspirations-Gemeinden, 1688–1850', *Zeitschrift für historischen Theologie* 24–5 (1854–5): Mathias Benad, *Toleranz als Gebot Christlicher Obrigkeit* (Hildesheim 1983): Hans Schneider, Introduction to N. L. von Zinzendorf, *Werke* Reihe 2 Bd. 18, *Berichte der Büdingischen Grafschaft zur Vertreibung der Herrnhuter aus der Wetterau* (Hildesheim 1978).
52. *Geistliche Fama* ran from 1733–43. A file may be reconstructed from incomplete sets in the university libraries at Göttingen and Halle, and the Landesbibliothek at Stuttgart.
53. *Selbstbiographie*, *Works* 12. 228, 230–31, 243–4.
54. Ibid., *Works* 12. 235.
55. Ibid., *Works* 12. 256.
56. Ibid., *Works* 12. 259.
57. Grossmann, *Edelmann*, p.100.
58. *Selbstbiographie*, *Works* 12. 266.
59. Ibid., *Works* 12. 247, 336.
60. Ibid., *Works* 12. 300.
61. Ibid., *Works* 12. 341.
62. *Die Göttlichkeit der Vernunft*, *Works* 8. 6, 16, 12.
63. Buddeus's title (Grossmann, *Edelmann*, p.15). Baumgarten succinctly described the *Tractatus* as 'one of Spinoza's most godless books'. Sigmund Jacob Baumgarten, *Geschichte der Religionspartheyen* (Halle 1776; repr. Hildesheim. 1966), p.129.

64. Edelmann had spotted a copy in the catalogue of a Berlin book auction, a treasure which did not turn up very often, and requested it. He was instantly attracted to Spinoza (who had received only passing mention in the *Göttlichkeit der Vernunft*, finished four months earlier) in a consignment of books received from Pinell on 24 June 1740. *Selbstbiographie*, *Works* 12. 334, 350.
65. See e.g. *Sponza in der Frühzeit seiner religiösen Wirkung* ed. K. Gründer and W. Schmidt-Biggemann, *Wolfenbütteler Studien zur Aufklärung* Bd. 12 (Heidelberg 1984): Hermann Timm, *Gott und die Freiheit. Studien zur Religionsphilosophie der Goethezeit* Bd. 1, *Die Spinozarenaissance* (Frankfurt 1974).
66. Hirsch, *Geschichte der neuern evangelischen Theologie* 2. 411–3. Edelmann also figures largely in Fritz Mauthner's monumental *Atheismus und seine Geschichte im Abendlande* (Stuttgart/Berlin 1922) 3. 220–228.
67. *Moses mit aufgedeckten Angesichte*, *Works* 7, Anblick 2. 34. Edelmann resolved to rescue Knutzen from oblivion by reprinting material which came his way in *Moses*. The first serviceable edition of Knutzen was by Werner Pfoh, *Mathias Knutzen, ein deutscher Atheist und revolutionärer Demokrat des 17. Jahrhunderts* ([East] Berlin 1965).
68. *Moses mit aufgedeckten Angesichte*, *Works* 7, Anblick 1. 2.
69. Ibid., *Works* 7, Anblick 1. 28.
70. Ibid., *Works* 7, Anblick 1. 29.
71. Ibid., *Works* 7, Anblick 1. 38, 43: Anblick 2. 11–17.
72. Ibid., *Works* 7, Anblick 1. 44, 47, 57.
73. Ibid., *Works* 7, Anblick 1. 94.
74. Ibid., *Works* 7, Anblick 2. 3–7.
75. Ibid., *Works* 7, Anblick 2. 41.
76. Ibid., *Works* 7, Anblick 2. 61.
77. Ibid., *Works* 7, Anblick 2. 91.
78. Ibid., *Works* 7, Anblick 3. 5–8, 123–4.
79. Ibid., *Works* 7, Anblick 3. 145–6.
80. Ibid., *Works* 7, Anblick 1. 139.
81. J.H. Pratje, *Historische Nachrichten von Joh. Chr. Edelmanns, eines berüchtigen Religionsspötters, Leben, Schriften und Lehrbegrif ...* (2nd edn Hamburg 1755).
82. Grossmann, *Edelmann*, p. 136.
83. Especially in *Die Erste Epistel St Harenbergs* (1747), *Works* 11. 413–578.
84. See above, n. 35. Also Gerhard Reichel, 'Die Anfänge der Brüdergemeine in Neuwied', *Unitas Fratrum* 18 (1986) 7–24.
85. Grossmann, *Edelmann*, p. 149.
86. *Abgenöthigtes Jedoch Andern nicht wieder aufgenöthigtes Glaubens-*

Bekenntniss, *Works* 9. 24.

87. Ibid., *Works* 9. 64, 71.
88. Ibid., *Works* 9. 101.
89. Ibid., *Works* 9. 122, 136.
90. Ibid., *Works* 9. 143, 182, 221.
91. Ibid., *Works* 9. 293, 297, 261–2.
92. The pamphlets of these years are printed in *Works* 9.
93. Grossmann, *Edelmann*, p. 167.
94. On this whole subject, including Edelmann's autobiography, see Hermann Hettner, *Geschichte der deutschen Literatur im achtzehnten Jahrhundert* (7th edn Braunschweig 1925) 3. i. 223–243: Georg Misch, *Geschichte der Autobiographie* (Frankfurt 1907–69): Günter Niggl, *Geschichte der deutschen Autobiographie im 18. Jahrhundert* (Stuttgart 1977), pp. 12–13.
95. Karl Wolfgang Becker, 'Die Wahrheit nach meinem besten Vermögen zu bekennen. Johann Christian Edelmanns Autobiographie', *Goethe Almanach* 1970, pp. 168–208, especially pp. 201–2.
96. Walter Grossmann, 'Edelmann und das öffentliche Schweigen des Reimarus und Lessing', *Zeitschrift für Kirchengeschichte* 85 (1974) 350–368.
97. Bruno Bauer, *Geschichte der Politik, Kultur und Aufklärung des 18. Jahrhunderts* (Berlin 1843–4; repr. Aalen 1965) 1. 204–236.
98. *Marx-Engels Collected Works* (London 1975–) 2. 320, 348.

3

John Wesley and England's 'Ancien Régime'

DAVID HEMPTON

Eighteenth-century British history so long illuminated and shaded by the work of Sir Lewis Namier has witnessed a remarkable resurgence of historical inquiry in the past decade. In particular there have been important studies made of the aristocracy, political ideology, Anglican and dissenting religion, criminality and the law, urban growth, commerce and consumerism, and the growth of manufacturing.[1] Much of this research was understandably compartmentalized, and the time was clearly ripe for a major new work of synthesis and interpretation. This was provided by Dr Jonathan Clark whose book *English Society 1688–1832* has occasioned almost equal amounts of criticism and praise. The wider merits and demerits of Dr Clark's book have been exhaustively debated elsewhere[2], but for present purposes it is what he said about John Wesley and the Evangelical Revival that is of most interest.[3]

As part of his wider scheme of presenting eighteenth-century English society as pre-industrial, hierarchic, aristocratic and confessional, he states that Wesley inherited almost intact the political theology of mainstream Anglicanism. As against those who regard Wesleyan Methodism as essentially a liberal, egalitarian and progressive ideology, Clark emphasizes Wesley's belief that God, not the people, was the origin of all civil power and that obedience to the king was the duty of all citizens of Britain and its colonies. Stung by dissenting criticism of his views and fearful of Wilkesite radicalism and American rebellion, Wesley wrote a clutch of loyalty tracts between 1772 and 1782 in which he eulogized the monarchy, castigated rebellious

Americans and disaffected Englishmen, rejected the libertarian rhetoric of radical dissenters and developed a full-blown English patriotism against foreigners and papists.[4] Some dissenters detected in all this a return to 'the good old Jacobite doctrines of hereditary, indefeasible, divine right, and of passive obedience and non-resistance'.[5] A new Sacheverell seemed to be on the loose and even Burke repudiated Wesley's court-inspired propaganda. Dr Clark stresses that Wesley's 'loyalty tradition' was also the official ideology of early nineteenth-century Methodism enabling Methodists, evangelical Anglicans and the Church of England as a whole to make common cause against revolutionaries, radicals and republicans. 'This conclusion was all the more remarkable', suggests Clark, 'in that Methodism was deliberately directed towards the poor.'[6] Clark thus finds himself as an unlikely supporter of E.P. Thompson in stating that Wesleyan Methodism, though numerically insignificant compared to the wider Church of England, stoutly defended the old order in both church and state against attacks from secular and religious radicals of all persuasions.[7] This conclusion is all the more noteworthy from Clark's viewpoint because it indirectly shows that religious populists were at least as conservative as Anglican bishops and that genuine religious radicalism made its presence felt through a small but influential coterie of rational dissenters and the great numerical weight of Irish catholics.

The interpretation just outlined has, of course, many merits, not least its attack on a growing tradition of Methodist scholarship more interested in what Wesley anticipated than in what he did, but its main drawback is a lack of subtlety in exploring Wesley's motives, assumptions, inconsistencies and wider principles, which not only help to explain, but add important conditions to his bold public statements. In saying this one is mindful of Henry Adams' remark about that other complex and elusive eighteenth-century octogenarian, Thomas Jefferson. Almost every other statesman, he wrote, could be portrayed with 'a few broad strokes of the brush', but Jefferson 'only touch by touch with a fine pencil, and the perspective of the likeness depended upon the shifting and uncertain flicker of the semi-transparent shadows'.[8] Wesley too requires careful etching and for some of the same reasons. Men of principle who live long enough to become men of affairs, and who write more than is entirely wise, are rarely models of consistency. The aim of this essay then is not to set up a radical Wesley in opposition to the conventional establishmentarian portrait, but merely to draw attention to aspects of Wesley's life and work which are not so easily encapsulated by Dr Clark's broad brush strokes. Of particular importance are Wesley's attitudes to those four cornerstones of British society and ideology in the eighteenth century: the constitution, the Church of England, property and the law. These issues have been selected, not because they conveniently suit my interpretation of Wesley's views, but because of their centrality to the theory and practice of the eighteenth-century state, and are therefore a proper test of Wesley's attitudes in the round. In each of these areas Wesley's principles have important radical elements within them and his views are generally more instrumental and pragmatic than his more colourful dogmatic statements would suggest. As with most writers of trenchant prose what is most quotable in Wesley's works is not always the most representative of his actual opinions in so far as they can be determined.

I

Wesley and the English Constitution

The High Church Toryism of Wesley's family background and Oxford connections is well known and has been justifiably re-emphasized by his most recent biographer who locates the central consistencies of Wesley's political views in the scriptural principle of 'obedience to the powers-that-be, which could be glossed by the old High Church and Tory views of divine right, suitably adapted to the Hanoverian dynasty'.[9] It is nevertheless assumed too easily that his later 'political' writings confined largely to the period 1767–82, are merely pro-Hanoverian versions of his earlier views. Wesley's rejection of the Jacobite cause and acceptance of the Hanoverian dynasty was influenced partly by the work of the repentant non-juror William Higden and by Wesley's quirky interpretation of the English monarchy's dynastic lineage;

but there is more to it than that. Wesley's enthusiasm for the Hanoverian monarchy was based also on the conviction that the Glorious Revolution had ushered in an unprecedented era of civil and religious liberty. In his *Thoughts Upon Liberty* Wesley set out to defend *both* liberties as fundamental to humankind. 'Religious liberty', he wrote, 'is a liberty to choose our own religion, to worship God according to our own conscience, according to the best light we have. Every man living, as man, has a right to this, as he is a rational creature.'[10] Since religious liberty is based on God's creation of a rational humanity it is 'an indefeasible right' and superior to all other rights, including those of property. It is precisely because Hanoverian monarchs were better protectors of religious freedom than their Stuart predecessors that Wesley is so fulsome in praise of them. The same is true of civil liberty which Wesley, after Blackstone, defined as 'a liberty to enjoy our lives and fortunes in our own way; to use our property, whatever is legally our own, according to our own choice'.[11] The threat to such liberties in the England of the 1770s, according to Wesley, came not from king or parliament but from mobs and misguided patriots. This judgment, whatever its merits, should not detract from the fact that Wesley supported limited monarchy in eighteenth-century England as the best way of defending civil and religious freedom; hence his support for it is purposeful and instrumental as much as it is theoretical or dogmatic.

A similar concern for the liberty of the person characterizes Wesley's *Thoughts Upon Slavery*. Borrowing from Blackstone once again he states that slavery is 'against the plain law of nature and reason' and is thus inconsistent with 'any degree of natural justice'.[12] But Wesley's opposition to slavery goes beyond Blackstone's strictly legal rebuttal to embrace higher notions of racial equality and human compassion.[13] Moreover he subjects the commercial, climatological and necessitarian defences of slavery to remorseless criticism, even stating that slave islands would be better 'sunk in the depth of the sea, than that they should be cultivated at so high a price as the violation of justice, mercy and truth'. In a spirited defence of natural rights Wesley concluded that 'liberty is the right of every human creature, as soon as he breathes the vital air; and no human law can deprive him of that right which he derives from the law of nature'.[14]

Every person then, according to Wesley, regardless of creed, colour or social status had the right to civil and religious liberty and to the protection of the law. Equally, Wesley saw no theoretical or practical justification for extending such freedoms into the political sphere. He flatly rejected Lockean ideas of popular sovereignty and subjected Richard Price's *Observations on the Nature of Civil Liberty* to withering criticism.[15] He countered Price's statement that government originated from the people and was dependent on their consent by employing the historical argument that the enfranchized had always been a select minority (adult propertied males) and that there was 'not a single instance, in above seven hundred years, of the people of England's conveying the supreme power either to one or more persons'.[16] A year later in his *Calm Address to the Inhabitants of England* Wesley followed up his attack on the Radical Dissenters.

> Do you imagine there are no High Churchmen left? Did they all die with Dr Sacheverel? Alas, how little do you know of mankind! Were the present restraint taken off, you would see them swarming on every side, and gnashing upon you with their teeth. There would hardly need a nod from that sacred person whom you revile, or at least lightly esteem. Were he to stand neuter, in what a condition would you be within one twelve months! If other Bonners and Gardiners did not arise, other Lauds and Sheldons would, who would either rule over you with a rod of iron, or drive you out of the land. Know the blessings you enjoy.[17]

No clearer statement could be made of Wesley's rejection of the 'persecuting' tradition of English religion and his defence of the Hanoverian monarchy as the custodian of religious liberty.

If religious liberty in England was threatened by irresponsible dissenters (unitarian or Calvinist) provoking a High Church reaction, civil liberty was equally in danger from Wilkesite radicals, American revolutionaries and the chronically disaffected. Jonathan Clark has convincingly shown how this 'contagion of disaffection' in the 1770s drew out Wesley's conservatism in the same way as the French Revolution influenced the evangelicals in the 1790s, but even here Wesley's conservative reaction is based on a distinctive view of liberty. The libertarian rhetoric of ribald Wilkesites he repudiated as bawling cant, the American cry for liberty was in his opinion a cry for independence and the liberties demanded by the mob he dismissed as licentiousness. Above all he did not see how English liberties could be improved by alternative forms of government especially those instigated by violence or dependent upon the will of the people.

Putting labels on Wesley's political theology, whether Tory, Whig, mainstream Anglican, conservative, progressive or whatever, ultimately conceals as much as it reveals. He believed that God was the origin of all power and that the Bible was his revealed will. He loved his king, his country and the constitution, but above all he had an exalted view of civil and religious liberty which he sought to defend against violence and anarchy. Like Burke, Wesley was more concerned with duties than with rights and with God's providential ordering of society than with the collective wisdom of democracy. Therefore an emphasis on obedience to established authorities and on reciprocal duties in all human relationships promised greater rewards of happiness and security for humankind than could be guaranteed by revolutionary enthusiasm. Although opposed in principle to revolutionary change, however, he retrospectively endorsed the Dutch revolt against Catholic Spain in the sixteenth century, and by 1784 he had accepted the American revolution as a *fait accompli*. But Wesley's position was no mere adaptation of Pope's phrase that 'whatever is, is right', because his approval went only to changes that resulted in more, not less, civil and religious liberty.[18] This fundamental concern for human liberty, absent in Dr Clark's treatment of Wesley, has led Leon Hynson to the conclusion that over a period of fifty years Wesley's political theology underwent a subtle change in emphasis from a primary focus on divine right, passive obedience and non-resistance to a primary concern for human liberties as ushered in by the Glorious Revolution and maintained inviolate by the Hanoverian dynasty.[19] Thus, Wesley's support for the established order in the period 1772–1782 was based not only on his residual and suitably amended Toryism, but also on his appreciation of the rights enjoyed by the freeborn Englishman. This is also the framework within which his anti-French and anti-papist sentiments, especially evident in 1778, are best understood.

Wesley was generally careful not to allow his innate sympathy for some popular causes to manifest itself in public opposition to the king and his ministers. His Toryism, though tinged with the kind of anti-whig radicalism described by Linda Colley, never spilled over into overt Jacobitism or into a sustained attack on Walpolean corruption.[20] Similarly, his early sympathy for the plight of the American colonists was almost embarrassingly subjugated to a full-blown defence of the mother country amidst understandable allegations of plagiarism (Wesley borrowed some of Dr Johnson's ideas and prose) and of being a weathercock.[21] With such evidence in mind Dr Clark states that Wesley inherited almost intact 'the political theology of mainstream Anglicanism', but Wesley's political observations, as has been shown, also follow a more tortuous path than some of his more propagandist writings would suggest.

II

Wesley and the Church of England[22]

'In a Christian commonwealth', Burke told the House of Commons in 1792, 'the church and the state are one and the same thing, being different integral parts of the same whole.'[23] Burke's high view of the church-state connexion as Jonathan Clark has shown was neither original nor out of step with a substantial corpus of Anglican literature thrown up in the period of the French Revolution.[24] Wesley, as is well known, lived and died within the established church and maintained a profound veneration for its forms, liturgies and doctrines. But Wesley's support of the Church of England, always more impressive in thought than in deed, was neither static nor entirely unconditional. Indeed there is a profound ambiguity at the heart of his opinions on religious establishments. On the one hand he valued the ecclesiastical discipline, historical traditions (including the writings of great Anglican churchmen) and social utility of the Church of England, while on the other he regarded state patronage of religion as one of the 'mysteries of iniquity' that destroyed the spirituality of the Early Church. The greatest blow against 'the whole essence of true religion' he wrote, 'was struck in the fourth century by Constantine the Great, when he called himself a Christian, and poured in a flood of riches, honours, and power upon the Christians; more especially upon the clergy'.[25] The connexion between establishment, wealth and corruption was never far from Wesley's mind and he reserved his severest remarks for those 'indolent, pleasure-taking, money-loving, praise-loving, preferment-seeking Clergymen' whom he regarded 'as the pests of the Christian world; a stink in the nostrils of God'.[26] To overcome the inconvenience of devotion to the established church while disapproving of many of its bishops and priests, Wesley stated that the essence of the church was to be found in its articles and Homilies, not in its personnel. Consequently he rejected the divine right of episcopacy as a Tudor innovation and the doctrine of apostolical succession as historically unsustainable.[27] His defence of the episcopal church was therefore essentially pragmatic, leading Maldwyn Edwards to the conclusion that Wesley was 'a rebel in thought as well as in action, and only a sleepy, loosely disciplined Church would have tolerated his shock tactics so long'.[28]

Since Wesley viewed the Church of England as primarily an instrument of the gospel, not a divine right institution of state, he worked out quite early on what his sticking point would be if ecclesiastical discipline was used against him. In 1775 he told the Cornish evangelical, Samuel Walker, that he *meant* no separation from the church.

> It is from a full conviction of this that we have, (1), preached abroad; (2), prayed extempore; (3), formed societies; and (4), permitted preachers who were not episcopally ordained. And were we pushed on this side, were there no alternative allowed, we should judge it our bounden duty rather wholly to separate

> from the Church than to give up any of these points. Therefore if we cannot stop a reformation without stopping lay preachers, the case is clear – we cannot stop it at all.[29]

Henry Rack has shown that whereas Charles Wesley's self-declared 'chief concern on earth was the prosperity of the Church of England; my next, that of the Methodists; my third, that of the preachers', his brother's priorities were almost the reverse.[30] For John, the cause of vital religion and the need to sustain his holy mission took precedence over the laws, forms and discipline of the Church of England. Wesley was nevertheless aware that connexionalism might easily become Congregationalism, and he used Methodism's position within the established church as a defence against the atomization of his societies. 'I see clearer and clearer', he wrote, 'none will keep to us unless they keep to the Church. Whoever separate from the Church will separate from the Methodists.'[31] Indeed one of the most persistent of the early Anglican attacks on Methodism was that its breaches of ecclesiastical order would result in the same sectarian avalanche as overwhelmed the puritans. Taking the Elizabethan Presbyterian, Thomas Cartwright, as his example, John Smith told Wesley that despite his best intentions 'strict order once broken confusion rushes in like a torrent at a trifling breach'.[32] Wesley's response was to draw a distinction between the anabaptist enthusiasts and the learned and pious puritans whom he greatly admired; 'Nor did they separate from the Church, but were driven out, whether they would or no.'[33]

At the root of Wesley's ambivalence about the Church of England was his biblically inspired belief that the true church in England was 'the congregation of English believers' and his experience told him that such a body was by no means co-terminous with the established church.[34] One possible strategy available to him therefore was to bring together the evangelicals within the Church of England in an alliance with the Methodists, but once this had failed by the end of the 1760s it was clear that Wesley's desire to follow his own version of authentic Christianity overrode his scruples about church order. In that respect he was a reluctant rebel, never seeking confrontation with the church, but always prepared to implement ecclesiastical innovations as circumstances dictated. Thus, even before the turning point in relations between Anglicans and Methodists effected by the Deed of Declaration in 1784, 'John Wesley had effectively separated from the Church of England by founding a closely-knit connexion of preachers and societies administering vast properties subject to no Anglican oversight except that of one priest with no official care of souls and sitting very loose to episcopal authority.'[35] As long as the Methodists continued to attend Anglican worship and sacraments, and as long as the bishops declined to enforce church discipline, Wesley's affection for the church remained unaltered, but it was the filial affection of a child with a mind of its own rapidly approaching separation from the parental home.

III

Wesley and Property[36]

'The chief end of political or civil society', wrote Locke, 'is the preservation of property', and while most of Locke's political ideology went unread or unheeded by practising politicians in eighteenth-century England, his defence of property rights was admirably suited to a governing élite composed of a tight privileged ring of landowners. With power based on the ownership of large estates, legal privileges, and a remarkable degree of political control of elections and high offices of state, English magnates have been described as 'the most confident, powerful and resilient aristocracy in Europe'.[37] This social élite was neither easy to penetrate from outside nor entirely closed to fortunes made elsewhere. Not only did English landowners facilitate commercial development by exploiting their mineral resources, taking responsibility for roads and laying down ground plans for urban building projects, but they also contributed to a 'consumer revolution' through their demand for fine decorative goods such as furniture, porcelain and silverware.[38] Thus, eighteenth-century England has been regarded as both an 'aristocratic society' and as a great age of commercial expansion and consumer demand.[39] Into this kind of society Wesley brought a distinctive and remarkably radical attitude to property and commerce which for convenience may be divided between his injunctions to his own followers and his attitudes to the wider economy.

Most interpretations of Methodism's economic teaching and influence published in the last quarter of a century have drawn attention to Wesley's emphasis on thrift and hard work. 'Without industry', he wrote, 'we are neither fit for this world, nor for the world to come.' Hence it is suggested that Methodist discipline and acquisitiveness were symbiotically linked to the early development of industrial capitalism.[40] Wesley and his followers are thus portrayed as exemplars of the protestant ethic – old puritans made new. Whatever the merits of this argument in relation to the Methodist movement as a whole during the industrial revolution, it will simply not do for Wesley's own teaching and example. Both W. J. Warner, and more recently John Walsh have drawn attention to the fact that Wesley's economic teaching was scarcely a model of acquisitive capitalism.[41] After providing for necessities Wesley repeatedly urged Methodists to give away the rest, otherwise they would be guilty of robbing God and the poor, corrupting their own souls, wronging the widow and the fatherless, and of making themselves 'accountable for all the want, affliction, and distress which they may, but do not remove'.[42] In addition, Wesley told his followers to think nothing of the future, to demand no more than a fair price and to make sure that excessive wealth was not passed on to their children.

There is yet another dimension to Wesley's economic opinions, for Walsh has drawn attention to Wesley's early attraction to the primitive church and its practice of the community of goods.[43] In contrast to conventional Anglican teaching he did not think that such practices were of necessity confined to the apostolic period, though he was realistic enough to recognize that material altruism was doomed unless it was based on Christian love and koinonia of the highest quality. But as with much of his economic teaching, Wesley found that persistent human acquisitiveness was against him and he was forced to retreat into the mediaeval solution of voluntary proverty for a self-denying spiritual élite. Even so his sermons never lost their anti-materialistic bite – at times close to desperation – as he viewed with dismay the first fruits of Methodism's upward social mobility.[44]

Wesley's rigorous teaching to his followers on the spiritual dangers of acquisitiveness and conspicuous consumption was carried over into his general attitudes to economy and society in eighteenth-century England. In his *Thoughts on the Present Scarcity of Provisions* Wesley blamed the country's economic ills on luxury, waste, engrossing, distilling and taxes. With opinions based on empirical observations rather than on economic theory, Wesley's pamphlet is a thinly veiled attack on what Edward Thompson has called the 'theatrical materialism' of the rich. Horses and carriages, useless pensions, extravagant waste and an insatiable thirst for luxury are all condemned as 'thousands of people throughout the land are perishing for want of food'.[45] As A.C. Outler has shown Wesley also repudiated Adam Smith's view that surplus accumulation was the basis of economic well-being.[46] Wesley's intensely ethical and biblicist stance, combined with a conviction that all great spiritual movements surged from the poor, left no room for the complacency of the country house. This is made clear in a remarkable letter to Sir James Lowther, owner of substantial estates in Cumberland, director of the South Sea Company, colliery and harbour developer, borough patron and one of the wealthiest and most parsimonious men in England. Wesley's point by point rebuttal of an earlier letter from Lowther is a classic statement of his social and economic philosophy.

> (2). It is true men of fortune must mind their fortune – but they must not love the world. (3). It is true, likewise, you can't go about to look for poor people – but you may be sufficiently informed of them by those that can. (4). And if some of these are never satisfied, this is no reason for not relieving others. (5). Suppose, too, that some make an ill use of what you give – the loss falls on their own head. You will not lose your reward for their fault. (8). I rejoice likewise that you have given some hundreds of pounds to the hospitals, and wish it had been ten

> thousand. (9). To the support of the family I did not object, but begged leave to ask whether this could not be done without giving ten thousand a year to one who had as much already.[47]

Herein is encapsulated Wesley's spiritual distrust of riches, his characteristic refusal to distinguish between the deserving and undeserving poor, his advocacy of a *sacrificial* charity and his suspicion of hereditary wealth. All this was within a framework of belief which held that the bounty of the earth was a God-given responsibility of stewardship and that eternal rewards were immeasurably more valuable than worldly luxury. Wesley was, of course, no philistine and on occasions he was attracted by the aesthetic trappings of wealth, but in general terms he was as opposed to the conspicuous consumption of the landed élite as he was to the growing consumerism of English society. To conclude, Warner is probably correct to suggest that Wesley's twin emphases on industriousness and charity was 'incapable of mass realization',[48] but that should not distract from the genuinely radical elements in both his instructions to his followers and his reflections on eighteenth-century English society.

IV

Wesley and the Law

'It was a shibboleth of English politics', state Brewer and Styles, 'that English law was the birthright of every citizen who, unlike many of his European counterparts, was subject not to the whim of a capricious individual but to a set of prescriptions that bound *all* members of the polity'.[49] Wesley's belief in civil and religious liberty and his opposition to all forms of violence resulted in a high regard for the law in so far as it was properly applied and administered. But he also recognized that early Methodism teetered on the brink of legal irregularities with respect to the penal legislation of Charles II's reign.[50] Edward Gibson, Bishop of London and a leading authority on ecclesiastical law, stated that the Methodists were in defiance of the government and the courts by posing as Anglicans while behaving as dissenters. In his opinion Methodist claims to be free from penal legislation without fulfilling the conditions laid down by the Toleration Act were merely a legal manifestation of Methodist antinomianism.[51]

Wesley's response was superficially straightforward and formed the basis of his societies' legal defence before magistrates for half a century. Methodists were not dissenters, therefore the Toleration Act was irrelevant to them. The Conventicles Act was designed to 'provide remedies against sedition'. Methodists were not seditious, quite the reverse. Field preaching was legal in theory and safe in practice because it was conducted in daylight to known crowds which were much smaller than opponents alleged. Similarly, if ordination was properly understood to be for a gospel ministry, not to a specific location, then itinerant preaching was not an offence against the church.[52] Such principles were, of course, easier to defend in learned debate than in English localities, especially during periods of foreign warfare and domestic instability. As time passed, therefore, Wesley grudgingly accepted the inconveniences of Methodism's uncertain legal position, and from at least 1748 (though more commonly from the late 1750s) Methodist preachers and owners of meeting places applied for certificates under the Toleration Act as a safeguard against intimidation.[53] Wesley refused to accept, however, that registration amounted to separation from the church; rather it was a device to protect life and property from the licence of the crowd.

Despite the registration of preachers and meeting houses the extent of toleration enjoyed by Methodists in English localities depended less upon known laws, which were seen to be ambiguous and subject to confusing jurisdictional disputes,[54] than on the degree of social acceptance accorded to the Methodists themselves. Wesley found this inconvenient, but not intolerable, despite periodic splenetic outbursts about the inadequacy of religious toleration accorded to his followers. In an oft-quoted letter to Wilberforce he bemoaned the fact that Methodists were neither accepted as Anglicans nor afforded relief as dissenters under the Act of Toleration[55]. But behind the spleen Wesley knew well that he had at times used Methodism's ambiguous position under the law as a device to keep potential separatists in check. The truth is that Wesley recognized the fact that the Methodist structure created peculiar legal problems, but so long as his societies were not unduly restricted he was content to put up the best possible legal defence and accept the consequences.

Whatever the complexities of the law with regard to preachers and conventicles, the great majority of cases against early Methodism which came before local courts was concerned with public order, assault, riot and damage to property. Opponents of the Methodists alleged that they disturbed the peace by breaking known laws, while Methodists in turn claimed they were victims of mobs unrestrained by those responsible for protecting civil and religious liberties. Encouraged by social superiors in the belief that since there was 'no law for the Methodists' mobs were virtually indemnified against prosecution, costs and damages, early Methodists were frequently victims of ritual humiliation and petty violence.[56] As is the fate of new religious movements, Methodists were accused of virtually everything from excessive puritanism to sexual licentiousness and from financial corruption to the breaking up of families and communities.[57] Wesley frustratingly discovered that local constables and quarter sessions could not be relied upon to protect his followers against 'the clamour either of the great vulgar or the small'.[58] But unlike the confusing legal debates surrounding the implementation of the Conventicles Act, Wesley was unequivocal in his repudiation of mob violence and untiring in his efforts to seek legal redress. His strategy was to attempt to overcome local prejudices by taking as many cases as he could afford to the court of King's Bench to establish that there was 'law for the Methodists'.[59] As case law built up Wesley used it to warn future protagonists and to remind local officials that their tenure in office depended upon their ability to maintain public order.[60]

In the period 1740–70, therefore, Wesley could do no more than appeal to those in authority to apply the laws they professed to live by. In that respect he used his knowledge of the law and social contacts from his Oxford days to seek protection for popular pietists from ruffians of all social ranks. In general terms Wesley had confidence in English law and its interpretation by metropolitan courts, but he had correspondingly little confidence in local justice when animated by violence and prejudice. As with his defence of the Hanoverian dynasty and the eighteenth-century constitution, Wesley valued English law primarily as a bulwark against the licence of the crowd and the curtailment of civil and religious liberty. In that respect, as in many others, Wesley shared Blackstone's patriotic view of English law as the very essence of freedom in 'the only nation in the world where political or civil liberty is the direct end of its constitution'.[61]

Allowing for the fact that Wesley's views were neither static nor entirely consistent, the striking feature of his attitude to the constitution, the Church of England, property and the law is that in each case his veneration for institutions was dependent on their achievement of certain ends. His primary concern, therefore, was not with theory but with performance. Thus the constitution and the Hanoverian dynasty defended civil and religious liberties against radicals, revolutionaries, anarchists and mobs. The Church of England, notwithstanding its carnal and wordly clergy, was, through its homilies, articles and traditions, the custodian of religion, pure and undefiled. The ownership of property conferred duties more than privileges, so that Wesley's preoccupation was with the distribution of resources, not their acquisition. Finally English law was not only the birthright of every English citizen, but the ultimate protection of the security of the person against intolerance, prejudice and violence. In addition, Wesley had a lifelong dislike of human exploitation, whether of Caribbean slaves or the English poor. The corollary to all of this was that he profoundly disliked any ideology or system which in his opinion contributed to human bondage, including Roman Catholicism,[62] high Calvinism,[63] popular sovereignty and inhumane commercialism. Much of the radicalism – as well as the conservatism – inherent in Wesley's thought stemmed from his willingness to obey biblical injunctions and Early Church practices with unremitting rigour even, as was the case with his teaching on the community of goods and celibacy, when they were inappropriate to the circumstances confronting him.[64]

In conclusion, Jonathan Clark is probably right to emphasize Wesley's conservative political theology, particularly in his period of polemical warfare against the disaffected at home and abroad in the 1770s and 1780s, and to rebut those who would place Wesley too neatly in the tradition of enlightenment liberalism. He may even be correct to state that the *effect* of Methodism in the generation overshadowed by the French Revolution was to reinforce the passive obedience of the poor.[65] But as the preceding pages have shown, Wesley could hardly be regarded as an impeccable exemplar of the mainstream Anglican tradition in the eighteenth century. Perhaps the point at which Wesley most obviously departs from that tradition is the greater weight he gives to the writings of the primitive church and Early Church Fathers in constructing his ideology of authority in church and state. Ironically, this was to be true of yet another Oxford Movement some hundred years later. Wesley's lifelong devotion to primitive Christianity and vital religion imbued his opinions with a degree of pragmatism and radicalism which can only be etherized at the cost of historical credibility. If not a self-conscious rebel, Wesley was far from a comfortable conformist.

Notes

1. For a survey of some of this material see Linda Colley, 'The Politics of Eighteenth-Century British History', *Journal of British Studies*, 25, 1986, pp.359–79. See also Jeremy Black (ed.), *British Politics and Society from Walpole to Pitt 1742–1789*, Macmillan 1990.
2. Joanna Innes, 'Review Article: Jonathan Clark, Social History and England's "Ancien Regime"', *Past and Present*, 115, May 1987, pp.165–200.
3. J.C.D. Clark, *English Society 1688–1832*, CUP 1985, pp.235–47.
4. *The Works of John Wesley*, XI, pp.14–163.
5. Bernard Semmel, *The Methodist Revolution*, Heinemann 1974, p.66.
6. Clark, op. cit., p.242.
7. E.P. Thompson, *The Making of the English Working Class*, Gollancz 1963, pp.350–400.
8. Merrill Petersen, 'Thomas Jefferson: A Brief Life', *Thomas Jefferson* ed. Lally Weymouth, Weidenfeld and Nicolson 1973, p.14. R.P. Heitzenrater, *The Elusive Mr Wesley*, 2 vols, Abingdon Press, Nashville 1984, vol.1, pp.11–36.
9. Henry D. Rack, *Reasonable Enthusiast: John Wesley and the Rise of Methodism*, Epworth Press 1989.
10. John Wesley, *Thoughts upon Liberty*, 1772, Works, XI, p.37.

11. Ibid., p.41.
12. John Wesley, *Thoughts upon Slavery*, 1774, *Works*, XI, p.71.
13. Ibid., pp.74–9.
14. Ibid., p.79.
15. John Wesley, *Some Observations on Liberty Occasioned by a Late Tract*, 1776, *Works*, XI, pp.90–118.
16. Ibid., p.103.
17. John Wesley, *A Calm Address to the Inhabitants of England*, 1777, *Works*, XI, p.13.
18. For a fuller discussion of these points see David Hempton, *Methodism and Politics in British Society 1750–1850*, Hutchinson 1984, pp.20–54.
19. Opinions expressed in an excellent unpublished typescript by Leon Orville Hynson, 'Human Liberty as Divine Right: A Study in the Political Maturation of John Wesley'. See also his 'Church and State in the Thought and Life of John Wesley', unpublished Ph.D. thesis, University of Iowa 1971.
20. Linda Colley, 'Eighteenth-Century English Radicalism before Wilkes', *Transactions of the Royal Historical Society*, 5th Series 31, 1981, pp.1–19; and *In Defiance of Oligarchy: The Tory Party 1714–1760*, CUP 1982, pp.112–5.
21. Heitzenrater, op. cit., vol.2, pp.116–27.
22. The standard work on this subject is Frank Baker, *John Wesley and the Church of England*, Epworth Press 1970.
23. Clark, op. cit., p.250.
24. Ibid., pp.247–76.
25. *The Works of John Wesley*, 2, *Sermons*, ed. A.C. Outler, Abingdon Press 1985, pp.462–3.
26. *The Works of John Wesley*, VII, p.303.
27. *The Letters of John Wesley*, 4, p.140.
28. Maldwyn Edwards, 'John Wesley', *A History of the Methodist Church in Great Britain*, vol.1, ed. Rupert Davies and Gordon Rupp, Epworth Press 1965, pp.71–2.
29. *The Works of John Wesley*, vol.26, *Letters* II, ed. Frank Baker, Clarendon Press 1982, p.595.
30. Rack, op. cit., p.302.
31. Baker, *Wesley and the Church*, p.135.
32. *Works*, 26, *Letters* II, p.189.
33. Ibid., p.135.
34. *Minutes of Some Late Conversations between the Rev. Mr Wesley and Others*, June 27 1744 in *Works*, 8, pp.280–1. See also Frederick Dreyer, 'A Religious Society under Heaven: John Wesley and the Identity of Methodism', *Journal of British Studies*, 25, 1986, pp.62–83,

in which he states that Wesley, both as an Anglican and a Methodist, 'thought of the church as a voluntary association that derived all the legitimacy it possessed from the agreement of its members', thereby rejecting notions of compulsory membership.

35. Baker, *Wesley and the Church*, p.283.
36. The most recent and authoritative discussion of Wesley's views on the ownership and distribution of property is to be found in John Walsh, 'John Wesley and the Community of Goods', *Protestant Evangelicalism: Britain, Ireland, Germany and America, c. 1750– c. 1950* ed. Keith Robbins, *Studies in Church History*, Subsidia 7, Basil Blackwell 1990.
37. Roy Porter, *English Society in the Eighteenth Century*, Allen Lane 1982, p.70.
38. Neil McKendrick, 'The Consumer Revolution of Eighteenth-Century England', *The Birth of a Consumer Society: the commercialization of Eighteenth-Century England* ed. Neil McKendrick, John Brewer and J.H. Plumb, Hutchinson 1983, pp.9–33. See also J.V. Beckett, *The Aristocracy in England 1660–1914*, Basil Blackwell 1986.
39. Joanna Innes, op. cit., pp.165–200. See also, Paul Langford, *A Polite and Commercial People: England 1727–1783*, Clarendon Press 1989.
40. Thompson, op. cit., p.355. Thompson's work has been particularly influential in this respect.
41. Wellman J. Warner, *The Wesleyan Movement in the Industrial Revolution*, Longmans 1930, pp.136–247. John Walsh, 'Methodism and the Common People', *People's History and Socialist Theory* ed. Raphael Samuel, Routledge & Kegan Paul 1981, pp.354–62.
42. Warner, op. cit., p.210.
43. According to Dr Walsh, Wesley's 'idealized image of the primitive Church provided stark contrasts with the acquisitiveness of Walpole's England, of which, as an old-fashioned Tory, he disapproved strongly' (Walsh, 'The Community of Goods', p.30).
44. *The Works of John Wesley*, vols.1–4, *Sermons*, ed. A.C. Outler, Abingdon Press 1984–5. See especially Sermon on the Mount VIII and numbers 50, 87, 108 and 131.
45. John Wesley, *Thoughts on the Present Scarcity of Provisions*, 1777, *Works*, XI, p.57.
46. A.C. Outler (ed.), *The Works of John Wesley*, vol.1, pp.92–3.
47. *Works*, 26, *Letters* II, pp.544–5.
48. Warner, op. cit., p.152. Hempton, *Methodism and Politics*, pp.231–4.
49. John Brewer and John Styles (ed.), *An Ungovernable People: The English and their Law in the Seventeenth and Eighteenth centuries*, Hutchinson 1980, p.14. See also Joanna Innes and John Styles, 'The Crime Wave: Recent Writing on Crime and Criminal Justice in

Eighteenth-Century England', *Journal of British Studies* 25, 1986, pp. 380–435.
50. J. S. Simon, 'John Wesley and Field Preaching' and 'The Conventicle Act and its relation to the Early Methodists', *Proceedings of the Wesley Historical Society*, XI, 1918, pp. 54–63 and 82–93. For a more comprehensive treatment of Methodism's early legal difficulties see David Hempton, 'Methodism and the Law, 1740–1820', *Bulletin of the John Rylands University Library of Manchester*, vol. 70 no. 3, 1988.
51. *Observations upon the Conduct and Behaviour of a Certain Sect Usually Distinguished by the Name of Methodists*, London 1744. Published anonymously but widely attributed to Edmund Gibson.
52. John Wesley, *A Farther Appeal to Men of Reason and Religion*, 1745, *The Works of John Wesley*, vol. 11, *The Appeals*, ed. G. R. Cragg, Clarendon Press 1975, pp. 178–83.
53. F. Baker, *Wesley and the Church*, p. 174 and J. M. Turner, *Conflict and Reconciliation*, Epworth Press 1985, p. 15.
54. See 2 Burr. 1041, Rex v. Moreley, 1760 and 4 Burr. 1991, Rex v. Justices and Clerk of the Peace for the County of Derby, 1766. For a more detailed discussion of the relationship between King's Bench and Quarter Sessions in this period see Norma Landau, *The Justices of the Peace, 1679–1760*, University of California Press 1984, pp. 345–53.
55. *Letters*, VIII, pp. 230–1, July 1790.
56. John Walsh, 'Methodism and the Mob in the Eighteenth Century', *Popular Belief and Practice* ed. G. J. Cuming and Derek Baker, *Studies in Church History*, 8, 1972, pp. 213–27.
57. Lambeth Palace Library Mss, Secker Papers, vol. 8, Methodists.
58. *Works*, 26, *Letters* II, p. 206.
59. *Journal*, V, p. 184.
60. *Works*, 26, *Letters* II, pp. 324–7, 335–7, 340–1 and 474–5. For a case involving the dismissal of local officials see P.R.O., KB 122, Great Dogget of Trinity Term in the 24th of George II, 240.
61. William Blackstone, *Commentaries on the Laws of England*, vol. 1, London 1830, p. 6 and pp. 143–4.
62. Hempton, *Methodism and Politics,* pp. 30–43.
63. Semmel, op. cit., p. 44. Wesley thought that the doctrine of irresistible grace made man 'a mere machine'.
64. Henry Abelove, 'The Sexual Politics of Early Wesleyan Methodism', *Disciplines of Faith* ed. Jim Obelkevich, Lyndal Roper and Raphael Samuel, Routledge and Kegan Paul 1987, pp. 86–99.
65. The evidence here is a good deal more ambiguous, and the issues more complex, than Clark allows. See W. R. Ward, *Religion and Society in England 1790–1850*, Batsford 1972, pp. 7–104, and Hempton, *Methodism and Politics*, pp. 55–115.

4

Frederick Lucas, *The Tablet* and Ireland – A Victorian Forerunner of Liberation Theology

SHERIDAN GILLEY

> 'I have even dreamt of the Tablet ... I had somewhere ... picked up a receipt for making ink as used in the Tablet Office. It was as follows. Take wormwood, gall, Jesuits bark, Irish black thorn & crab-stick, salt, & gunpowder, an ounce of each: pound them well with a sledge-hammer, saturate them with double distilled vinegar, put all these ingredients into a good sized bottle & fill up with holy water.'
>
> Revd James Jones to Wiseman, 16 March 1848

In James O'Shea's recent history of priests and politics in post-famine Co. Tipperary, the name of Frederick Lucas stands next in the index to Lucifer,[1] and some might consider this fair comment on his famous contest with Archbishop Cullen over the role of the priest in politics. This essay is intended to show what no Irish historian has shown before, the English-and European-religious background which plunged Lucas into Irish history.[2] Perhaps his religious outlook has been overlooked because so much Irish historiography is written by political historians for whom religion can be taken for granted, as natural an environ as the air; and it is only the modern secular-minded English who love to dwell on the peculiarities of the Victorian Christian: of say, Mr Gladstone, whose barque was always in danger of being blown off course in a gale of polemical passion, or on an altogether lower level, Charles Newdigate Newdegate, MP, whose whole long career was ruled by an obsession with getting the British government to introduce an inspectorate for nunneries.[3]

Certainly Frederick Lucas has been a minor puzzle to Irish historians, but the problem is resolved by the principle that his passion for Irish freedom was the fine flower of his commitment to Catholicism. As a Roman Catholic, albeit an English one, he came a good deal closer to the self-understanding of most ordinary Irish Catholics than any English secular radical. He died a martyr to Irish divisions, and it was said of him that he became 'more Irish than the Irish themselves'.[4] To the countless thousands who attended requiem masses in his memory, he was very near to Irish hearts, as a militant Hibernophile at the very centre of English Catholicism, though one whose religion carried him away from the mainstream views of ordinary Englishmen. The purpose of this essay, then, is to show the Catholic inspiration of his involvement in Irish politics, of how his Catholicism dictated his view of Ireland. And the reader after completing it may not like him better, and even feel a little sorry for Paul Cullen.

Lucas was born a religious outsider in 1812, as the son of a London Quaker corn merchant; but it was this class of person, commercially-minded and moderately liberal in politics, and opposed to the Tory Party and the established Church of England, who defined one of the two principal schools of opinion in the coming England of Victoria. There were only fourteen thousand members of the Society of Friends in the country, and their numbers were kept low by the most rigid ban on intermarriage with the members of other denominations exercised by any church, as any Quaker who wed a non-Quaker was expelled from the Society. Most of them were kept out of active politics by their own tradition of passive and acquiescent quietism.[5] But Quakers figured among the principal industrial entrepreneurs of the age, and were opposed to social distinctions of rank and privilege and to state regulations and restraints on commerce and trade. The new style of Quaker leadership is summed up in Frederick Lucas' older brother Samuel, a corn merchant like his father and a journalist like his brother, a crusader against the corn laws and an apostle of universal secular education. He became editor of the Victorian *Morning Star* – no relation to the modern paper of that name – which disseminated the *laissez-faire* principles of the

Manchester School of free trade. Samuel married Margaret Bright, sister of John Bright the Quaker MP and manufacturer; and Margaret was a prominent proponent of votes for women and temperance reform, and a crusader against the state regulation of prostitution.[6] Frederick himself attended the so-called 'Godless' University College, London, set up to provide a tertiary education for non-members of the Church of England. He distinguished himself as a brilliant conversationalist and debater, and like many another Victorian journalist, was called to the Bar. As a Quaker liberal member of a rising middle class, he might seem to be at the remotest social pole from the Church of Rome, with its aristocratic leadership of English noblemen and gentlemen and its massive Irish pauper following in the slums of urban England.

There was, however, also an English Catholic middle class, as John Bossy has shown in his recent attempt to link Quakerism and Catholicism as English varieties of non-Protestant middle-class Dissent.[7] There were certainly ties between Quaker and Catholic communities where both were strong, in northern England. The world's first passenger railway, between Stockton and Darlington, was a joint Catholic-Quaker enterprise, a party of Friends and two priests presiding over the laying of the first rails;[8] and Darlington was where Lucas received his schooling at the local Quaker Academy, a Quaker schooling being one thing he shared with his future Catholic foe, Paul Cullen.

The theological divide between Catholics and Quakers was more obvious than the social, and of Lucas' conversion to Catholicism at the age of twenty-seven – a conversion which also drew his fiancée to the church – it might be said that the theological ground that he then traversed exceeded all ordinary distances of religious travelling. His own published justification[9] to the Society of Friends was that the Quaker doctrine of the inner light was that of Catholic mystics like St Theresa, and that Quakerism itself had been a recall to religious unity against the religious disunity created by Protestantism, back to a religion given directly by God. The Catholic faith had this essentially Quaker quality of the spiritual union inspired by the Holy Ghost, and Lucas supports Professor Bossy's analysis on one point, that

Quakers were not Protestants because like Catholics, they did not claim to base their religion solely on scripture. Nor, declared Lucas, could a Quaker who trusted his own inner light deny Lucas his right to follow his own inner light and become a Catholic.

At another point, however, Professor Bossy's framework of interpretation ceases to be useful, as he describes the affinities between Quakerism and the reserved, devotionally Quietist, moderate and eirenically-minded English Roman Catholicism of the era before 1830; while Lucas was converted to a much more aggressive, militant and distinctively Romanist religion, with a strong stress on the pope's authority and infallibility and on devotion to the Virgin Mary.[10] It was this tender, ardent, romantic neo-Ultramontane devotionalism, with its central image of the Virgin and Child, which moved Lucas closer to the Irish; as in his declaration that his favourite daily prayer was the favourite Irish one, the Rosary. The popular propagation of this more distinctively Catholic Catholicism was especially the work, not so much even of the priesthood as of lay journalists like Louis Veuillot, editor of the French *L'Univers*, a sort of Ultramontane *Daily Mail*; and there was an English precedent for the type to hand, in the warlike editor of the *Catholic Magazine*, William Eusebius Andrews. It may have been the combative debating quality in Lucas which led the Mayfair Jesuit Father Lythgoe, who received him into the Roman Catholic Church in 1839, to put him forward in 1840 as founding editor of the new Catholic newspaper *The Tablet*. It certainly seems rather extraordinary that the establishment of the first major English Catholic weekly should have been entrusted to a twenty-eight year old of only a year's standing as a Catholic, and in 1843, Lucas took the controversial step of placing the publication under the Virgin's special patronage, under a drawing of the Mother and Child and the superscription of the oldest of prayers to Mary, *Sub tuum praesidium confugimus, sancta Dei Genitrix*: 'we flee to thy protection, O holy Mother of God'. One of Lucas' favourite themes was pure horror of the surviving English Catholic reserve about so pronouncedly popish a devotion. He thought that much English Catholicism showed a want of a properly aggressive

Catholic spirit, a want of Catholic spirit which he was also to denounce in denouncing the attitudes of many English Catholics to Ireland. In short, he was a religious militant before he was a political militant, and his Irish political militancy was the outcome of the novel English militancy of his Catholicism.

The renewal of a militant nineteenth-century Catholicism by this double devotion to the Pope and the Virgin is a general European phenomenon. Lucas' Irish political attitudes were grounded in his understanding of the church's proper attitude to the political forces unleashed by the French Revolution. Most Latin Catholics had been hostile to the Revolution – indeed this opposition had often taken the form of genuinely popular movements, extending to a majority of the population; but Lucas shared the 'Liberal Catholic' view[11] that the church had been crippled by its connexions with royal and aristocratic power and privilege in much of Catholic Europe, especially in France[12] and Austria;[13] and that in the Rhineland, Poland, Belgium and above all Ireland, the church had achieved its modern vitality by espousing the democratic cause. There is an underlying conservatism in this view, for by democracy in the favourable sense Lucas meant clerical peasant democracy, but this also implied on the European stage – at least outside central Italy, for which Lucas made a counter-revolutionary papal exception – the church had a duty to support peoples and not princes; and that for good religious reasons. For whether radical or conservative in its politics, nineteenth-century Catholicism had a general characteristic, that it became more assertively, belligerently Catholic, more committed to the defence of the church against secular or anticlerical liberalism and Protestant heresy; and in these conflicts, radical Catholicism had this advantage, that in Rhenish Prussia or post-partition Poland or Ireland, it offered a religious sanction for Catholics to confront non-Catholic authority, by presenting the general rights of Catholics as one with the freedom of the church.

In Ireland, the freedom of the church for Lucas was one with the rights of Irish Catholics, and a blow for the church was a blow for Irish freedom.[14] In his journalism, Lucas freely drew on the analogies with Belgium, Poland and Prussia: a fair sample of his internationalist understanding of the matter appears in a book by a M. de Jailly, which he freely translated from the French in 1845, *How to enslave a Church; or, the Religious Tyranny of Prussia over her Protestant and Catholic Subjects, particularly in the Rhenish Provinces,*[15] a denunciation of the Caesaropapist Frederick William III's attempts to force an amalgamation of the Lutheran and Calvinist Churches under the Crown, and to induce the Catholic Church in the Rhineland and Prussian Poland to relax the ban on mixed marriages between Protestants and Catholics: allegedly in order to provide Catholic brides in these regions for a new immigrant officialdom of Prussian bureaucrats.[16] As Lucas gleefully reported it, the Prussian government made the fortunate mistake of gaoling the Catholic Archbishops of Cologne and Posen for defying it, and of fining or imprisoning the Catholic priests who insisted on obeying their authority. Lucas's prince-prelate *par excellence* was the Archbishop of Cologne, the Baron Clemens August von Droste-Vischering, (or Droste zu Vischering) whom the German journalist Görres hailed as a modern Athanasius; and the result, as Lucas understood it, was a democratic mass movement like the Irish one, against heretical rulers in support of the martyr-clergy. Lucas drew the moral that if the church defied the state and suffered persecution for the Catholic cause, then it would be popular and its directives would be enforced from below by the people. Let the church exert its infallible authority in conflict with the state, and Catholic democracy would support the church against state authority. Catholic authority needed the sanction of Catholic democracy, and would enjoy this sanction when the clergy fought with honest intransigence for the Catholic cause.

The church therefore needed democracy: but democracy needed the church. Only the church had the power to stop democracy from running to French revolutionary excess; and only the church could sustain a fight for the democratic cause against a tyrant like the king of Prussia. God, Lucas concluded, in the person of his author, 'had bound up the liberal cause with that of the church, had given them the same adversaries and the same interests, so that one could not triumph without serving the other ...'[17]

What Lucas disliked in Prussia was what he disliked in England: the idea of a church as a creature and servant of the state in which the highest authority is state authority; in which the state corrupts the church by appointing careerist priests and bishops and by claiming the right to define religious truth. Indeed to Lucas as to other Liberal Catholics like Lamennais, the infallibility of the Pope, the independence of the Pope, was the very *magna carta* of the freedom of the church against all attempts by the state to control her. Take away the Pope, and the church becomes enslaved to the state, as in the Gallican Church before the Revolution, in Protestant Prussia and Orthodox Russia and Anglican England. The danger for Catholics lay in the church's entanglement with the pre-revolutionary order of wealth and privilege, in the machinations of those aristocratic, worldly and time-serving clergy like the aristocratic cathedral chapter of Cologne or the renegade Archbishop von Spiegel, 'one of those men, such as, from the time of him who delivered Christ into the hands of the princes and Pharisees, have always been found ready to betray the church'.[18]

To Lucas, the Catholic ecclesiastical Judas was ever to hand: as in Prussia, to obey the state and to conduct mixed marriages. Lucas drew the moral from his book, for Ireland: the work, he said, in his Preface, was:

> a true, living, and comprehensive picture of the mode in which that constant problem of worldly governors – 'How to enslave a church' – is worked out, after the most approved fashion of modern plausibility and deceit. It is also a true picture of the detestable baseness with which even Children of the Sanctuary, anointed Priests of God, at times are found to earn for themselves everlasting infamy by playing the part of Judas to those modern Pilates, who are as ready as ever to scourge Christ, and deliver him to be crucified, while, in a tone between mockery and curiosity, they ask the question – 'What is truth?' Not less do these pages set forth a third lesson teaching us how, amidst the general cowardice of a whole race and nation, the dauntless resolution of one old archbishop may rescue affairs from ruin, breathe life and vigour into a down-trodden church,

and make the standard of St Peter float once more proudly and gaily over the crumbling and smoking ruins of overthrown conventicles.[19]

One aspect, then, of Lucas' populist Liberal Catholic Ultramontanism was an open eye for the likely *trahison des clercs*, to use the later phrase, of Catholic clerics ready to deliver their Lord for scourging to the English Pilate.

Such, essentially, was to be his view of Wiseman in England; in some degree, of Murray in Dublin; but supremely, of Archbishop Cullen. Cullen turned out to be no Droste-Vischering; he therefore had to be von Spiegel.

A religious politics so conceived takes on a dimension of otherworldliness, and for Lucas implied by the mid 1840s a near total estrangement from the 'worldly' and 'unCatholic' spirit of the English politics of party. When it came to English Whigs and Tories, he found it difficult to decide the measure of iniquity between them. In milder mood, in the first *Tablet* in 1840, in his 'brief confession of political faith',[20] he retained a mild preference for the Whigs, who had supported the Catholic claims, but he saw no essential difference in English domestic affairs between Whigs and Tories, both being committed to a mixed aristocratic and democratic constitution, and to the ascendency of Anglicans over Catholics. Lucas was to develop a Tory temperament like Dr Johnson's: 'if you want the Whigs to do you right – for Heaven's sake kick them!'[21] he was to declare, and he had a truly Tory Christian contempt for those Whigs who lacked even the merit of professing a false religion. The Tories, however, were spokesmen for Protestant Orange bigotry and the established Church of England and Ireland; indeed many Tories, Lucas said, were hardly sane. It was, therefore, difficult to decide the relative merits of Tory hatred of Catholicism and Whig contempt for it, and Lucas' increasing Catholic detachment from the passions of English party politics meant an easy transition to the view that all English governments were untrustworthy for Catholics and all were oppressors and coercers of Ireland. Even at the beginning of his journalistic career, Lucas declared that of Ireland, 'it is difficult to speak with moderation … We are no Repealers; but we look upon the cry for Repeal to be the most natural for the inhabitants of a country which has been governed with such fatal disregard of all the plainest rules of justice and prudence'.[22] Lucas incurred O'Connell's displeasure by arguing against Repeal on the ground that even if the union was bad for Ireland, it was good for Catholicism: indeed the *Irish* Catholics had won Catholic Emancipation for the English Catholics through the Union, and, he concluded, '*The Irish Catholics owe the English Catholics no Political Gratitude Whatever* ... The debt is all the other way ... The English peer is debtor to the Irish peasant ...' The implication was that peasants were to be preferred to peers, as in the eyes of the God who had made more of them.

Lucas' English Catholic preference of peasants over peers was not obvious to O'Connell in 1841, as the Liberator exploded[23] over the English Catholic prejudice apparent in *The Tablet*'s advertisement for a Catholic cook, specifying that 'An Irish person will not suit': (it transpired that the would-be employer was Irish). Nor should too much be read into Lucas' denunciation of the Catholic squire Sir John Gerard in Lancashire for influencing his tenants to vote for a Tory Protestant against another English Catholic gentleman, Charles Towneley, a Liberal.[24] Most English Catholics, even aristocrats, were formally Whigs, and Lucas saw Gerard's activity against the backdrop of Lord Stanley's Irish voters' registration bill which good Whigs thought likely to increase Tory landlord power in Irish elections. The peer to crystalize most of Lucas' attitudes was John Talbot, Earl of Shrewsbury and Waterford, an Irish landowner and sometime Whig supporter of O'Connell over Catholic Emancipation, now tending to the Tories and author in 1841–42 of three published Letters to Ambrose Lisle Phillipps.[25] The first letter was devoted to a description of those interesting young mystical females who enjoyed the *stigmata*, the 'Estatica' of Caldaro and the Addolorata of Capriana, for whom the noble Earl had braved the Alpine passes to meet in person; but his second and third letters to Phillipps, while deploring the excesses of evicting Irish landlords, also defended the sacred rights of property and denounced Repeal as tending to Chartism and democracy, and considered the Repealer clergy as a 'political priesthood ... far removed from the meek and peaceful spirit of Christianity'.[26] Shrewsbury had influence in Rome through the marriage of his two daughters to members of the black papal aristocracy, and he took the conventional Latin Catholic counter-revolutionary line: 'Has the revolutionary party', he asked, 'in any country ever yet been the religious one? In France, Spain, Portugal? Were they not quite the reverse?'[27] Shrewsbury in his own eyes was leader of the English Catholic laity as a munificent patron of the genius-enthusiast Augustus Pugin's Gothic church-building programmes,[28] and he was associated with his correspondent Ambrose Phillipps, later called Phillipps de Lisle, a Leicestershire squire converted to Catholicism by the revelation that Antichrist was Mahomet and not the Pope, in a crusade to convert England by converting its ruling élites to a neo-mediaeval Gothic Christianity.[29] Like their ecclesiastical patron Bishop Nicholas Wiseman, Coadjutor to the Vicar Apostolic of the central District, and later Cullen's English equivalent as an Ultramontanizer of the Catholic Church in England, the English Gothic Catholics took a wholly sympathetic and highly ecumenical view of the English Tractarians as men leavening the Church of England with the principles of Catholicity. These High Churchmen were from Lucas' anti-ecumenical standpoint some of the most Hibernophope High Tory members of the Anglican Church, and while he had read some Anglican divines – he had a particular affection for Bishops Butler and Berkeley – neither the Dissenting background which he had admittedly outgrown nor his aversion to state-supported church establishments gave him any affection for the Church of England.[30] The Tractarians' approaches to Catholic doctrine were no doubt welcome, but they could do no real good except by submitting to the Church of Rome. Wiseman was of Irish descent, though born in Spain and educated for the priesthood in England, and was co-founder with O'Connell and the London Irish barrister and journalist Michael Joseph Quin of the London-based *Dublin Review*. But Wiseman, like Shrewsbury, found O'Connell's Repeal campaign a large embarrassment in the task of winning friends among the Tractarians and making them Roman Catholics. To Lucas, such hopes were largely moonshine. He agreed with O'Connell's attack on Shrewsbury especially as a 'pious fool' dangerous to religion[31] and in Lucas, the English Catholic convert-makers found their major *English* embarrassment, as *The Tablet* ploughed a furrow hostile to English peers, unsympathetic to Tractarians and increasingly sympathetic to Ireland.

This complicated conflict enlivened one of the more interesting episodes in early Victorian journalism. In February 1841, Lucas' Bermondsey Catholic leather-seller proprietors, the Keasleys, went bankrupt, and the paper was bought by Lucas' Tory Protestant printer, Cox. Cox objected to Lucas' anti-Tory politics and his total independence of proprietorial influence, and with his solicitor Innis, Cox made a private raid via a ladder, at 2 a.m., on the newspaper's offices to seize its books and papers.[32] In an editorial reversal of Wapping, Lucas repelled a further assault from Cox's printing employees with a guard of Irish labourers; and Cox employed Michael Joseph Quin of the *Dublin Review* to edit his own *Tablet* newspaper, to which Lucas published his *True Tablet* as rival. Wiseman began by offering his patronage to both papers, but privately he deplored to Shrewsbury Lucas' 'wild democratic principles'[33] and wrote a public letter to the *True Tablet* withdrawing all connexion with the newspaper in protest against Lucas' attacks on the Irish politics of the noble Earl,[34] who, Lucas insisted, was using every opportunity to blacken the *True Tablet* among English Catholics in Rome.[35] Quin in *The Tablet* described Lucas as 'incompetent, dishonest, treacherous, mendacious, and blasphemous'.[36] 'No paper', declared Lucas, 'of which Mr Cox is proprietor, Mr Quin the editor and Mr Innis the attorney can possibly succeed ... I stamp them beneath my heel as we crush cockroaches ...'[37] The outcome was decided by O'Connell, who had fallen out with the *Dublin Review* and Quin over a paragraph published in the *Review* regretting the vehemence of the Liberator's attack on Shrewsbury, and O'Connell's letter of support for Lucas against Quin won the *True Tablet* an instant five hundred subscribers. Cox's sole interest in Catholic journalism was financial, and when *The Tablet* and its sequel *The Catholic* were failures, he withdrew, to Wiseman's regret, leaving the field free to Lucas.

Lucas' alliance with O'Connell was sealed by the Englishman's conversion to Repeal early in 1843, after a first-hand inspection of Irish peasant misery;[38] and the relations between O'Connell and Lucas were further strengthened in 1843 when the *Dublin Review* and Wiseman became embroiled in a public row with O'Connell over whether O'Connell had, as he claimed, given Quin £1100 in the early days of the *Review*, the *Times* supporting the *Review* and *The Tablet* O'Connell.[39] After O'Connell's reconciliation with Wiseman, the *Dublin Review* kept a straight bat to Irish issues, even turning down a contribution from Shrewsbury. *The Tablet* had no such inhibitions, and established an alliance with Irish nationalism which lasted until the end of Lucas' brief life, with a blithe contempt for the inactive English Catholic lay politicians, whom Lucas on one occasion threatened *en bloc* with hell fire.[40]

This certainly impressed O'Connell: 'Lucas is the best Englishman, the best in his sentiments and views towards Ireland I ever knew', he declared[41] and Lucas' criticism extended to the English Catholic failure to press for Irish interests in England: as in the Earl of Arundel and Surrey's suppliant approval in the Lords in 1843 for Sir James Graham's education bill, essentially for providing an Anglican-controlled education for children working in factories.[42] Here militant Catholic and radical attitudes neatly coincided: confirming Wiseman's anxieties over *The Tablet's* tone, its enthusiasm for Ireland and its harangues against Tractarians and Catholic noblemen. Wiseman with his senior bishop, Walsh, in the Midlands, and Dr Sharples, the Coadjutor in Lancashire, tried in 1843 to get their fellow-bishops to warn their congregations against the newspaper. The outcome was a sharp rebuke to Lucas from Bishop Thomas Griffiths in London, deploring *The Tablet's* attacks on eminent ecclesiastics and its mixing of religion and politics.[43]

There was a sense in which Lucas accepted the distinction: the authoritative church had the sole power to define dogma, and with that, the laity had no right to interfere. But to Lucas, it was in the nature of Catholicism to refuse to distinguish the things of earth from those of heaven;[44] and education, or indeed any issue before parliament, was a matter of legitimate lay concern, especially where the Bishops were themselves divided, as over

Irish education, in which Lucas sympathized with Archbishop John MacHale of Tuam in his ferocious opposition to the Irish National Schools. To Lucas, MacHale was the Irish Athanasius or Archbishop Droste-Vischering, and Lucas' first major foray into Irish politics came with the Charitable Bequests Act of 1844, a bill supported by English Catholic peers like Arundel, Beaumont and Camoys,[45] while the Irish episcopate divided over whether to accept a commission to administer bequests which was half-Catholic and half-Protestant. The episcopal minority in favour, led by Archbishop Daniel Murray of Dublin, was denounced by Lucas with unmeasured severity as he extolled the majority and MacHale. 'The minority of the bishops', Lucas thundered, 'have set a terrible precedent. They have adopted a frightful resolution of allying themselves with the Castle against a majority of their own brethren ... They have taught the laity ... to despise the authority of the episcopacy; they have taught the government to despise and vanquish it. The secret of the weakness of the Church in Ireland is now revealed and patent. It can no longer be esteemed a bulwark against authority. It is no longer in any sense of the word a Church ... There is no longer a Church of Ireland ...'[46] When three Irish bishops, one of them Dr Murray, and two Catholic laymen, joined the Commission, Lucas predicted that they would soon be replaced by 'five Catholic Judases'.[47] In this, he insisted, he was not interfering in religious matters; rather, he was upholding the authority of the church and of the majority of bishops against an episcopal minority who in refusing to defy the English state, were betraying their own priests and people.

The Irish hierarchy divided yet again in 1845, when Murray and an episcopal minority expressed themselves willing, with a long list of proper safeguards, to accept the so-called 'Godless' Queen's Colleges as proper places for a Catholic's education. Here, as in the matter of the Charitable Bequests Act, Lucas' instincts were all on the side of MacHale as an opponent of any system of education other than a fully Catholic one for Catholics.[48] Indeed, he went further than MacHale, in deploring the English grant to the Irish seminary of Maynooth: a grant not, of course, involving mixed education, but in his own eyes, compromising the purity of Catholicism.[49] In short, Lucas regarded the Murray school of Catholics as lacking in the spirit of a true Catholicism, and as in Prussia, so in Ireland, and among the Irish in England: Lucas perceived an essential division *within* Catholicism, between on the one hand, the great mass of Catholics, priest and laymen; on the other, a Quisling Catholic minority prepared to sacrifice Catholic rights to the English Protestant state, a minority which included the more 'worldly' or timid or conservative Catholics and a number of Irish Catholic bishops. Lucas, therefore, had consistent sets of Catholic allies and enemies: his allies were a vigorous Catholic authority like MacHale's united to a Catholic democracy; his enemies were those well-to-do and privileged Catholics, especially peers and prelates, ever ready to compromise Catholic interests and betray the rights of Ireland. One aspect of the problem was simply the influence of certain English Catholic aristocrats, which Lucas tried to shake in June 1847 by establishing the Westminster Association of St Thomas of Canterbury as a rival to the aristocracy-dominated Catholic Institute, which was to be a thorn in the side of Bishop Wiseman, now Vicar Apostolic in London. It has perhaps been insufficiently appreciated by Irish historians that Cullen had caught a tartar, that Lucas was a man made to tangle with authority, a militant MacHaleite hostile to Murray, a hater of English Whigs and Tories, a bishop-baiter already well-blooded with the gore of Bishop Wiseman. The sword raised against Cullen was forged through a long series of battles in the 1840s, and its owner always knew his side.

It will be evident that Lucas' so-called 'Liberal Catholicism' did not involve any liberality to Protestantism, though he was always kind to well-affected Protestants. Nor did his 'Liberal Catholicism' have any affinity with economic liberalism, with the principles of political economy and *laissez-faire*.[50] Lucas seems to have outgrown this aspect of his Quakerism early, under the influence of his London friend Thomas Carlyle, who like William Cobbett, had a romantic view of the corporate collective character of mediaeval Catholic society, in which they believed that poverty and not property had been regarded as holy and there had been abundant monastic charity for the poor; in which usury and exploitation were regarded as sin, and economic self-interest was regulated and confined by the church's teaching on a just price for goods and a just wage for labour. In short, Lucas had imbibed and propagated the contemporary propaganda, much of it by non-Catholics, which denounced the evils of industrialism by depicting a past Catholic polity as a just social order curbing mercantile greed by the moral law. Lucas' friendship with Carlyle did not last as long as his relations with Carlyle's exact ideological obverse, John Stuart Mill; but Carlyle's influence was the more profound one. No more than Carlyle did Lucas want to destroy inequality. 'On the contrary, he regarded the social hierarchy as part of an order established by Divine Providence.'[51] Rather, his vision was of a conservative inegalitarian social order, a kind of passionate paternalist anti-industrialism in a Catholic rural Eden before the Fall. This had its Protestant equivalent among those Tory Evangelicals like Shaftesbury concerned to regulate the working hours of women and children by enlightened legislation from above. But Catholic paternalism was given a cutting edge by Ireland, and the great failure for Lucas of the principles of *laissez-faire* was the Irish Famine. He was especially bitter about the discontinuance of Peel's relief measures by the subsequent Whig administration of Lord John Russell, and of Russell's policies, Lucas declared that 'the mode of thought inspired by our economic literature is so inhuman in its nature, that the mind which adopts its logic becomes tainted, and hardened, and defiled beyond the possibility of cure'.[52]

Lucas' conservative economic antiliberalism was in no sense quietist, indeed it was a call to political action, and a sanction for denouncing the sins of the rich for failing in their duty to the poor, while predicting the revolutionary consequences of this failure. This was not intended to exhort the poor to revolution or to encourage them to seize the property of others; rather, it indicated that the poor would rise in rebellion against the rich unless relieved by a loving Catholic charity. Lucas was one of the founders in 1844 of the Society of St Vincent de Paul to promote the duty of almsgiving to the poor, especially the immigrant Irish poor;[53] though he declined the presidency of the Society which passed to an English Catholic gentleman. Similarly religious and paternalist in inspiration were his crusades to secure the appointment of Catholic chaplains and the introduction of Catholic services into English prisons and workhouses, the army and navy. But Lucas did not hesitate to invoke the severest sanctions of the gospel against the rich, that those who failed to relieve the poor would go to hell. This is the message of his most famous 'Ethiopian sermon' of 1846 on the Irish Famine: 'Under the penalty of hell! Think well of it!'[54] 'In how many hundred or thousand Irish cabins, more squalid than the beast-stall in Jewry, is Christ now perishing for want!' With high sarcasm, Lucas lashed the failure of English Catholics to give on any sort of scale commensurate with the magnitude of the disaster, and declared that in 'this tremendous and sweeping affliction, the Quakers – the Society of Friends – ... They – and we almost say they only – have behaved like Christians ... have exerted themselves ... to relieve the wants of the destitute in proportion to their means.'[55] Lucas concluded later that:

> The English people of the middle and upper classes are Pharisees to the very marrow of their bones. With full bellies, roofs wind-and water-tight, warm hearths, soft beds, and a balance at the banker's, enough (as they think) to ensure (sic) them against Providence itself, they sit arrogantly on the crimes of starving, naked, heart-broken, men. Even their very alms-deeds are too often blasted by pride. This people, among whom it has passed into a proverb that poverty is a crime, and which, without discrimination of circumstance, or temptation, is pitiless as only Pharisees can be; this people, which in the midst of its riches has forgotten God, and in His place has reared up a ghastly idol, in which, as in an enchanted mirror, it beholds and worships a golden image of itself; this comfortable, purse-proud, luxurious, money-making nation, as a matter of course, has decided against the poor; pronounced the Irish savages; their crimes without excuse; their religion a Thuggery; their priests instigators to murder.[56]

This last complaint came not just from Protestant Pharisees but from those English Catholic peers with whom Lucas had crossed swords already, the Earls of Arundel and Shrewsbury. In a public letter to Archbishop MacHale in 1847, the Earl of Arundel echoed the Protestant charge that Irish priests had incited their flocks from the altars to murder evicting landlords.[57] The accusation was rebutted by MacHale in public letters to Arundel and Lord John Russell,[58] and repeated, in the case of the murder of Major Mahon in County Roscommon, in further public letters from Shrewsbury to the Bishop of Elphin and to MacHale.[59] MacHale's reply to Shrewsbury occupied eight columns of *The Tablet*, and described the Earl's letter, in virulent clericalese as 'among the most extravagates of the extravagantes of lay pretension' by Catholic peers who 'were lending themselves ... to the foul conspiracy against the lives of the Catholic people and the character of the Catholic Hierarchy'. The Earl himself reminded the Archbishop 'of the sincerity of Herod's homage to our divine Redeemer, who sought for an opportunity to destroy his victim', and was charged with insulting the majesty of Rome, with calumniating the entire Catholic Church in Ireland and with grieving and scandalizing the whole Christian world.[60] This might seem odd language in which to extol the meek and peace-loving character of the Irish clergy, but like the Archbishop, Lucas stressed the counter-revolutionary role of the Irish Church in preventing a wholly explicable violence. Lucas' own view was that it was the landlords who were guilty of murder by their evictions. All of this was to help confirm Shrewsbury's view of *The Tablet* to Wiseman, that the paper was 'the great scandal of our Religion, the disturber of our Peace, & the opprobrium of our Age'.[61]

The view was Wiseman's already. The Bishop had promised closer episcopal control of *The Tablet* to Shrewsbury,[62] who through his Roman relations put pressure on Wiseman to disclaim any responsibility for Lucas' opinions. Wiseman's letter of reassurance to the Cardinal Secretary of State promptly found its way into an Italian newspaper: an act which Lucas treated as a declaration of war.[63] 'I am really glad', wrote Shrewsbury to Wiseman, 'that Lucas has attacked you, because I trust it will finish him up.'[64] But it proved impossible for Wiseman to get the

English bishops to act. As a layman, Shrewsbury was obnoxious to the most impressive in the hierarchy, Ullathorne, for his attacks on MacHale, and Phillipps' question to Ullathorne later in the year – 'Are we to be governed by the bishops or ... by a hired writer who scribbles his anathemas without judgment and without charity'[65] – was equally open to the objection that Phillipps himself was writing as a layman, with his own history of difficult relations with the clergy.

Shrewsbury's complaint to Wiseman was two-fold, that Lucas was 'out & out Irish, & puts it forth that all who do not go *his* lengths are Anti-*Irish*', and that Lucas was a '*communist*' for arguing 'that the people of Ireland should live on the *soil* of Ireland' with a right to its benefits. 'This', he darkly added, 'is *their* notion of tenant right – of *fixity of tenure*'.[66] Wiseman did not regard the Irish tenantry as likely Communists: that danger was greater, he thought, in the towns of England. But Lucas was also in dispute with Wiseman in 1848, over the bishop's support for a government bill to establish diplomatic relations between Great Britain and Rome. The Irish hierarchy took fright at the measure as a backstairs means of increasing British influence on the Church in Ireland, and it was also opposed by the English bishops Briggs and Ullathorne, with the vociferous support of Lucas and the Association of St Thomas. The Catholic supporters of the principle of the Bill included Arundel and Shrewsbury, who were loudly hissed at the Association's meeting in London to protest against it: drawing from Wiseman an indignant pamphlet expressing a special horror that an English Catholic assembly should have received the hallowed names of Howard and Talbot 'with "hisses", "groans", or derisive "laughter"'.

Briggs and MacHale carried their hostility to the proposal in person to Rome, and though the Bill received the royal assent, political developments in England and Rome rendered it a dead letter. The incident, however, enabled Lucas to point up Wiseman's isolation from the Irish hierarchy and from some of his own episcopal colleagues, but Wiseman dissuaded Shrewsbury from placarding the churches with his protests when in 1849, Lucas and his Irish ally Thomas Doyle, the Provost of Southwark and builder of St George's Cathedral, ridiculed

Shrewsbury's son-in-law, Prince Doria-Pamfili-Landi, who was Pius IX's minister for war, for fleeing to Gaeta after having allegedly urged the Pope to go into battle against Austria and to introduce constitutional government in Rome.[67] The affair only increased Wiseman's anxiety to establish a Catholic weekly rival to the disreputable *Tablet*, and though this failed for lack of funds, he supported the new weekly *Rambler*, established by converts from Anglicanism in January 1848, in the hope of setting it up as *The Tablet*'s rival. This prelatical partisanship was an embarrassment to the *Rambler*'s editor, John Moore Capes, who in any case removed the element of competition in turning the organ into a monthly in September.[68] Wiseman's hostility, however, was an element in Lucas' decision to remove himself and his newspaper to Dublin in 1849, and Wiseman pronounced its metropolitan epitaph: 'No time should be lost in determining, so as to stop the gap, the moment Lucas leaves the field, or some other violent man may take possession.'[69]

A 'violent man': there was some ground for the opinion in Lucas' public argument, that as British rule in Ireland had no proper legal basis, the Irish had a legal right to rise against it. Lucas thought it quite impractical to exercise the right – so that the clergy properly opposed it. This did not, however, make his language less inflammatory: 'Nothing short of bloodshed', he declared, 'can stir these selfish Whigs.'[70] The Young Irelanders he regarded as well-meaning idealists, driven to take up arms by the people's suffering; and he urged their acquittal, alleging the unfairness of the trials that convicted them.

> The truth is [he wrote in 1849], that under this precious Whig Government, of which so many English and Irish Catholics are members, every man who dislikes [it] holds his life on the tenure of the Attorney-General's employers not choosing to murder him. Writing, as I do, in Dublin, I am not committed to Newgate, and strangled after the lapse of a few days, simply because Mr Monahan does not think it prudent to have me strangled. If I did, if I were charged with shooting the man in the moon, he would find a sheriff to pack a jury, a judge to charge, jurors to convict, a hangman to adjust the noose, and

> Whig journalists to attest the honesty, impartiality and veracity of the court and the delicacy of the hangman.[71]

Lucas especially applauded the acquittal of the Young Irelander Charles Gavan Duffy, with whom he had already formed a close friendship, and it was with Duffy and Sir John Gray, the Protestant Nationalist editor of the *Freeman's Journal*, that Lucas formed in 1850 the Tenant League which made him for the first time a notable figure in Irish politics. The radicalism of its proposals should not be exaggerated, for all the landlord attacks on it for its Communist interference with private property: indeed Lucas' defence of Tenant Right brings out the essentially anti-capitalist conservatism of his political opinions, for he located the fount of all Irish ills in the commercial exploitation by a landlord class of tenants milked for rent on the tenants' own improvements to the land. It was, insisted Lucas, this exploitation which made the Irish peasant a radical, where peasantries elsewhere, as in France and Germany, were as they should be, the lawabiding upholders of authority and tradition. Lucas' ideal social order was rural, not urban; it was one governed as his friend Carlyle had put it, not by the cash *nexus* but by the *nexus* of personal relations, by landlords who were benevolent fathers to their tenants and were bound to them in the bonds of obedience from below and benevolence from above, in Christian charity and love. Nothing delighted Lucas more than the sight of a prosperous small-holding, of every man under his vine and fig-tree, of a cottage and farmyard full of healthy peasant children and abustle with honest yeoman labour. Nothing horrified him more than the post-Famine desolation of the Irish countryside, with mile on mile of derelict huts whose occupants had fled or died of hunger, often standing as witness to an evicting landlord. The Tenant League queried *laissez-faire* by urging state intervention to exempt the Irish peasant from paying rent on the value of his own improvements on the land: but the end in view was, if not full peasant proprietorship, at least the kind of security and reward for honest labour which made men less revolutionary and not more so. The result would be one that the most ardent reactionary like the Orange Lord Roden could wish: 'we are endeavouring', wrote Lucas, 'to plant in every acre of Ireland a conservative spirit, and root out from every part of the land the principles of revolution by making every family in Ireland so satisfied with their position that they will have no motive or wish for change ...'[72] This was a radical means to a conservative end; and the landlords who denounced Tenant Right as Communism, would see a true Communism arise when the landless peasant had been driven to the slums of England and left only the Communist hope of change by violent revolution.

Lucas' Tenant League following corresponded not so much with his outcast favourites, the poor of Christ, as his sociological ideal of a yeomen-farmer class, for the League was strong, not among the subsistence potato farmers and labourers devastated by the Famine, especially in the West, but by the more prosperous and market-oriented wheat and barley growers hit in 1849–50 by falling yields and falling prices.[73] Indeed at first they were joined by the Presbyterian tenants of the North, but this 'League of North and South' was destroyed after 1850 by a virulent outbreak of Protestant No Popery, and by a corresponding new militancy in Irish Catholicism.

It was here, however, that Lucas' tragedy began, in the return to Ireland in 1850 of the former Rector of the Irish College in Rome, Paul Cullen, from 1849 Archbishop of Armagh and from 1852 Archbishop of Dublin. Cullen looked like Lucas' kind of Catholic prelate, an Ultramontane with great influence in Rome determined to make papal authority effective in Ireland and to Romanize the doctrine, devotion and discipline of the Irish Church; a firm opponent both of mixed education and of formal diplomatic relations between Rome and Ireland; a bishop wholly indifferent to Protestant opinion and like MacHale quite content to earn the unmitigated loathing of English Whigs and Tories. Cullen quickly decided that 'Lucas is the only man that knows how to write a line in our defence',[74] and their relationship was seemingly strengthened, when Lord John Russell showed the Whigs in what Lucas always regarded as their true No Popery colours by denouncing the restoration of the English Catholic hierarchy in 1850.[75] The government proposed and passed an Ecclesiastical Titles Act in 1851 denying Catholic bishops the right to use the titles of their dioceses, and Cullen in reaction founded a Catholic Defence Association which had the support of the Irish MPs known from their defence of Catholic interests as the 'Irish Brigade' or 'the Pope's Brass Band'. The Brigade's union with the Tenant League in 1851 seemed to promise the fusion of Irish grievances with Catholic ones; and it was into their crusade that Lucas now put his heart and soul.

In fact, the union was tenuous from the first. The Presbyterian supporters of the League had no interest in Catholic grievances, the wealthier Catholics none in tenant right. Lucas was made suspicious of the Association by its unwillingness to make him an officeholder and by its appointment as its Secretary of Henry Wilberforce, an English Catholic convert clergyman; and the parliamentary committee of the Association actually put up a rival candidate before, under the auspices of the League, Lucas was elected MP for County Meath in 1852.[76] He was, however, to be happy in his constituency. Bishop Cantwell of Meath and his clergy had been overwhelmingly pro-Repeal from 1841, and were unusually strongly committed to political agitation on behalf of agrarian reform throughout the 1850s and 1860s. Lucas noted with approval the large number of prosperous middling-sized farms in his constituency, and the flood of vocations which they produced to swell the numbers of the clergy, in a partial realization of that kind of Catholic peasant republic which was nearest to Lucas' own heart.

The Tenant League, however, turned out to be a false dawn for a new national movement, and during the following quarter of a century, Irish elections were to be decided as much by local issues as by national ones. At a national level, the unity of the Independent Opposition was broken in 1853 after two of its leading members, John Sadleir and William Keogh, the 'Corruptionists' as Lucas called them, joined late in 1852 Lord Aberdeen's administration. Keogh was an emotional and unstable lawyer of such iron-bound alcoholic capacities that one English electoral competitor who opposed him in a drinking contest had to be shipped home in a violent fit of *delirium tremens*.[77] Sadleir, however, was the greater villain of the two, being succinctly described in the *Dictionary of National Biography* as an 'Irish politician and swindler'. He committed suicide in 1856, when it was discovered that he had embezzled two hundred thousand pounds from small investors in his bank in Tipperary. Sadleir and Keogh might seem a world away from Shrewsbury; but both men typified for Lucas, even before their apostasy, the kind of worldly treachery in the hope of place and office which he had never ceased denouncing among Catholics in England.

Cullen had called down the special blessing of Mary Immaculate on Keogh, and now disgraced himself in Lucas' eyes by failing to condemn the lawyer's treason to the cause. The elements in what followed, Lucas' great public feud with Cullen, are complicated, and it is only one of the ironies about it that an Englishman should have made so powerful a contribution to the Irish nationalist anti-Cullenite black legend. Lucas opposed revolution in Ireland, but had shown every sympathy for Irish revolutionaries. Everyone knows, of course, that Cullen's counter-revolutionary attitudes had been formed by first-hand experience of the Roman revolution of 1848, and he was especially suspicious of the affinities between Mazzini's Young Italy and Young Ireland. Cullen's *bête noire* was Lucas' Young Irelander friend Charles Gavan Duffy, whom Lucas claimed to have restored to a devout Catholicism, and who was to describe Lucas as 'the man of subtlest intellect save one, and of the most practical ability without any exception, among the English converts to Catholicity'.[78] 'Lucas says Duffy is a saint,' Cullen noted sourly. 'He may be so far as I know, but ... When I hear of the sanctity of some of these gentlemen I always recollect ... the Romans in 1848.'[79] I have already said that Lucas agreed with Cullen on the ultimately counter-revolutionary character of Catholicism, and the Archbishop did not object to priestly involvement in politics to defend Catholic morals and religion. Cullen can be easily caricatured as a cold and cautious ecclesiastic, suspicious and reserved, 'Paul the prudent', who had no politics except church politics, and who placed the interests of Catholicism before Ireland. It would be truer to say that his vision of a holy Catholic Ireland of yeomen farmers and the poor can hardly be distinguished from that of Lucas, and that like Lucas, he was an O'Connellite nationalist, committed to a peaceful constitutionalism which was bound to conflict with the revolutionary nationalism of Young Ireland. I think it wrong to say with Emmet Larkin that 'Cullen's politics were religious and Catholic in scope; Lucas' were less sectarian and more national.'[80] Lucas' politics were just as Catholic as Cullen's, even if he identified more closely Irish national interests and Catholic ones. Then there is that loaded word 'sectarian'. *Neither* was a sectarian in the sense that both were willing to work with Protestants of goodwill; *both* were sectarian, if one means by this the attitude that there is nothing more important on earth than the Catholic religion. Cullen did differ from Lucas on a number of points of greater detail. First, he thought that the Young Irelanders, and Duffy especially, were not good Catholics; in that, he was very largely wrong. Second, Cullen's political methods were subtle if not always successful, and when it came to method, he was a pragmatic opportunist, and not, like Lucas, a conviction politician. Indeed Cullen's own political involvements were probably more considerable than MacHale's, and while he discontinued Murray's attendance at levées at Dublin Castle, he was inching back to an alignment with the Whigs and Peelite Tories: endeavouring as early as 1853 to extract concessions from the Aberdeen administration on the education of Catholic soldiers' children, and failing to persuade Lucas that this was proper policy. In brief, he was flexible where Lucas was rigid; or, it might be said, he was unscrupulous where Lucas was principled. Third, while Cullen was by no means indifferent to the conditions of the tenantry, he regarded the Tenant League's proposals not as religious dogma but as a secular programme on which good Catholics might legitimately disagree. And fourth, he thought that Lucas' work of keeping the parish priesthood in a ferment in support of Tenant Right undesirable and only likely to cause landlord retaliation, and he wanted to curb the more colourful excesses of priestly activity in urging or intimidating their flocks on how to vote in elections.

Cullen's national synodical regulations of 1854 to the clergy not to make political denunciations or to hold political meetings in chapels were in line with earlier such directives agreed both in Dublin and in Rome. They were, of course, ignored by bishops like MacHale and Cantwell, though echoed by some like the bishop Walsh of Ossory who muzzled the Tenant League's original Callan curate-founders. Such episcopal discouragement hastened the League's decline, which was more directly a consequence of the lightening of the economic distress which had produced it. Lucas decided, however, to appeal against Cullen's instructions to Rome, where the dispute became embroiled with Archbishop MacHale's running battle over the control of the Irish seminaries. Lucas arrived in the city in 1854 just in time for the papal definition of the Immaculate Conception, an experience varied with a tour of Naples in the company of John Stuart Mill. He was received by the Pope in two lengthy private audiences, and at the Pope's request prepared a massive 'Statement' denouncing Cullen's reign of terror against Tenant League priests in Ireland. Cullen's influence, however, was supreme in Propaganda, and Lucas, already ill with heart-disease, returned to England to die. He was only forty-three.

Lucas' 'Statement', which occupies much of the second volume of his *Life*,[81] is a detailed defence of the Callan curates against the Bishop of Ossory and a detailed denunciation of Cullen's policies and political involvements, especially his collaboration with English Whigs and Liberals, and of his refusal to accompany Lucas on his Catholic crusade for Tenant Right. The paradox of Lucas' position was that it was the layman who was seemingly the clerical, who wanted more priestly involvement in politics, not less, and who exhorted the priesthood to give a particular political party and programme the awesome sanctions of religion. 'The politics of the Irish priests', wrote Lucas, 'are to protect the lives, the faith, and the dearest interests of the Catholic poor:'[82] there was no essential distinction between Catholic lives and Catholic faith, as Cullen seemed to claim, and what Cullen appeared to define as a secular issue, Tenant Right, was to Lucas a religious one. The clergy, Lucas argued, were right to use 'that political influence which, being devoted to the interests of religion and the poor, increases the love of the people for the priest, and makes more indissoluble the bond which unites them to religion'.[83] To withdraw priests from politics even as far as Cullen wished to take them was, Lucas thought, to weaken the popular attachment to Catholicism, to make Irish politics secular politics, to abandon the government of Ireland to the English and to leave Irish Catholics a prey to worldly politicians like Sadleir and Keogh or to the very anticlerical revolutionaries whom Cullen claimed most to fear. For all his Ultramontane opinions, it was Cullen who seems to stand nearer the modern secular liberal in making clear if subtle distinctions between the sacred and the profane, where Lucas the layman stood for the traditional theocratic position that the religious imperative should govern the whole of life. Indeed, the ultimate logic of Cullen's position was to confine the priesthood as a sacred caste to the sanctuary and, increasingly, to consign politics to a new breed of Irish lay politicians, both of them developments which were to follow. In this, Lucas might seem crude, where Cullen was supple: that Lucas was the backward-looking reactionary who wanted martyr-priests and bishops whose authority was a defiance of state authority and whose very authoritarian power was converted by their defiance into a statement of the popular will. Lucas wanted an authoritarian church to uphold a Catholic democracy, and people's priests to direct the people. This is like liberation theology in its definition of all politics as religious politics; it is unlike liberation theology in wishing to preserve a church authority internally untainted in its hierarchical structures and dogmatic teaching by the external political democracy which it upholds. Perhaps, however, the greatest irony for Lucas was that Cullen, the prelate who most clearly stood for Ultramontanism in Ireland, turned out to be such a political disappointment, by refusing what might have made him spiritually great, the role which Lucas so wanted him to play, of tribune for his church and people.

Notes

A version of this paper was read at the Irish Historians in Britain Conference in the University of Liverpool, and to the Church History Seminar in King's College, London.

Abbreviations:	*T*	= *The Tablet*
	UC, WP	= Ushaw College (Co. Durham), Wiseman Papers

The opening quotation from James Jones' letter to Wiseman is taken from UC, WP, 515; cited by Susan Acheson, *Catholic Journalism in Victorian Catholic Society, 1830–1870, with special reference to the 'Tablet'*, M. Litt., University of Oxford 1981, p.159.

1. James O'Shea, *Priests, Politics and Society in Post-famine Ireland: A Study of County Tipperary, 1850–1891*, Wolfhound Press, Dublin 1983, p.365.
2. The principal biography is that of Edward Lucas, *The Life of Frederick Lucas, M.P.*, 2 vols, The Catholic Truth Society, for the author, London 1887. It tends to chronological vagueness, but it captures the spirit of the man.

   Of his other biographers, one, Christopher James Riethmüller (*Frederick Lucas: A Biography*, Bell and Daldy, London 1862), was an old University College friend whose attitudes to his Irish and Catholic activities were rather uncomprehendingly English and liberal Protestant. (See especially pp.102–8, on his Irish policy and pp.126–7, on his mistakes and failures, as the 'noble errors of an unselfish enthusiasm'.) On the other hand Riethmüller, who wrote within only seven years of Lucas' death, is a valuable guide to his attitudes, the more sharply focussed because the author did not agree with them.

   The essay by John J. Horgan, 'Frederick Lucas, M.P., The Founder of the Tablet' in *Great Catholic Laymen*, Catholic Truth Society of Ireland, Dublin 1905, pp.203–246, is heavily dependent on Edward Lucas. There is, apparently, no Frederick Lucas correspondence in the Lucas family papers in the Hertfordshire County Record Office (letter of the County Archivist to the author, 17 March 1986). See also notes 4, 6.

   Among modern works, I would especially acknowledge my indebtedness to the thesis by Susan Acheson, for which see the reference to the opening quotation.
3. See Walter L. Arnstein, *Protestant versus Catholic in Mid-Victorian*

England: Mr Newdegate and the Nuns, University of Missouri Press, Columbia and London 1982. Professor Arnstein is, of course, an American.

4. 'Frederick Lucas', in Joseph Gillow (ed.), *A Literary and Biographical History, or Bibliographical Dictionary of the English Catholics ...*, 5 vols, Burns & Oates 1885–1902, vol.iv, p.340.
5. Elizabeth Isichei, *Victorian Quakers*, OUP 1970, pp.188–193: though Lucas' biographer remarks that 'On the question of Catholic Emancipation Lucas was, like the rest of the Society of Friends in England, on the side of the Catholics' (Edward Lucas, op. cit., vol.I, p.22).
6. See *Dictionary of National Biography*.
7. John Bossy, *The English Catholic Community 1570–1850*, Darton, Longman & Todd 1975, pp.392–396.
8. Leo Gooch, *The Durham Catholics and Industrial Development 1560–1850* M.A. thesis, University of York 1984.
9. Frederick Lucas, *Reasons for becoming a Roman Catholic; addressed to the Society of Friends*, Dolman, London 1839.
10. 'Lucas was not only a Roman Catholic, not only what is called an Ultramontane, not only an advocate for the extreme claims of the Papacy, but ... a Catholic of the twelfth century ... His imagination had appropriated to itself all that world of the Middle Ages ... Lucas dwelt habitually in such a supernatural atmosphere, and many wonders and extravagances, which most modern Catholics would be inclined to apologise for and explain away, were to him perfectly in order ... Once convinced of the infallibility and miraculous gifts of Rome, he ... appeared to take delight in the most questionable parts of her history ...' (Riethmüller, op. cit., pp.82–3).
11. On his admiration for Lamennais' great disciple the Comte de Montalembert, see Riethmüller, op. cit., p.84.

    There was, however, for Lucas, one abiding exception to this rule: that the need for the Papacy's independence overrode the claims of the Roman people. 'In comparison with the rights of the Church', he wrote, '... I think no more of the rights of the Romans than I think of the rights of a dozen of oysters when I am hungry ...' (Edward Lucas, op. cit. vol.I, p.328).
12. '... the Bourbons in France, just like the Whigs in Ireland, wishing to create a submission ... of once more governing France through Rome' (Edward Lucas, op. cit. vol.I, p.303).
13. On Lucas' hostility to Austria, see Edward Lucas, op. cit. vol.I, p.265.
14. See for example, his letter to Riethmüller on becoming an MP in 1852. 'I go into the House of Commons ... having cast upon me ... the defence of the two noblest causes in the world; that of a religion ... and ... the noblest population, that ever existed on the face of the

earth ...' (p. 107).

15. James Duffy, Dublin 1845.
16. On Lucas' hostility to mixed marriages in England, against their English Catholic defender, C. E. Jerningham, see Edward Lucas, op. cit. vol. I, p. 122.
17. *Tyranny of Prussia*, p. 196. Cf. Riethmüller, op. cit. pp. 83–4: 'Retrograde in religion, he was progressive in politics, and no man looked forward with more hope and confidence, to the spread of free institutions, and the establishment of popular rights.' Though neither 'a revolutionist, or even a democrat, in the common sense of the word', with an aristocratic affection for a liberty 'based on legal and historical foundations', 'he held it to be the true policy of the Church of Rome (subject always to the assertion of her religious supremacy) to ally herself with the reforming and popular party in every nation, and to take the lead in the general enfranchisement of Europe.'
18. Lucas, *Tyranny of Prussia*, p. 110.
19. Ibid., pp. viii-ix.
20. *T*, 16 May 1840.
21. Edward Lucas, op. cit. vol. I, p. 318.
22. Cited ibid., vol. I, p. 35.
23. *T*, 31 July 1841.
24. *T*, 26 June 1841.
25. *Letter ... to Ambrose Lisle Phillipps Esq. Descriptive of the Estatica* (sic) *of Caldaro* (Maria Morl) *and the Addolorata of Capriana* (Domenica Lazzari), London 1841. (A second edition of 1842 included visits to the 'Estatica' of Monte Sansavino (Domenica Barbagli), London 1842; *A Second Letter to A. L. Phillipps ... on the Present Posture of Affairs*, London 1841; *A Third Letter to A. L. Phillipps ... chiefly in reference to his former letter, 'On the present posture of affairs'* London 1842.
26. *Second Letter*, pp. 18–19.
27. *Second Letter*, p. 18.
28. Denis Gwynn, *Lord Shrewsbury, Pugin and the Catholic Revival*, Hollis & Carter 1946.
29. E. S. Purcell and Edwin de Lisle, *Life and Letters of Ambrose Phillipps de Lisle*, 2 vols, London 1900.
30. Riethmüller, op. cit. p. 147.
31. *True T*, 19 February 1842; Acheson, op. cit., p. 174.
32. I am following here the account in Bernard Ward, *The Sequel to Catholic Emancipation*, 2 vols, Longmans 1915, vol. II, pp. 40–1
33. Wiseman to Shrewsbury, Feast of St Stanislaus, 7 May 1842, UC, WP, 856; cited Acheson, op. cit., p. 175.
34. *True T*, 30 April 1842.

35. *True T*, 23 April 1842.
36. Ward, op. cit., p.42.
37. *True T*, 23 April 1842: cited Acheson, op. cit., p.175
38. Ward, op. cit., p.47.
39. Ambrose Macaulay, *Dr Russell of Maynooth*, Darton, Longman & Todd 1983, pp.175–178.
40. *T*, 4 November 1843.
41. W.H. O'Neill Daunt, *Personal Recollections of O'Connell*, vol.III, p.263; cited Horgan, art cit., p.203.
42. Edward Lucas, op. cit., vol.I, pp.114–122; Ward, op. cit., pp.50–53.
43. Griffiths to Lucas, November 1843; cited Ward, op. cit., pp.47–48.
44. Acheson, op. cit., p.170.
45. Edward Lucas, op. cit., vol.I, p.167.
46. *T*, 23 November 1844; cited Ward, op. cit., p.78.
47. Ibid., p.79.
48. Macaulay, op. cit., pp.100–101.
49. '... he not only offered to give up the grant, but urged the Catholics to reject it, and to take their stand altogether on the voluntary principle ...' (Riethmüller, op. cit., p.113.
50. 'I do not know', wrote his biographer-brother, 'which feeling prevailed most in Lucas' mind, hatred or contempt, for the politico-economical principles of the Manchester School. Both feelings with him were as strong as a man of his calibre could possibly entertain' (Edward Lucas, op. cit., vol.I, p.233). Cf. pp.390–391: 'He would, however, only instance the Factory Act, the Truck Act, Acts controlling pawnbrokers, markets, builders, cab and boat proprietors, shipowners, and even emigrants themselves, to prove that nothing could be further from the practice or intention of the Legislature than to leave the weak and defenceless to the tender mercies of "free competition".'
51. Edward Lucas, op. cit., vol.I, p.17.
52. Ibid., p.225.
53. A.G. Mahoney, *The Origins of the Society of Saint Vincent de Paul and its Establishment in England and Wales*, Thesis, St Mary's College, Strawberry Hill, Twickenham 1967.
54. Edward Lucas, op. cit., vol.I, p.239.
55. Ibid., pp.237–238, p.242.
56. Cited Edward Lucas, op. cit., vol.I, pp.292–293.
57. *T*, 25 December 1847; cited Ward, op. cit., p.136.
58. Ward, op. cit., pp.137–140.
59. *T*, 8 January 1848; Ward, op. cit., p.141.
60. *T*, 29 January 1848.
61. Shrewsbury to Wiseman, 25 March 1848, UC, WP, 549; cited Acheson, op. cit., p.177.

62. Wiseman to Shrewsbury, 17 November 1847, UC, WP, 909; cited Acheson, op.cit., p. 164.
63. Richard J. Schiefen, *Nicholas Wiseman and the Transformation of English Catholicism*, The Patmos Press, Shepherdstown 1984, p. 166.
64. Shrewsbury to Wiseman, 7 March 1848, UC, WP, 914; cited Schiefen, op. cit., p. 166.
65. Phillipps to Bishop Ullathorne, 1 December 1848, B. 1322 Birmingham Diocesan Archives; cited Acheson, op. cit., p. 181.
66. Shrewsbury to Wiseman, 16 March 1848, UC, WP, 916; cited Schiefen, op.cit., p. 167.
67. Schiefen, op. cit., pp. 169–171.
68. Josef L. Altholz, *The Liberal Catholic Movement in England: The 'Ramber' and its contributors 1848–1864* Burns & Oates 1960, pp. 12–13.
69. Wiseman to Shrewsbury (copy) November 1849, UC, WP, 954A; cited Schiefen, op. cit., p. 171. It should be added that Wiseman wrote Lucas an affectionate note as he lay dying (Riethmüller, op. cit., pp. 123–4).
70. Edward Lucas, op. cit., vol. I, p. 313.
71. Ibid., pp. 316–317.
72. Ibid., p. 398.
73. K. Theodore Hoppen, *Elections, Politics, and Society in Ireland 1832–1885*, Clarendon Press 1984, p. 480; Paul Bew, *Land and the National Question in Ireland, 1858–82*, Gill and Macmillan 1978, p. 34: 'The League was not a direct response to the famine. In the South it represented instead the short-term reaction of relatively prosperous grain farmers to a cyclical depression: when agricultural prices rose in 1853 there was a subsequent loss of tenant interest.'
74. Cullen to Bernard Smith, 17 January 1851; cited Desmond Bowen, *Paul Cardinal Cullen and the Shaping of Modern Irish Catholicism*, Gill and Macmillan 1983, p. 245.
75. Lucas told his friend Riethmüller that 'I prefer the hostility of the Whigs, and penal laws, to their friendship, which I believe to be radically and necessarily treacherous ... I would willingly – if I could afford it – have paid down 1,000 *1*. to purchase Lord John's letter with its consequences' (Riethmüller, op. cit., p. 102).
76. *T*, 12 June 1852; cited J.H. Whyte, *The Independent Irish Party 1850–9*, 1958, p. 36.
77. Hoppen, op. cit., p. 431. On the idiosyncrasy of his religion, see *Memories of Father Healy of Little Bray*, Macmillan 1904, pp. 111–139.
78. Sir Charles Gavan Duffy, *Young Ireland: A Fragment of Irish History, 1840–1850*, D. Appleton and Company, New York 1881, p. 382. The 'subtlest' was obviously Cardinal Newman.

79. Cullen to Bernard Smith, 18 December 1852; cited Emmet Larkin, *The Making of the Roman Catholic Church in Ireland, 1850–1860*, The University of North Carolina Press, Chapel Hill 1980, p. 220. The letter is quoted differently in Bowen, op. cit., p. 246.
80. Larkin, *The Making of the Roman Catholic Church*, p. 200. Cf. Lucas: 'In Parliament and in politics I have no secular object to pursue; and if the Church should really proclaim that Irish Catholic politics are merely or mainly a secular business, a pursuit of secular ambition, … I, and every man who shares my opinions, will of course feel our function has come to an end …' (Edward Lucas, op. cit., vol. II, p. 159).
81. Edward Lucas, op. cit., vol. II, pp. 139–441.
82. Ibid., p. 151.
83. Ibid., p. 170.

5

Manning versus Newman: A Reconsideration

JOHN COULSON

In 1890, the year of Newman's death, J.E.C. Bodley had the following conversation with Cardinal Manning: 'I gather', said the Cardinal, 'that you are under the impression that Doctor Newman is a good Catholic.' Bodley replied that 'such was my vague belief'. 'Either you are ignorant of the Catholic doctrine,' retorted the Cardinal, 'or of the works of Doctor Newman.' After asking which of Newman's books I had read, he proceeded to tick off on his tapering fingers in his usual way, ten distinct heresies to be found in the most widely read works of Doctor Newman.

In spite of, even because of, Newman's success in the *Apologia*, we find Manning writing to Monsignor Talbot, the Pope's close adviser, on 25 February, 1866: 'What you write about Dr Newman is true. Whether he knows it or not, he has become the centre of those who hold low views about the Holy See, are anti-Roman, cold and silent ... In one word it is Worldly Catholicism, and it will have the worldly on its side, and will deceive many.' In the following year, on 25 April 1867, Talbot warns Manning that the laity are beginning 'to show the cloven foot' by putting into practice 'the doctrine taught by Newman in his article in the *Rambler*' (On Consulting the Faithful in Matters of Doctrine). It is then that Talbot asks the notorious question, 'What is the province of the laity? To hunt, to shoot, to entertain. These matters they understand, but to meddle with ecclesiastical matters they have no right at all.' Talbot concludes by warning Manning that Newman 'is the most dangerous man in England ... He will make use of the laity against your Grace.'

This reputation of being, not merely disloyal and rebellious, but a heretic did not leave Newman until he was created Cardinal by the new Pope Leo XIII in 1879. How then does one account for the persistence throughout their lives of expressions of affection which culminate in Manning's panegyric at Newman's funeral, when he speaks of 'my love and veneration for my brother and friend of more than sixty years?'

In their youth, both men were Evangelicals. Something of what Manning gained from Newman and the Tractarians is to be seen in a letter from Henry Wilberforce of 1 August 1834 to Newman: 'He (Manning) says that a year and a half ago he did not know that there was such a thing as a church.' The relationship with Newman is recorded and begins with dining in Oriel in the autumn of 1830. Although he was much impressed by Newman's criticism of the Church of England, he did not join Newman in the Church of Rome until 1851. Instead he married Caroline Sargent in 1833. The marriage was tragically brief, Caroline dying of consumption in 1837. How much his marriage meant to him can be seen from his grief when a bag containing her letters to him was stolen when he broke his journey to Rome at Avignon. Aubrey de Vere writes in his Recollections that the expression of grief in his face and voice were such 'as I have seldom witnessed'. Later on at dinner, Manning noticed 'at a small table not far distant there sat a maid-servant, alone and neglected. The future Cardinal rose and did for her all that her master and mistress had forgotten to do. He brought a waiter to her, became her interpreter, and took care from time to time that nothing should be wanting to her dinner.' Far from wanting to suppress his love for Caroline, it is reported by Friedrich von Hügel that, as he lay dying, Manning felt beneath his pillow and pulled out a small, worn volume which he handed to Cardinal Vaughan saying, 'into this little book my dearest wife wrote her prayers and meditations. Not a day has passed since her death on which I have not prayed and meditated from this book. All the good I may have done, all the good I may have been, I owe to her. Take precious care of it.'

This is the quality of feeling, even passion that lies beneath the mask of ecclesiastical severity. After Caroline's death, he tried to lose himself in work, being appointed Archdeacon of Chichester in 1841.

He was in the mood to test the Anglican establishment to destruction as he found it increasingly unable to satisfy his radical political convictions and sympathies. In 1851 Manning joined the Roman Church some six years after Newman and in the same year as Newman agreed to found a Catholic University in Dublin. He resigned some six years later. Instead of a place where clergy and laity might meet and act upon each other what the bishops wanted was not a university but a lay seminary. Newman resigned as Rector in 1857, the year in which Manning was appointed Provost of Westminster. Within eight years he was to become Archbishop. On the other hand, Newman's experiences in Dublin led him to distinguish between the Pope's infallibility in matters of doctrine, and his sagacity. If the Pope intended a university in Dublin was it bound to succeed? Circumstances obliged Newman to regard assertions of Papal authority with caution in distinction from Manning's enthusiastic ultramontanism. Already the seeds of future conflict were being sown. Newman's next attempt on behalf of an educated laity, far from improving matters made them much worse.

Lord Acton and Richard Simpson had been editing what might be called the voice of liberal Catholicism, *The Rambler*, whose critical tone had so offended the bishops that they threatened to close it down. The current row was over primary education. To avoid condemnation Newman's bishop, Ullathorne, persuaded Newman, much against his will, to take over the management of the periodical. In the interest of conciliation, and in order to put the issues in perspective, Newman contributed an article, 'On Consulting the faithful in matters of Doctrine' (1859). Newman argues that since in the case of the Immaculate Conception the laity were consulted, there was every reason to anticipate 'such an act of kind feeling and sympathy in great practical questions'. The present issue concerned the quality of education in Catholic schools, and their relationship with the government.

Newman's argument now takes a historical turn – to the fourth century and to the Arian heresy, during which time 'the body of the bishops failed in their confession of the faith. It was the faithful who remained firm.' Thus, 'the ecclesia docens is more happy when she has ... enthusiastic partisans about her ... than when she cuts off the faithful from the study of her divine doctrines, and the sympathy of her divine contemplations, and requires from them a fides implicita in her word, which in the educated classes will terminate in indifference, and in the poorer in superstition.' Newman concludes by asserting that when pastors and the faithful come together in consultation, 'there is something in the *pastorum et fidelium conspiratio*, which is not in the pastors alone'.

Reaction was mixed. Bishop Brown of Newport wrote to Rome charging Newman with heresy. Then followed a tragic set of misunderstandings. Requests for clarification from Rome were sent to Cardinal Wiseman and Bishop Ullathorne but not delivered to Newman, whose silence was misinterpreted as wilful stubbornness. If he would not explain, why did he not retract? Newman was under a cloud and judged to be a rebel who refused to answer Rome. The impression this caused is summed up by Cardinal Barnabo – 'Le pape est beaucoup peiné.'

It is here that Newman and Manning part company. Earlier on Manning had suggested a way out: 'The article in *The Rambler* has been many times in my mind, and I wish you would write and print a sermon on the office of the Holy Ghost in the Church in which you could bring out *in ordine theologico* what *in ordine historico* as in *The Rambler* is confusing to common readers.' In other words, play safe and leave history to the historians, and in your capacity as a theologian practice non-historical orthodoxy. The two friends began to move into opposite camps. To Manning Newman's judgment had been shown to be defective and untrustworthy. Although the issues which divided them continued to grow, Manning never ceases to express his affection for Newman the man, and former leader of the Tractarians. It will not do to dismiss the matter as a clash of personalities, whatever that may mean, but there were differences of temperament. To borrow a distinction from Coleridge, Manning was 'a man of commanding genius ... Such men are driven to express their preconceptions on the world without, in order to present them back to their own view with the satisfying degree of clearness, distinctness and individuality.' Manning was at his best in action, as is testified by his rapid rise to power in the church he joined in 1851, and ruled as Cardinal Archbishop from 1875.

On the other hand, Newman was what Coleridge calls a man of the greatest genius. Such men 'appear to have been of calm and tranquil temper in all that related to themselves. In the inward assurance of permanent fame, they seem to have been either indifferent or resigned with regard to immediate reputation' (*Biographia Literaria*, chap II). Keats calls this quality 'negative capability, that is when man is capable of being in uncertainties, Mysteries, doubts, without any irritable reaching after fact and reason'.

For Newman, even theology 'is ever running into mysteries, which reason can neither explain nor adjust. Its lines of thought come to an abrupt termination, and to pursue them or complete them is to plunge down the abyss. But logic blunders on.' Of the reception of his views on such thorny questions as Catholic education, residence at Oxford and above all on the need for an educated laity, Newman wrote: 'I say as far as I see, and I don't see any of those further conclusions which others draw from me. Such sayings then are not hints on my part of something I see beyond, but ultimate points of vision.' Here is the boundary between the poet-theologian, and the genius of Archbishop Manning who wrote, 'I am not, like Newman, a poet, or a writer of autobiography, but a priest, and a priest only.'

Newman's first clash with Manning was over the higher education of Catholics. Newman had agreed to go to Dublin in 1851 to establish a Catholic university. But he soon discovered that what the Pope wanted was not necessarily bound to succeed. St Peter may have spoken, but there was no guarantee that what the Pope wanted would be achieved. By March 1867, Newman concluded that such a university was a 'speculative perfection, which cannot be carried out in practice'. Furthermore he was unable to avoid the conclusion that mixed education in the higher schools is as much a necessity now in England, as it was in the East in the days of St Basil and St Chrysostom. What the bishops wanted was not a university but a lay seminary. It was in an 'open university, when complemented by a strong mission', that students would be safest rather than in 'a close Catholic college'. The diocesan bishop Ullathorne agreed and encouraged Newman to buy land in Oxford suitable as a site for an Oratory. Manning opposed this solution in principle. He would have nothing to do with mixed education whether it be for the poor or the rich. Accordingly he established a 'Catholic university' in Kensington. Newman, when invited to take part, declined. The 'university' began with fourteen students, but by the next year was bankrupt.

Mixed education exposed its subjects to worldliness, and Catholics were not allowed to go to Oxford or Cambridge until 1895, some twelve years after permission of a comparable kind was granted to Italian laymen. Manning's education policy was to exclude even the religious orders, particularly the Jesuits, in order to have the direction of all education entirely in the hands of the archdiocese. The results at the primary end of the scale were substantial. Elementary schools grew from 11,000 in 1865 to 19,000 in 1889 and 21,800 in 1892. 10,000 were rescued from the work houses with their narrow Protestantism, while 4,500 waifs and strays were housed in Catholic institutions.

The fundamental source of disagreement between the two was focussed on the role and function of the papacy and especially on its temporal power. A strong maximizing or ultramontane position was adopted by Manning, while Newman (as one might suppose) adopted a cautious or minimizing position. As recently as 1842 a priest visiting Rome noticed that when the Pope walked down the road, no one bothered to raise their hats. It had been taken for granted that the Pope's authority rested upon his possession of the papal states. Sir Thomas More, for example, in the early days of his association with Henry VIII had said, 'the Pope is a prince as you are Sire'. Thus, when the papal states were threatened by Garibaldi and the Risorgimento, the underlying question – what is the basis of papal authority? – was forced to the surface. To Pius IX the papal states were a seamless robe – the patrimony of Christ. This was a claim bound to encourage such exaggerated claims as that when the Pope thought it was God thinking within him. Manning firmly held to the ultramontane claim that the temporal power of the Pope should be made a doctrine *de fide*. Newman objected on the grounds that the issue had come like thunder in a clear sky to a church unprepared for such a discussion. Given the threat directly posed by the inevitable encroachment of the Risorgimento, however, the Vatican Council of 1870 grounded the Pope's authority in the exercise of his office, so that when he spoke *ex cathedra*, his decisions were infallible. Because of the haste with which it was reached, Newman held that it should be treated with a wise minimism: 'Future Popes will explain and in one sense limit their own power ... Hitherto he has done what he would, because its limits were not defined – Now he must act by rule.' Manning regarded such interpretations as failing in loyalty to the Pope in his difficulties.

A firm Ultramontane, Manning held that to believe was as easy as to obey, and that to disobey authority was to be disloyal to the Pope in particular. In such circumstances it was easy to fall into heresy; and one's duty is to hate heresy no matter how much one might have strong feelings of affection for the heretic – a distinction which accounts for Manning's behaviour to Newman during their lives in the Roman Church.

Manning's vision of the church as the church of the poor reached its climax in the celebrated dockstrike of 1889. Today we have become accustomed to the claim that the poor are where the church must be. What is noteworthy is the degree of passionate radicalism with which Manning practised this precept. He speaks of himself as being 'on the side of labour' and as sharing the sufferings of the poor. To see London as Manning saw it was to encounter the abomination of desolation: 'no one knows the depth of the sufferings of women save the doctor or the priest'. Newman, too, had his vision of the lowest class of the cities rising from the depths and becoming 'the new scourges of God'. It is the passion with which such views were held which distinguishes Manning from both Newman and his successor at Westminster, Herbert Vaughan. When Vaughan tried to water down Manning's social and political concerns, he received a stinging rebuke: 'God so loved the world that he sent his only begotten son – but that is a detail!' Manning suffered with those he saw suffer. Unlike many of his fellow Catholics, he did not retreat into the church, but offered it as a means of arbitration and fruitful compromise. To the charge that he was advocating socialism, he replied, 'I do not know whether it means socialism to you. To me it means Christianity.' He had not time for doctrinaire politics; 'socialism is to society', he wrote, 'as rationalism is to reason.' Later, in 1890, he asserted, 'There is no justice, mercy, or compassion in the Plutocracy: that is my creed.'

Manning's concern for working people, and their concern for him reached its climax with his successful arbitration in the dockstrike of 1889. By contrast it is often suggested that Newman was indifferent to such achievements, but this is to overlook a letter of congratulations which Newman dictated to Manning on 29 September 1889. Manning replied by return, expressing his 'hearty' thanks, saying that he prayed for Newman daily and ending 'yours affectionately'. In 1892 Manning himself died. The route of his funeral procession from the London Oratory to the cemetery at Kensal Green was lined by working people in honour of such a man and such an advocate.

The theological problems which had divided Manning and Newman remained, namely, how to rethink the Christian faith in a culture each day growing more remote from the circumstances in which the faith had originated. There was tension between the deductive application of traditional teaching, and the experience of faith arrived at inductively. This was the programme of Modernism; and any theologian who strove to resolve such a tension put his orthodoxy at risk, especially if (as now in the case of Frs Küng, Schillebeeckx and Curran for example) he is a priest, or member of a religious order, or a teacher in a Catholic faculty or seminary. It is the layman teaching in an open university who is least affected by the double loyalties which afflict clerical theologians.

The layman is faced by a different agenda which places theology alongside its contributory disciplines. The effect can be both positive and negative. It is positive, for example, when the literary tradition enables him to understand more richly how successfully the symbolic language of poetry and imagination retain and make intelligible the primary sources of religious experience.

John Kent has been at home with both sides. Not only has he

made a significant contribution to Newman studies, but he has also turned to face the changing of the questions by trying, for example, to examine the extent to which accelerated social change has affected denominational identity. Does the 'vision glorious' of the Oxford Movement survive its confrontation with the indifferent and unromantic landscape of industrial Britain? Will the movement of reform deriving from the Second Vatican Council meet the same fate as the Modernists? Does the ecumenical movement stem from weakness rather than strength?

The range of the questions which confront the lay theologian is such that to prevent his or her sliding into simple scepticism theologians like John Kent have sought to preserve a 'wise minimalism' as opposed to a maximal polemic. Is it then better to believe too little than too much?

Here the paths divide. For the Catholic his religion is more than a philosophy or set of beliefs. It is also at once a spirituality and an institution. Its elements co-exist in various states of tension.

It has taken a century for the tension between the 'commanding genius' of a Cardinal Manning, and the 'ultimate points of vision' of a Cardinal Newman to be acknowledged for what it is – a sign not of heresy but of growth. In the words of Manning's successor at Westminster, Cardinal Basil Hume:

> The responsibility of the teaching authority within the Church to safeguard the authentic teaching of the Christian Gospel has to be maintained; and at the same time the duty of the theologian to speculate has to be asserted. From time to time the two will clash; better this than indifference and apathy.

6

The Religion of Matthew Arnold

HENRY D. RACK

It has been a distinctive feature of John Kent's work that he has always been sensitive to the historical and social conditioning of theology and here he has been very much the historian's theologian. He has also applied a well-cultured and ironical eye to party historians and theologians and has sought to come to terms with the realities of religious experience under its many disguises. Matthew Arnold has been a congenial spirit here as indicated by a neat combination of two famous aphorisms made by Professor Kent to me many years ago: 'Religion is morality touched by emotion, recollected in tranquillity.' This essay is offered as a tribute to an author who has given refreshment and enlightenment to the honorand as well as to me over the years. It is submitted in the spirit of Schleiermacher who in *The Christian Faith* claimed that he did not wish to be the founder of a theological 'school' but that 'in my thinking I have never had any other aim than that of communicating my thoughts by way of stimulus, for each to use in his own fashion'.[1]

I

T.S. Eliot dismissed Arnold as a religious writer in a slighting sentence which seems to have had all too much subsequent influence on English views of him: 'In philosophy and theology he was an undergraduate; in religion a philistine.'[2] Eliot also perpetuated the savage caricature of Arnold's theology given by the philosopher F.H. Bradley. Bradley quoted Arnold's description of God as 'the Eternal not ourselves that makes for righteousness' and mockingly commented: 'The habit of washing ourselves might be termed "the Eternal not ourselves that makes for cleanliness" or "early to bed and early to rise" as "the Eternal not ourselves that makes for longevity" ... the Eternal in short is nothing in the world but a piece of literary claptrap.'[3] Although many English critics have admired Arnold's literary and social criticism they have tended to write off his religious essays if only because, as one anthologist remarked, they were the one part of his work which may have been significant for Arnold's day but 'no longer retain their significance for ours'.[4] Those taking this line may not be greatly impressed by the fact that *Literature and Dogma* appears to have sold best of all his writings during his lifetime, though for the historian this is a point of some significance.

Theologians and historians of doctrine have also generally agreed to ignore or dismiss him.[5] He was, after all, uncomfortably radical in theology and at the same time defective in metaphysics. But one could always pass over him as a mere layman and in no sense a professional theologian. Furthermore, was he not too witty and sarcastic about traditional orthodoxies to be taken as a sincerely religious man at all? He has suffered neglect and misunderstanding as a serious contributor to theology in much the same way as Erasmus. Both men, however, only satirized what they regarded as nonsensical or morally objectionable so as to clear the ground for a defensible and practical religious reality; both, too, were dedicated to the pursuit of practical 'righteousness'.

One notorious example of Arnold's irony at the expense of traditional orthodoxy indicates how easily he caused offence. He pictures the traditional view of the atonement thus:

> Imagine a sort of infinitely magnified and improved Lord Shaftesbury, with a race of vile offenders to deal with, whom his natural goodness would incline him to let off, only his sense of justice will not allow it. Then a younger Lord Shaftesbury, on the scale of his father and very dear to him, who might live in grandeur and splendour if he liked, but who prefers to leave his home, to go and live among the race of offenders, and to be

> put to an ignominious death, on condition that his merits shall be counted against their demerits, and that his father's goodness shall be restrained no longer from taking effect, but any offenders shall be admitted to the benefit of it on simply pleading the satisfaction made by the son. Then, finally, a third Lord Shaftesbury, still on the same high scale, who keeps very much in the background, and works in a very occult manner, but very efficaciously nevertheless, and who is busily applying everywhere the benefits of the son's satisfaction and the father's goodness.

This, Arnold says, is precisely the Protestant theory of justification and he acknowledges that awe and love induced by the story can indeed transform people's conduct. But, he asks, 'Is it *sure*? Can what is here assumed be *verified*?'[6] This is his objection to such doctrines as the basis for conduct. Talk like this seemed to some religious people to be blasphemous and the reference to the Evangelical hero Lord Shaftesbury made it doubly offensive. One may still feel that Arnold was at least guilty of bad taste in this case yet also reflect that the doctrine caricatured had its own elements of moral and intellectual affront.

North American scholars, particularly literary critics, have tended to be much more appreciative of Arnold as a religious writer. However, until about the 1970s, their problem seems to have been that they have been determined to claim him as a good humanist rather than as a 'liberal' or 'radical' Christian. They have felt that he still retained remnants of a Christian supernaturalism inconsistent with what they have felt to be his basically humanistic position. As a result of this reading they have judged his religious thinking to have fallen into illogicalities and inconsistencies.[7] But within the last ten to fifteen years more positive appreciations have appeared of Arnold as a religious thinker particularly relevant and congenial to those concerned with religious values in a 'secularizing' age.[8]

The purpose of this essay is a limited one. I shall be concerned mainly with Arnold's directly religious writings, though I am well aware that they cannot be detached from his literary and social writings which would have to be read along with them for a fuller treatment of his religious teaching. Although I shall indicate some of the difficulties which have been found in Arnold's attempt to reinterpret Christianity I shall not attempt a full defence of his position. The main purpose of the essay is to show that in intention at least Arnold was certainly not a 'mere' humanist; that he stood firmly in the Christian tradition; and that he at least raised questions which continue to be central to any modern attempt at a tenable Christian theology.

II

First of all, a brief summary of Arnold's religious teaching. He thought that Christianity, and a Christianity based on the Bible, was likely to be for the foreseeable future the main source of religion and ethics for the English people. 'Two things about the Christian religion must surely be clear to anyone with eyes in their heads. One is that men cannot do without it; the other, that they cannot do with it as it is.'[9]

What does he mean? Religion, he believed, must rest on something 'verifiable' – on some empirical evidence and not on metaphysical speculation. The empirical evidence for religion must be moral or religious experience. But traditional theology offers instead a set of elaborate, abstract descriptions of God as the great personal First Cause, Governor of the Universe, Trinity. Its scheme of salvation is based on the Fall, Original Sin and the death of Christ to appease the Father (as in the Lord Shaftesbury story).[10] Traditional Christian apologetic rested mainly on the so-called 'evidences' of miracle and fulfilled prophecy which were supposed to prove that Jesus was the Son of God and so the bearer of revelation and salvation.[11] Arnold's objection to this whole style of argument is that it has no basis in direct experience and therefore cannot be verified (and was in any case open also to damaging moral historical and scientific criticism).

The alternative is to get at the actual experiences which the Bible records, experiences which he thought *could* be experientially verified. 'Liberal' Christians of the nineteenth century tended to do this by way of biblical criticism – literary, historical, scientific. Arnold took much of this for granted at a time when many of his conservative contemporaries were not seriously trying to come to terms with it. But while he certainly took such criticism for granted (after doing his homework on it) he also thought that much of it by itself was barren and 'not edifying'.[12] To understand the Bible and to benefit from reading it (he thought) one must read it not like a scientific or philosophical or historical or theological treatise. Rather, one should read it as a literary, poetic work, one which gives imaginative images of great moral and religious experiences and truths.[13] Read it in this way and you will be able to grasp the living experience which it embodied. For Arnold the real object of religion is 'conduct' which is 'three-fourths of life' and this 'conduct' or 'righteousness' is the 'special object of biblical religion'. The other quarter is what he called 'culture' – in this context the capacity to read the Bible in Arnold's 'literary' way so as to get at its true spiritual and moral message.[14]

If you read the Bible in this manner much of the traditional dogma dissolves away. Even the term 'God' does not refer to a mysterious metaphysical being but is rather a 'literary term' 'thrown out at a not fully grasped object of the speaker's consciousness, and men mean different things by it as their consciousness differs'.[15] Arnold suggests that a more exact way of describing the actual experience which men label as 'God' might be 'the Eternal not ourselves that makes for righteousness'.[16] This is because what we actually experience is some force outside ourselves which impresses a moral imperative upon us.

If, as he says, the real object of religion is conduct and if conduct is three-fourths of life, then what is the difference between morality and religion? 'Religion ... is ethics heightened, enkindled, lit up by feeling; the passage from morality to religion is made, when to morality is applied emotion. And the true meaning of religion is not simply *morality*, but morality *touched by emotion*.'[17] 'The very power of religion lies in its bringing emotion to bear on our rules of conduct – to enable us to dwell on and pursue what otherwise we would be distracted from by the rest of life.[18]

The Hebrew people were particularly concerned about

righteousness and in experience found 'the very great part of righteousness which belongs, we may say, to *not ourselves*'; that is, they were conscious of standards and demands of righteousness which did not originate in themselves but from beyond.[19] It was this direct experience of the demand from outside (and not metaphysical speculation) which led them to believe in what Arnold calls an 'Eternal not ourselves that makes for righteousness'. Although the Hebrews used all kinds of anthropomorphic terms for God – picturing him in human, personal terms – yet they knew that all these images were only words 'thrown out at a vast object of consciousness' which they did not fully grasp.[20] But all that experience directly shows is that God or the Eternal is 'the *enduring* power not ourselves, which makes for righteousness'.[21]

Unfortunately, later in Old Testament times they added what Arnold calls *Aberglaube* – 'extra belief' going beyond the verifiable certainties of moral experience.[22] Hence one gets apocalyptic and messianic ideas and God becomes a 'magnified and non-natural man'. To get rid of this and return to the basic religious experience it was necessary to have a fresh application of emotion and better sanctions for conduct. These were supplied by Jesus. He stressed 'dying to oneself', self-renunciation, self-examination; and the motive for following this way is 'ardent affection' and gratitude towards Jesus.[23]

But alas! – *Aberglaube* comes in again as Christianity develops. Men used miracles instead of moral experience to 'prove' Christianity.[24] The language of the Bible came to be treated as 'scientific', dogmatic propositions. God was seen again as a 'magnified, non-natural man'; the Son was related to him in terms of atonement by penal substitution and as part of the Trinity. But the real message of Jesus was the 'word of the Cross' and 'dying', 'losing', self-renunciation as the main part of righteousness.[25] 'Faith' for the Christian is 'the being able to cleave to a giver of righteousness, appealing to our higher and real self, not to our lower and apparent self'.[26]

So Arnold condemns popular religion for its literalist view of God, atonement and salvation. For him (to take a central example of reinterpretation), 'resurrection' really means that Christ's death made an epoch of victory for him and his cause which thereafter reigns indestructibly. For Jesus the final act of 'sacrifice' and 'resurrection' was already present in the work of his lifetime, a spiritual and moral 'dying and rising' from the lower to the higher self.[27] Unfortunately his followers turned this into a physical miracle of rising from the dead but we can see Jesus' real message living on in Paul's teaching. 'The three crucial themes of Paul's theology', says Arnold, are not, therefore, as popular theology renders them in terms of 'calling, justification, sanctification' but rather 'dying with Christ, resurrection from the dead, growing into Christ' all in a non-physical moral sense.[28]

To complete this account of Arnold's reinterpretation of Christianity some indication can be given of how he applies it to the institutions of the church, prayer and worship. The Church of England has its place as 'the great national society for the promotion of what is commonly called *goodness*' – very much in the manner of Thomas Arnold of Rugby.[29] As to worship: 'Catholic worship is likely, however modified, to survive as the general worship of Christians, because it is the worship which, in a sphere where poetry is permissible and natural, unites most of the elements of poetry.'[30] On prayer, he says, 'There is, then, a real power that makes for righteousness; and it is the greatest of realities for us' and prayer 'deals with this reality'. It is 'an energy of inspiration towards the Eternal not ourselves that makes for righteousness'.[31] So prayer and worship for Arnold is not the kind of auto-suggestion it is often now suggested to be but has an object distinct from the human subject.[32] Arnold is quite explicit here: 'Everything turns on its being at *realities* that this worship and its language is aimed. And its anthropomorphic language about God is aimed at a vast, though ill-comprehended reality.'[33]

III

Arnold's approach to the Bible and dogma obviously reflects the cumulative effects of historical and scientific criticism since the seventeenth century which had been belatedly sharpened and publicized for the English by the controversies over Colenso and *Essays and Reviews*. But equally important were the doubts raised in some minds over the same period by legalistic doctrines such as atonement by penal substitution; justification by imputed grace and eternal punishment. *Essays and Reviews* is often seen as an expression of biblical criticism but several of the rather heterogeneous group which produced it were equally concerned to reinterpret traditional salvation doctrine in moral rather than legal terms, though Arnold criticized them for their undue concentration on 'scientific' biblical criticism.[34] His own approach was more in the tradition of Coleridge and Thomas Arnold though he went further than either of them in his critical approach to the historicity of the text.

Arnold's contention that the Bible is properly understood by reading it in a 'literary' manner and with the help of 'culture' rather than as a dogmatic handbook of formal propositions may be thought by now to be part of the conventional wisdom of biblical study; nor was he the only one in his own day to make the point. Such a view had, however, more far-reaching implications than may appear at first sight. Traditionalists looked for precise dogmatic knowledge based on literal historical facts and proof-texts (a habit of mind still clinging to theologians who would feel insulted if accused of biblical literalism). Arnold offered moral knowledge of a much less clearcut kind. The point is partly that the nature as well as the content of 'revelation' were altered by Arnold's prescription, for the 'literary' approach meant treating the language of the Bible as a poetic or symbolic mode of discourse rather than as the conveyance of literal historical or scientific 'facts'. It conveyed a different kind of truth and in a different way. Yet contrary to what is sometimes claimed, Arnold was as anxious as any literalist to find 'truth' in religion and he did so in terms which show the force of contemporary fashions for seeking 'scientific' facts and certainties when he spoke of finding a 'verifiable' and 'empirical' basis for religion.

This is one of the most significant though also one of the most criticized parts of Arnold's prospectus. Still, whatever one thinks of his success or lack of success in putting Christianity on to a new and verifiable basis, it is important to recognize what he was trying to do and why. He was convinced that the traditional apologetic from prophecy and miracle which had been the orthodox eighteenth-century weapons against Deism and still had a considerable vogue in conservative nineteenth-century circles was bankrupt in face of naturalistic historical and scientific knowledge. Nor were the abstract dogmas of the Trinity and the Evangelical plan of salvation in any better case. They were, Arnold thought, intellectual constructions with no real basis even in the 'revelation' they claimed to expound. The solution was to turn from the sphere of the intellectual to that of the emotional; to 'internal' evidence of a primarily moral kind. Here Arnold was an example of an important general trend in nineteenth-century theology.[35] But the desire for something scientifically 'verifiable' rather than a recourse to a merely individual experience of faith remained strong. Hence Arnold hoped that he had found 'facts' of an empirical kind in direct emotional and moral experience which could be 'verified' by their practical results in conduct.

As a piece of apologetic this was far from adequate. To Arnold the content and meaning of the moral experiences he described were self-evident, directly 'read off' from the experience. In reality, no apologetic seems possible on the basis simply of direct 'religious experience' as evidence of God's existence, character and will.[36] We would now recognize that 'raw' or 'shapeless' experiences are all that are immediately given; or rather that they are immediately perceived and given a 'shape' in terms of the traditions in the minds of those who experience them. An early Methodist visionary is likely to see Christ crucified for the justification of a believing sinner and is not likely to see the Virgin Mary in the way characteristic of a nineteenth-century Roman Catholic. Schleiermacher managed the remarkable feat of extracting a liberalized Protestant dogmatics from the initial 'feeling of absolute dependence' – a concept which itself has a distinctly Lutheran ring about it. Nor do good effects in conduct infallibly prove the truth of the doctrines on which they are supposed to be founded. Arnold was, in reality, standing upon a subjective act of faith. He could not *demonstrate* that he was directly in contact with a transcendental reality. It may still be maintained that his simple moral findings were a more plausible reading of experience than the grand abstractions and metaphysical convolutions of tradition, which was after all what he was mainly concerned to maintain. In any case, the fact that he wished to claim an experience of a moral transcendent and thought he could do so is of importance for any claim that he stood in the Christian tradition.

What is empirically grasped and verifiable in religion for Arnold is morality. As we have seen, he defined religion as 'morality touched by emotion'. From one point of view, as has already been remarked, this represents a response, by no means confined to Arnold, to the uncertainties created by the difficulties of miracle and prophecy apologetic and moral doubts about some aspects of traditional doctrine. To morality, however, Arnold added 'emotion' which lifts mere morality into religion. Here, too, he was by no means alone among Victorians in feeling that he needed to find some means of adding warmth to his morality as well as his metaphysics after abandoning some or all of the traditional religious tenets.

Many have doubted whether 'morality touched by emotion' will do as a full definition of religion. Myth, ritual, worship have often been more conspicuous features of religion than dogma and moral codes and Christianity has made much of revelation in history. On some occasions, indeed, in his early and later years Arnold wrote as if the 'religion' added to morality was a concession to human weakness and perhaps a temporary concession at that. Thus in 1853 he wrote to Clough:

> If one loved what was beautiful and interesting in itself *passionately* enough, one would produce what was excellent without troubling oneself with religious dogma at all. As it is, we are *warm* only when dealing with these last – and what is frigid is always bad. I would have others – most others – stick to the old religious dogmas because I feel that this *warmth* is the great blessing and this frigidity the great curse – and on the old religious road they still have the best chance of getting the one and avoiding the other.[37]

In 1880 he seemed to see poetry as man's best 'stay' with religion as a possible popular vehicle for it:

> Poetry, then, is more of a stay to us than art or science. It is more explicative than art, and it has the emotion which to science is wanting. But the grand sources of explication and emotion in the popular opinion, are philosophy and religion ...

However, he goes on:

> The reign of religion as morality touched with emotion is indeed indestructible. But religion as men commonly conceive it – religion depending on the historicalness of certain supposed facts, on the authority of certain received traditions, on the validity of certain accredited dogmas – how much of this religion can be deemed unalterably secure? ... Our religion has materialized itself in the fact – the supposed fact; it has attached its emotion to the fact. For poetry the idea is everything; the rest is its world of illusion, of divine illusion; it attaches its emotion to the idea, the idea *is* the fact. The strongest part of our religion today is its unconscious poetry. The future of poetry is immense, because in conscious poetry where it is worthy of its high distinction, our race, as time goes on, will find an ever surer and surer stay.[38]

Some of these sentiments sound very like the élitist double standards of eighteenth-century Deists – rational religion for the educated few and useful superstitions to keep the masses in order. Arnold answered this charge in 1863 when he wrote that he had been 'reproached with wishing to make free-thinking an aristocratic privilege, while a false religion is thrown to the multitude to keep it quiet'. In fact, he claimed, he spoke for those in all classes who desired 'edification'. When the educated minority 'enter the sphere of religion, they too ask and need to be edified, not informed only'.[39]

It has been pointed out that Arnold's attempt to preserve religion by assimilating it to the values of poetry was a further stage in a process which had begun with Wordsworth and Coleridge. Both poetry and religion as expressions of knowledge and truth seemed to be reduced to fiction and illusion by the claims of natural science in this period to exhaust the possibilities of truth by its methods and descriptions. Thus Wordsworth emphasized the value of poetry as a source of knowledge against science, though not as religion. Coleridge kept science, poetry and religion distinct, allocating them the appropriate faculties of 'understanding', 'imagination' and 'reason' in his special sense. Arnold, it is argued, went further by placing on poetry the responsibility for functions once performed by the exploded dogmas of religion and religious philosophy – hence his claims for the future of poetry.[40] What is more remarkable is that it seems that a number of other late Victorian sages, some of them strongly imbued with the values of science as the road to truth and antipathetic to God and religion, nevertheless also hoped that the 'poetic' use of the old religious terms would cater for certain continuing human emotional needs. But, then as later, the question arises whether religious 'poetry' can work religiously without the 'facts' it once expressed, or the old poetry be attached legitimately to any new 'fact'? For Arnold, like the rest, was in reality denying the historical, factual truth of things like the miracles, the physical resurrection of Jesus and his divine status which had supported the old poetry and dogma.[41] For some, like T.S. Eliot, Lionel Trilling and I.A. Richards, Arnold had simply reduced Christianity to its 'subjective effects, its emotional kick, to what is useful but not "true" '. All that can be said of it, then, is that it is an unverifiable religious feeling. If this is so, it is a severe blow to Arnold's belief that he had found a way of 'verifying' his ideas in a way that traditional dogmas could not be.[42]

Yet Arnold certainly intended to make 'factual' and 'truth' claims for Christianity as he understood it, for what he called the 'natural truth' of Christianity shorn of miracles and the supernatural. This 'natural truth' was the phenomenon he described as 'The Eternal that works for righteousness'. This is the God of Jesus who 'explains what God would have of us ... The natural experiential truth of his explanations is their one claim upon us.'[43]

This truth is apprehended and expressed by his 'literary', 'poetic' language – the language (it has been argued) of what we would call image, symbol and myth. It covers areas which cannot be expressed by the language of literal fact. It should not be converted into 'scientific' statements as happens with traditional dogma. What is needed is a kind of demythologizing and for Arnold 'poetry is the means by which a people represent imaginatively their moral understanding of existence and their experience of God'. For him 'the idea is the fact, for the idea is grounded in authentic spiritual experience. But the idea can only be expressed imaginatively, figuratively, mythologically'.[44]

The notion that what raises 'morality' to 'religion' is the addition of emotion to strengthen us to do what we know to be right and that without this emotion morality is ineffective, is also worthy of more serious attention than it has often received. Here one recalls Braithwaite's version of Arnoldian religion as 'an empiricist's view of religious belief'. For Braithwaite, the essence of religion is also conduct, but the sanction for conduct, which also distinguishes different religions from each other, is to be found in the different sets of 'stories' used by religions to capture the emotions and the will for their precepts.[45] Close though this is to Arnold in some respects, it falls short of what Arnold was claiming. For Braithwaite the Christian stories are simply vehicles for expressing a moral purpose in religious terms, but for Arnold they were also statements of 'facts' which though not of the same type as 'scientific facts' could still be 'verified' in other empirical ways.[46]

It may well be contended that in the long run it is indeed the moral element which is fundamentally important in any religion and that whatever else is added (and Arnold did not deny that there were other elements in religion, such as the church, prayer and worship) should be subordinated to the service of morality. But that he was more than a moralizing humanist and was in a very positive relationship to the Christian tradition is shown by several points in his teaching. He had a very particular set of Christian values and stories in mind as the content of the experience and demands of the 'Eternal' and the focus of belief and worship was a transcendental object.

Even Lionel Trilling pointed out in answer to F. H. Bradley that Arnold was intending to refer to an external, transcendental force when he spoke of the 'Eternal not ourselves'.[47] It is true that Trilling went on to dismiss this as an example of Arnold's descent into an *Aberglaube* of the kind he had condemned in others. Similarly, Braithwaite, though comparing his own position with Arnold's, also sees Arnold's transcendent Eternal as an inconsistent piece of dogma rather than as the direct product of experience.[48] For our present purpose, the important point is that Arnold did add this and found it necessary. To Clough he had written 'There is a God, though not well conceived by all.'[49] Moreover, the 'religious' emotion and the morality are specific and placed in the Christian tradition by the shape and content they are given by reference to the teaching and person of Jesus.

What are we to say, however, about Arnold's 'transcendent' or 'Eternal not ourselves' in relation to the Christian idea of God? Humanists have been suspicious of it because logically, it is claimed, he should have kept to a system purely within the confines of this world and human experience. Arnold, however, claimed that human experience included just this sense of an other-worldly, transcendent element. He did not regard his 'Eternal not ourselves' as a mere speculation or a piece of *Aberglaube* but as an empirically observed fact. It is, moreover, seen as a transcendent force and not (as some have claimed) simply as a projection of human ideals in the manner of Feuerbach or, more recently, Don Cupitt.[50] Humanists have naturally been unhappy about this super-human transcendent. At best it has been seen as a 'transcendent within the human order alone' (a concept not without its own difficulties); at worst, an empty phrase concealing the 'disappearance of God'.[51]

Even if the existence of Arnold's 'Eternal' is not as obvious as he supposed, the idea is still of interest as well as, apparently, integral to his whole reinterpretation of Christianity. But is it a satisfactory equivalent for, or reinterpretation of the traditional *personal* God of Christianity? Many have thought not and that it is fundamentally unacceptable as Christian at all. A.C. Benson saw it as 'a literary Pantheism tinged with Idealism' and an 'unattractive substitute' for the personal Christian God.[52] Is this vague and rather abstract 'power' an improvement on the anthropomorphic but attractive traditional picture? Even Arnold, though ironic at the expense of the dogmatists' abstractions, had a certain sympathy with the warm humanity of Hebrew anthropomorphism. Does it, too, really stand the test of experience? Could it ever become the object for worship?

Arnold did not in fact take the 'Eternal not ourselves' as a fixed formula but rather as one suggested formulation of what experience renders to us. He was protesting against any claim directly to be able to experience God in the terms of a 'magnified non-natural man' or as the traditional Trinity. He did not, however, directly deny the possibility of a personal God: 'All we can say is that men do not know enough about the Eternal not ourselves that works for righteousness to warrant their pronouncing that entity a person or a thing.'[53] A recent writer on the relationship between the ideas of Arnold and George Tyrrell the Roman Catholic Modernist claims that Arnold was here the victim of his own divisive method. His commitment to feeling, poetry and religion was at odds with his commitment to empirical verification. His God can best be made explicit not by traditional metaphysics but by a close attention to experience. But in the end he offers nothing that one could recognizably call a 'God'.[54]

Yet even if this is a fair criticism of the inadequacies of Arnold's reasoning, the impersonality of his 'God' does not necessarily rule it out of the Christian tradition. There is much in early and mediaeval theology, especially of the mystical type, about God's Being, the Ground of Being, the Abyss of Being; and more recently Tillich's contention that this, rather than personality, is the ultimate experience of God. If one is to take seriously claims that non-Christian religions contain religious truth, the scope is enlarged for allowing such ideas at least to be one element in a full picture of God. That the more impersonal pictures often emerged in a mystical milieu suggests also that they correspond to some element in human experience of God, rather than being the produce of abstraction and a priori thinking. For mystical theologians, like Arnold, were using terms 'thrown out at a great though incomprehensible reality' which they believed they had experienced. Nor should theologians ever forget that all theological thinking about God is analogical and that the use of 'personal' language about him is subject to more difficulties than the Fathers dreamt of. Finally, one may perhaps ponder on the challenging thought in a recent book by Professor Kent. After claiming that Western religious creativity no longer works happily with orthodox Christian symbols (which was already part of Arnold's dilemma) he goes on to say that 'A second death of religious images not unlike that which took place in the eighteenth century but more complete, is occurring in Western culture, leaving the religiously-minded to grapple with ideas of *im*personal theism, of religion in a valid Buddhist style, which takes little account of older Western ideas about God.'[55]

In fact it is not quite true to say that Arnold has no personal element in his conception of God. Once again he follows the Christian tradition which has repeatedly stressed both at the level of theology and of personal piety that one can only give a shape to God by seeing him through the image of Jesus. This is what Arnold does when he ties his moral imperative to the shape of the teaching and example of Jesus. The problem here is the exact status he ascribed to Jesus as well as the fact that he never really makes clear the relationship he conceives to exist between God and Jesus. He does once remark, however, that the revelation of Jesus, as of the Old Testament, is of the 'Eternal not ourselves'. This is what 'I came forth from the Father' really means, and not the abstract doctrine of 'the godhead of the Eternal Son'.[56]

That Arnold gave Jesus not only a high but a supreme place as the model, in his life and teaching, of the morality and religion which he wished to recommend, is certainly clear. In his *Last Essays on Church and Religion* he wrote: 'I believe, then, that the real Jesus will continue to command allegiance … Christianity will remain because of its substantial truth. Those who fancied that they had done with Christianity will have to return to it again, and learn it better.'[57] One may perhaps contrast this with Benjamin Jowett's tendency in his later years to put Jesus at best on the same level as Plato, perhaps even rather lower than him.[58]

For some modern critics this is certainly not sufficient for Arnold to qualify as a Christian. Dorothea Krook, for example, firmly ruled that Arnold was in opposition to what she claimed to be the only tenably Christian position. Thus she says that

Christians accept Jesus' divinity as a revelation founded on the proofs by prophecy and miracle and they see him as fulfilling the prophecy of the Suffering Servant in Isaiah 53. But Arnold saw Jesus as deliberately adopting and elevating this highest point in Jewish thought and did not need to be divine to do this.[59]

The general question of when 'reinterpretation' of Christianity becomes a departure from it – a major problem since the nineteenth century – will be considered at the end of this essay. On the question of the person of Christ as raised by Krook two points can be made here. One is that Christians have always differed in their attempts to describe and define the meaning of Jesus' personality and his relationship to God. Today the question has become still more difficult and no consensus on it exists. Krook's attempt to approach the question by way of miracle and prophecy grotesquely ties it to a type of eighteenth-century apologetic which even conservative apologists today find difficult to defend as it stands. Such attempts to discredit any ventures in restating Christianity by arbitrarily defining what its nature 'must' be by reference to some arbitrary point in the past show either a profound ignorance of the history of doctrine or a determination not to allow Christianity to perpetuate its influence by making itself more intellectually credible. It is an old and depressingly familiar story.[60]

Secondly, there is a very great difference between those who do and those who do not accept Jesus as the supreme standard for faith and conduct. The former have a prima facie case for being considered as candidates for places in the Christian tradition; the case for the latter is at least problematical. Arnold is clearly in the first category. But for others in the West, at least since the time of the eighteenth-century Deists, a morality and religion centred on Jesus have ceased to be a living form of inspiration. It has become either intellectually unacceptable or simply no longer evokes a mental and emotional response. For Arnold this is clearly not the case – quite the contrary. But acceptance of Jesus as the model for religion, morality and life is consistent with a great variety of interpretations of him, in theology as in (for example) iconoraphy. (One is tempted to say that Arnold's image of Jesus as a person of 'sweetness and light' suggests the early Greek iconography of the beardless hero rather than the bearded Syrian ascetic or the Orthodox Pantokrator.)[61]

Since Arnold's presentation of an apparently impersonal 'Eternal' despite his attention to the person of Jesus, has often been taken to be defective as a focus for faith and devotion, it is worth saying something further about his personal attitude to worship and spirituality. What can be glimpsed of his personal piety is in fact interestingly suggestive for a modern spirituality. The literary and moral approach was naturally important for him. As Lowry says, 'The grace of God, he believed, often consisted in setting certain thoughts before the mind and in keeping off others'.[62] His published *Notebooks* with their cryptic collections of aphorisms in six languages, some of them repeated again and again, are an indication of his personal practice in the stimulation of moral and religious sensibilities.[63]

Perhaps a clue is offered, too, by the celebrated contrast between on the one hand Arnold's early 'aestheticism' and dandified 'poses' (some continued later in life), and on the other the high seriousness of his poetry as well as the commitment evidenced in his religious and moral writings and in the *Notebooks*. The contrast could no doubt be explained partly in psychological terms as an attempt to establish a personality distinct from that of his formidable father as well as to protect his poetic gift from his father's oppressive seriousness.[64] We know, too, that he felt that his was a difficult, almost impossible age for a poet and man of culture to express himself. He wrote to Clough in 1852:

> I am more and more convinced that the world tends to become more and more comfortable for the mass, and more uncomfortable for those of any natural gifts or distinction – and it is as well perhaps that it should be so ... I am sure however that in the air of the present times *il nous manque d'aliment* (we lack nourishment) ... Still, nothing can absolve us from the duty of doing all we can to keep alive our courage and activity.[65]

One might venture to suggest that Arnold was pursuing a kind of inward asceticism for which the traditional outward means and signs no longer seemed appropriate or meaningful. Like Kierkegaard's 'knight of the secret inwardness' (or indeed Kierkegaard himself) Arnold appeared outwardly like most of the world – the dandy, the wit, the school inspector, the family man; but inwardly concentrated on the Eternal. Or, as Newman put it, many decent people appear like the rest of humanity while inwardly they are trying to obey God and serve the world. 'Yet they all look about the same to human eyes, because true religion is a hidden life in the heart; and though it cannot exist without deeds, yet these are for the most part secret deeds, secret devotion, secret prayers, secret self-denial, secret struggles, secret virtues.'[66] Newman's 'hidden life' is interestingly echoed in the title of Arnold's famous poem on 'The Buried Life'. A. C. Benson saw a 'duality of disposition' in Arnold: 'a nature that agonized in the deeps of thought, and a nature that could live easily and cheerfully in daily life'. He thought that Arnold had 'disciplined his life into patience and acquiescence out of feverish discontent and limitless dreams'.[67]

Some will, nevertheless, feel that Arnold's church and worship ideas lack a fully Christian quality. The natural bent of his personal religion was individualistic rather than corporate which some will take to be in itself an indication of its inadequacy, even though he conceded the continuing need for corporate piety. Yet, as Professor Kent has remarked, the question of how far the church as an institution is primary or even central to the religious life of the Christian is, if not exactly an open question, at least one on which different opinions are possible, not least at the present time. The main practical question may be (as with modern reconstructions of Christianity like that of Don Cupitt) whether the rather impersonal God of moral ideals can be an effective object for prayer and worship for ordinary believers. Arnold's own answer seems clear enough on one point: 'Everything turns on its being at *realities* that this worship and language is aimed', even though the 'materialism' of traditional language is interpreted by Arnold in a non-materialistic way. For him, as we have seen, auto-suggestion is not enough; and the 'reality' at which devotion is aimed acquires a certain 'shape' through the form of Jesus.

IV

An attempt can now be made to answer the question whether Arnold's reinterpretation of Christianity is an adequate account of it, or at least whether it is within the Christian tradition and not the work merely of an inconsistent humanist.

Arnold had cut out most of the more 'supernaturalist' aspects of Christianity: miracle goes, even the miracle of the literal, physical resurrection of Jesus. For Arnold quite clearly makes 'resurrection' a symbol for the purely spiritual and moral process within the individual. 'Dying' and 'rising' mean dying to the old lower self and rising to the new higher self. This is what he says Jesus and Paul really meant by 'resurrection'.[68] There is no doubt that Paul did speak of dying and rising in the spiritual sense (see Rom. 6.4–12) but there is no doubt that he also believed in a literal resurrection as the source of the Christian hope. (T.H. Huxley, who liked Arnold's reinterpretation, nevertheless doubted whether Paul would have admitted this to be a valid reinterpretation of his ideas.)[69] Although one may choose to deny the title of 'Christian' to anyone who denies the physical resurrection it has to be said that a number of nineteenth-century Christians and even more twentieth-century ones have at least preferred to emphasize the spiritual dying and rising of believers and by-passed the physical question as insoluble.[70] Concepts of 'resurrection' in any case cannot be tied to the crudely physical as some appear still to suppose. As regards the 'supernatural' in general, it has been argued here that Arnold's 'Eternal' is intended to be an assertion of a transcendental power and being.

In the place that he gives to Jesus, Arnold is no more radical than some modern theologians. The demand that those who wish to see themselves as Christians are bound to traditional interpretations of the Person of Christ should be seen as unacceptable since these interpretations can only be seen as the forms in which inhabitants of past phases of culture have conceived of the figure in the Gospels – and the process was already at work within the

Gospels themselves. One may criticize modern solutions to the problem but not the attempt to reinterpret as such unless one subscribes to the myth of the special authority of the 'undivided' church of the early centuries.

Arnold's central concern with the problems of religious language and religious experience is at the heart of modern discussion of Christian doctrine. Whatever criticisms may be made of his attempt at finding 'verifiable' facts and his reinterpretation of theological statements as 'poetic' rather than 'scientific', he should be credited with having asked the relevant questions and with sketching, however inadequately, the lines along which answers should be looked for. The attempt to give literal meanings to Christian images is often mistaken and sometimes unconsciously dishonest or at least highly selective. (How many Christians *literally* believe in all the statements of the Nicene Creed?) From another point of view, indeed, Arnold's procedures do raise the question of how far one can reinterpret traditional language while still keeping it alive and effective as a vehicle for moral and religious experience.

Another major issue raised in the eighteenth century and becoming ever more pressing since has been the relationship between Christian truth or 'revelation' and historical fact. The ravages of modern gospel criticism have made this more pressing than ever before but the essential issue was already made clear in Lessing's famous aphorism that 'accidental truths of history can never become the proof of necessary truths of reason'.[71] Even if we knew much more than we do about the facts of the life of the historical Jesus, how do we extract doctrines from them? At times Arnold seems to dismiss the kind of religion which ties itself to uncertain historical facts in favour of the 'poetry' of moral ideas which are the real 'facts' of religious experience. (Perhaps significantly, he thought the words of Jesus had been preserved better than his deeds.) It is a delicate and unresolved question how far Christianity can survive without reference to a reasonably secure basis of historical evidence about Jesus himself. Arnold seems to have felt that it was facts of 'experience' that were necessary. In the last resort he was depending on a moral intuition of the 'Eternal not ourselves' and what this signified for our conduct.

Jesus' words were, in a sense, an extension and reinforcement of this original intuition.

Finally, Arnold's whole enterprise in reinterpretation, quite apart from particular details in it, raises the question of the continuity and identity of the Christian tradition. When does development of the tradition (which theologians of all traditions in fact implicitly accept if in different ways) become change? And when does change depart from the 'authentic' tradition? Some words of an eminent modern theologian seem relevant here, and not least to Arnold's claim to be a Christian theologian. 'I have not found myself able to propose any set of beliefs, or other distinguishing characteristics, which any Christian theologian must include or exclude ... I would want to suggest that any theology that emerges out of a serious attention to the Christian tradition has a prima facie claim to being considered a Christian theology. The important issue that then arises is not whether the prima facie claim to be called Christian is sound or not but whether or not it is true.'[72] Judged in this way it is impossible to deny Arnold a prima facie claim to be regarded as a Christian theologian. Whether or not his theology is 'true' is another and more difficult question to answer and has only been lightly touched upon in this essay. That it contains important hints of truth, if not always happily or adequately expressed, seems a reasonable claim to make for him. Even more plausibly it may be claimed that Arnold was, in terms of the questions he raised and the directions in which he sought answers, much more than a timebound religious dilettante. He has some claim to be called one of the fathers of modern English theology and perhaps a patron saint for modern spirituality.

Notes

1. F.D.E. Schleiermacher, *The Christian Faith*, T. & T. Clark 1928, p. viii (Preface to 1830 edition).
2. T.S. Eliot, 'The Use of Poetry and Use of Criticism' (1933) from *Selected Prose*, Pelican 1953, p. 175. The 'philistine' epithet was no doubt deliberately chosen for its ironic use by Arnold himself.

3. F.H. Bradley, *Ethical Studies*, OUP 1962 edn, p.317. For Eliot on Bradley and Arnold see *Selected Essays*, Faber 2nd edn 1951, pp.444ff. But for a defence of Arnold against these particular criticisms see Douglas Bush, *Matthew Arnold*, Macmillan 1971, pp.178ff.; William Robbins, *The Ethical Idealism of Matthew Arnold*, Heinemann 1959, pp.110f., 134f.
4. P.J. Keating (ed.), *Matthew Arnold: Selected Prose*, Penguin 1973, pp.7, 30.
5. For a more sympathetic account Bernard M.G. Reardon, *Religious Thought in the Nineteenth Century*, 1966, pp.324–7 and *Coleridge to Gore*, Longman 1971, pp.381–94.
6. *Literature and Dogma*, Longman 2nd edn 1873, pp.306f. (hereafter *LD*); R.H. Super (ed.), *Complete Prose Works of Matthew Arnold*, University of Michigan Press 1960–77, VI, pp.360, 459f., 575 (hereafter *Works*). The Lord Shaftesbury reference or the whole passage were often omitted in later editions. For Arnold's defence of the image, *God and the Bible* (*GB*) in *Works*, VIII, pp.151ff.
7. So Lionel Trilling, *Matthew Arnold*, Allen and Unwin 1939; endorsed as lately as 1980 by P.J. Creevy, 'The Poetry without the Prose', *Journal of Religious History* XI, 1980–1, p.451.
8. For example B. Hoban, *Matthew Arnold: A Life*, Weidenfeld and Nicholson 1981, pp.368–72; Ruth apRoberts, *Arnold and God*, University of California Press 1983; but especially J.C. Livingston, *Matthew Arnold and Christianity*, University of South Carolina Press 1986 (a detailed defence on similar lines to mine but read after this essay was completed).
9. *God and the Bible* (Popular Edition) Longman 1884, p.viii.
10. *St Paul and Protestantism* (*SPP*) in *Works* VI, pp.9, 11ff.
11. *LD*, chapters IV and V; *Works* VI, pp.232ff., 238ff.
12. G.W.E. Russell (ed.), *Letters of Matthew Arnold*, Macmillan 1895, I, p.176. See *Works* III, pp.52f., 73–5 for criticisms of the *Essays and Reviews* group and Colenso, but he recognized the need for German biblical criticism as a preliminary to biblical study and did his homework on it (*Works* VI, pp.157–62). What was needed beyond this was the 'edification' he found in Spinoza and Dean Stanley (*Works* III, pp.40–64). In fact Jowett and Rowland Williams reinterpreted Protestant salvation doctrine in moral terms very similar to Arnold's. See e.g., B. Jowell in *The Interpretation of Scripture*, Routledge n.d., pp.455, 501 from the dissertations to his Pauline commentary of 1859.
13. *LD* in *Works* VI, pp.152f.; *GB* in *Works* VII, pp.153f., pp.III, pp.65, 73f.
14. *LD* in *Works* VI, pp.175, 407–11.
15. Op. cit., p.171, 189.

16. Op. cit., p. 190n. and similar phrases in 180–6, 193, 196, 200; *GB* in *Works* VII, p. 156.
17. *LD* in *Works* VI, p. 176.
18. Op. cit., p. 216.
19. Op. cit., pp. 181f.
20. Op. cit., pp. 187f.
21. Op. cit., p. 200; *GB* in *Works* VII, pp. 156ff.
22. *LD* in *Works* VI, chapter II.
23. Op. cit., chapter III, pp. 228f.
24. Op. cit., p. 231.
25. Op. cit., pp. 243f., 220f.
26. Op. cit., p. 315.
27. Op. cit., pp. 319, 320; *GB* in *Works* VII, p. 397.
28. *SPP* in *Works* VI, p. 50; *LD* in *Works* VI, pp. 328–32.
29. *Last Essays on Church and Religion* in *Works* VIII, p. 65. The organization of the church is 'comparatively unimportant' (*LD* in *Works* VI, p. 344). It is 'not a corporation for speculative purposes, but ... for purposes of moral growth and practice' (*SPP* in *Works* VI, p. 92). But he defended the Establishment against Dissent while hoping for the comprehension of Dissent within it, e.g. in parts two and three of *SPP*. Here he followed Coleridge and especially Thomas Arnold. See also Jowett in E. Abbot and L. Campbell, *Life and Letters of Jowett*, Murray 1897, I, p. 385.
30. *GB* in *Works* VIII, p. 396f.
31. *LD* in *Works* VI, p. 190n.
32. For example in Paul Van Buren, *The Secular Meaning of the Gospel*, SCM Press 1963, pp. 188–90.
33. *GB* in *Works* VII, p. 397.
34. See note 12 above.
35. As seen in several of the *Essays and Reviews* group, for example Williams, Jowett and Baden Powell. All show a considerable Kantian influence directly or mediated through Coleridge's version of him. Cf. also W. Robbins, op. cit., pp. 83–5.
36. For a powerful cautionary exposition of the difficulties of the apologetic appeal to religious experience see F. R. Tennant, *Philosophical Theology*, CUP 1930, I, pp. 306–32.
37. H. F. Lowry (ed), *Arnold's Letters to Clough*, OUP repr. 1960, pp. 143f.
38. Preface to *The Hundred Greatest Men*, London 1880 (*Works* IX, p. 63) and in altered form in 'The Study of Poetry' in *Essays in Criticism* Second Series (*Works* IX, p. 161). For a criticism of Eliot's and Trilling's claim that Arnold here was simply replacing religion with poetry see George Watson, *The Literary Critics*, Penguin 1962, p. 157 quoted by B. W. Martin, *John Keble*, Croom Helm 1976, p. 172 who also sees

some limited parallels with Keble's 'sacramental' view of poetry and religion.

39. 'Dr Stanley' in *Works* III, pp.79f.
40. M.H. Abrams, *The Mirror and the Lamp*, OUP 1953, pp.334f. for this and a comparison with J.S. Mill.
41. For a discussion of these including such diverse figures as Frederic Harrison, Herbert Spencer and John Tyndall see P.J. Creevy, op. cit.
42. T.S. Eliot, 'Arnold and Pater' in *Selected Essays*, p.434; Lionel Trilling, op. cit., p.358, endorsed by Creevy, p.451.
43. Preface to the Popular Edition of *LD*; *Last Essays* in *Works* IX, p.181; J.C. Livingston, 'Matthew Arnold and his Critics on the Truth of Christianity', *Journal of American Academy of Religion* XLI, 1973, pp.391ff. for critique of Trilling.
44. Livingston, art. cit., pp.393, 395.
45. R.B. Braithwaite, *An Empiricist's View of the Nature of Religious Belief*, 1955.
46. Livingston, art. cit., pp.398f.
47. L. Trilling, op. cit., p.340; W. Robbins, op. cit., p.134.
48. R.B. Braithwaite, op. cit., pp.28f.
49. *Letters to Clough*, p.87.
50. B.M.G. Reardon, *Religious Thought*, pp.7f.
51. J. Hillis Miller, *The Disappearance of God*, Harvard University Press 1963, p.265 quoted in D. Bush, op. cit., p.178. Cf. D.J. DeLaura, *Hebrew and Hellene in Victorian England*, University of Texas Press 1969, p.xvii who claims that 'Arnold persistently appeals to a covert supernaturalism' but 'in the final reckoning he confessed his inability to fuse science and faith, ideas and morality, in a higher, post-Christian synthesis'.
52. A.C. Benson, *The Leaves of the Tree*, London 1910, p.299.
53. *GB* in *Works* VII, p.160.
54. N. Sagorsky, *Between Two Worlds*, CUP 1983, pp.123, 126f.
55. John Kent, *The Unacceptable Face*, SCM Press 1987, p.220.
56. *LD* in *Works* VI, p.311.
57. *Last Essays* in *Works* VIII, pp.161f.
58. Abbot and Campbell, *Jowett*, II, pp.310ff.
59. D. Krook, *Three Traditions of Moral Thought*, CUP 1959, pp.137, 220f.
60. Cf. Frederic Harrison's complaints about *Essays and Reviews* in *Westminster Review*, July 1860, pp.33–49; Alasdair Macintyre on John Robinson's *Honest to God* in D.L. Edwards and J.A.T. Robinson (eds), *The Honest to God Debate*, SCM Press 1963.
61. E. Mâle, *Religious Art from the Twelfth to the Eighteenth Centuries*, Routledge 1949, pp.21f., 23.

62. *Letters to Clough*, p.44n.
63. H.F. Lowry et al. (eds), *The Notebooks of Matthew Arnold*, OUP 1952, passim.
64. K. Allott, *Matthew Arnold*, British Council/Longmans revd edn 1962, p.16.
65. *Letters to Clough*, pp.122f.; cf. *Letters of Arnold*, I, p.213.
66. J.H. Newman, sermon on 'Christ Hidden from the World' in *Parochial and Plain Sermons*, London 1869, IV, p.243. For Kierkegaard's 'knight of the secret inwardness' see his *Concluding Unscientific Postscript*, Princeton University Press 1941, pp.446–52.
67. A.C. Benson, op. cit., p.308.
68. See above, notes 25 and 28.
69. L. Huxley (ed.), *Life and Letters of T.H. Huxley*, Macmillan 1900, I, p.329.
70. So Jowett and in more recent times Bultmann. See also Harry Williams, *True Resurrection*, Mitchell Beazley 1972.
71. G.E. Lessing, *On the Proof of the Spirit and of Power* in H. Chadwick (ed.), *Lessing's Theological Writings*, A. and C. Black 1956, p.53.
72. M.F. Wiles, 'The Criteria of Christian Theology' in *Working Papers in Doctrine*, SCM Press 1976, pp.192f.; and on the same problem D.A. Pailin, 'Authenticity in the Interpretation of Christianity' in M. Pye and R. Morgan (eds), *The Cardinal Meaning*, Mouton 1974, pp.127–59.

7

F. D. Maurice: Rebel Conservative

DAVID M. THOMPSON

At first sight Frederick Denison Maurice does not seem to be an obvious religious rebel. He was born in 1805, the son of Michael Maurice, a Unitarian minister and a strong political liberal. He died in 1872, a minister of the Church of England and Knightbridge Professor of Moral Philosophy in the University of Cambridge. His theological and political position was conservative: he defended the state as a divine institution; he defended subscription to the thirty-nine articles of the Church of England as a condition of university study; and he was not enamoured of contemporary developments in biblical criticism. He certainly abandoned, if he did not rebel against, his parents' religious and political position: but he seems to be a rebel moving in the wrong direction. Yet in the middle of his career he was a Christian Socialist who voiced his sympathy for the working classes; and he was dismissed from his position as Professor of Theology at King's College, London, which must surely count as prima facie evidence of religious rebellion! Little wonder that Olive Brose should subtitle her biography of Maurice 'rebellious conformist'.[1]

Maurice was also an isolated figure. Soon after his death his theology was strongly attacked in the *Fortnightly Review* by Leslie Stephen (who was also the author of the critical article on him in the *Dictionary of National Biography*). His loyal friend John Llewellyn Davies sprang to his defence, but even he admitted that Maurice never had a large following. 'Mr Maurice has left behind him no large or coherent body of followers,' he wrote. 'But those who could have been named as theological disciples of Mr Maurice were always few.'[2] The public attitude to

Maurice seems to have changed after the publication of the *Life and Letters* by his son in 1884. Henry Shorthouse noted his saintliness, pointing out that a boyhood friend had called him 'Christ-like'. E.S. Talbot, the first Warden of Keble College, Oxford, said that he stood out 'as one of the most remarkable figures in this century for the independence of moral and mental originality, for range and subtlety of thought, for the magic of personal influence'; though he also warned that it was dangerous to occupy a lonely position.[3]

Maurice was in fact someone who defied classification. One of the most misleading descriptions of him is that he was 'Broad Church'. John Tulloch took care in his influential *Movements of Religious Thought in Britain during the Nineteenth Century* (1885) to say that Maurice disowned that title, but he nevertheless regarded Maurice as being 'rightly identified with the great succession of liberal thinkers in the Church of England'.[4] The root of the difficulty in placing Maurice is that like Coleridge he reacted against both the new liberalism and the traditional orthodoxy of what was still popularly called Calvinism. He was therefore neither reactionary nor progressive. He found a resting place in a Platonic view of the nature of reality that enabled him to retain biblical language whilst interpreting it in an original way. Professor Christensen remarked that 'Maurice had an amazingly deft, and often ingenious, way of making the biblical texts say precisely what his Platonic conception of reality demanded that they say.'[5] To appreciate the significance of Maurice's Platonism is a greater help towards the understanding of his theology than the other comment often made about him, namely that he was a mystic. Dean Church noted that Maurice 'and his master Coleridge ... with all their imputed mysticism ... seem to me to say plain things as often as most people'.[6] R.H. Hutton showed characteristic insight when he remarked that

> Theologians of the ordinary type coming to the study of Maurice are not only apt to be bewildered as to his real meaning, but to feel themselves reproached for that external and 'notional' view of things divine which they find him

> rebuking as the lowest element in himself, whereas *they* had rather taken a pride in their masterly speculative apprehension of matters so transcendental.[7]

Maurice was also like Coleridge in that he left Unitarianism for the Church of England; but again like Coleridge he had a rather idiosyncratic view of it, which depended on his particular understanding of the link between church and nation in the providence of God. So Michael Ramsey's statement that Maurice 'was Anglican to the core' was misleading.[8] Like many converts he saw the church to which he had moved as the answer to certain difficulties, and that always influenced the way he explained it. Sometimes those who had been brought up in the Church of England found it difficult to recognize their church from Maurice's description.

John Kent has cited Maurice's belief that both church and nation were divine institutions as evidence for his conservatism. He sees the decline of belief in the supernatural from the eighteenth century on and the increasingly secular view of the state and society that resulted as providing the main challenge to the church in the modern period. In this context Maurice is classed with de Maistre, Lammenais and Coleridge as a romantic conservative provoked by a feeling of 'incipient cultural superfluousness'.[9] To be sure Maurice reacted against the French Revolution, but whether this is decisive evidence of cultural superfluousness is debatable. The basic problem is that his dependence on Plato cannot be regarded as simply a reversion to the supernatural, yet it is obviously not post-Kantian. Perhaps therefore he does deserve to be treated as a rebel, however conservative his conclusions may have been.

Maurice's theological movement began with his study of Plato under Julius Hare at Cambridge in 1823–24. From this he learnt many things, but in particular that

> there is a way out of party opinions; a principle which is not a compromise between them, but which is implied in both, and of which each is bearing witness. Hare did not tell us this … Plato himself does not say it; he makes us feel it.[10]

The possibility that there might be such a way through conflict of opinions was a source of hope to a young man who had been keenly affected by the divisions within his own family on the matter of religion. One by one his mother and sisters had broken with his father's unitarianism, and had adopted various forms of Calvinism. In the circumstances it is perhaps not surprising that Maurice yearned for a position which might do justice to the truth on each side. R. H. Hutton suggested that his change of faith was almost as much due to his passionate desire to find a centre of unity beneath religous feuds as to the impression made on him by the scriptures:

> He held that he had discovered this centre of unity when he had discovered the evidence of a growing divine purpose ... to draw man close to God, a purpose effected not by any unnatural convulsion of human nature, but by the descent of God into human nature, and by the taking-up of human nature into God.[11]

The decisive movement of his mind as it concerned the nature of God can be discerned from his letters between 1830 and 1832; and his baptism in the Church of England was a stage in that process, not the culmination of it. It began early in 1830, as he was finishing his novel, *Eustace Conway*, with a change of view about the significance of the death of Christ. Some time in February he wrote to his sister, Priscilla, that 'the death of Christ is far, very far, more than a mere peace-making, though that view of it is the root of every other. But it is actually and literally the death of you and me, and the whole human race.' Hence the only life human beings had was a universal life in Christ. In January 1831 he wrote, again to Priscilla, that he had come to see the significance of those biblical texts which spoke of Christ as the Light and Truth, manifested in darkness. Furthermore, 'it was pride, it was self, it was sin, which separated between me and God, which produced the darkness. Christ had taken that away, and therefore the true Light shineth'. About this time he read Thomas Erskine's *Brazen Serpent* and found it 'unspeakably comfortable'.[12]

He was baptized on 29 March 1831, and in October wrote to his mother of how he had come to see 'the necessity of taking our heavenly Father's love to us for granted, in order to be the ground and parent of love in Him to us'. 'It seems to me,' he continued, 'that all relations acquire a significance and become felt as actually living and real when contemplated in Him, which out of Him, even to the most intensely affectionate, they cannot have.' Finally in February 1832 he wrote two letters to his father which summarized the position he had reached. He had come to see communion with God as the desire of the characters depicted in the Bible: 'They wished to know God, not in a vague, loose sense, but actually to know Him as a friend.' The only way in which that longing could be satisfied was if 'the Infinite, Incomprehensible Jehovah is manifested in the person of a Man, a Man conversing with us, living among us, entering into all our infirmities and temptations, and passing into all our conditions'. Nor was it sufficient simply for God to be revealed in the life of a human being; he had to be seen in death as well:

> To pass through that state which had been proclaimed by God and always regarded by man as emphatically the punishment of that hatred and opposition to God; to pass through it and reappear again in the world with God's own glad tidings of pardon in his hand attested by that act; was absolutely necessary [on His part] before there could be any peaceful, comfortable feeling in man towards the Maker with whom he had felt himself at such issue.[13]

If therefore the Mediator was to manifest God, he must partake of God's nature. Not only that; if he was to effect mediation he must share his spirit with his disciples, and his spirit must therefore also partake of God's nature. Maurice therefore abandoned his father's unitarianism because it did not do justice to the biblical record.

What is striking about the way Maurice described his position, even at this early period, is that he was first convinced of the principle, then of an event or set of events to manifest the principle, and then that the life, death and resurrection of Christ were the events in question. In other words the story of Jesus assumed its significance as the particular manifestation of an underlying principle; and the validation of that story lay in the principle rather than the particularity. This is the sense in which Maurice's approach to theology was Platonic. In the light of that, the statement in the letter to Priscilla of February 1830 that the death of Christ is 'actually and literally the death of you and me' did not mean quite what it appeared to mean. He was not referring our present state to what was achieved historically by the death of Christ; rather he was saying that the death of Christ shows us what has always been true, because it is an eternal principle, 'that we are dead' and 'that we are risen'.[14]

Maurice became an Anglican after he went to Oxford in January 1830, and by 1832 he had decided to seek ordination. Although he graduated before the Oxford Movement began in 1833, he was initially sympathetic to Tractarian views, probably because of the significance they attached to the church. Early in 1834 he wrote to his friend Acland: 'I would wish to live and die for the assertion of this truth: that the Universal Church is just as much a reality as any particular nation is.' He went on to say that one could only believe in the reality of the nation if one believed in the reality of the church; that the church was 'the witness for the true constitution of man as man, a child of God, an heir of heaven, and taking up his freedom by baptism'; whereas the world was 'a miserable, accursed, rebellious order, which denies this foundation, which will create a foundation of self-will, choice, taste, opinion'.[15]

But this letter showed that he was not going to fit in easily with existing positions. At the heart of his understanding of the church lay his view of baptism, and on this he disagreed both with the kind of Calvinism represented by his mother, and later with Tractarianism as represented by Pusey. He was unable to accept the Calvinist view of election, and expounded his own view in an oft-quoted letter to his mother of December 1833:

> My text is this, 'Know ye not that Jesus Christ is in you?' ... The truth is that every man is in Christ; the condemnation of every man is that he will not own the truth; he will not *act* as if

> this were *true*, he will not believe that which is the truth, that except he were joined to Christ, he could not think, breathe, live a single hour.[16]

Maurice was attempting to comfort his mother because of her fear that she was not among the elect. What he said was an amplification of his earlier argument to Priscilla, but it was now sharply expressed in the statement that the difference between the believer and the unbeliever was not about the fact, but precisely in the belief of the fact – the fact being that 'Christ is the Head of every man'. Similarly condemnation came from failure to acknowledge the truth, and acts of self-will were understood as manifestations of this fundamental failure. R. H. Hutton summed up the controversial point here well when he noted that 'If the only difference between sin and righteousness is that men living in sin do not recognize their accomplished redemption, while men living in faith do, the sin would appear to be a sin of ignorance rather than of will.'[17]

Baptism was for Maurice the declaration of the true relationship between God and humanity. This insight was brought home to him in his pastoral ministry, as a curate in the country parish of Bubbenhall, Warwickshire, from 1834 to 1836, and as chaplain at Guy's Hospital from 1836 to 1846:

> It seemed to me that except I could address all kinds of people as members of Christ and children of God, I could not address them at all. Their sin, it seemed to me, must mean a departure from that state; it must be their true state, that which Christ had claimed for them ... I felt therefore much sympathy with those who spoke of baptism as bearing witness of the state into which men are redeemed.[18]

By 'those' he meant the Tractarians, but his sympathy was shattered by the publication of Pusey's Tract on Baptism (no. 67), in which Pusey expounded the view that post-baptismal sin deprived the baptized of their purity. This seemed to Maurice to take away with one hand what had been given with the other. Nevertheless his understanding of baptism remained one of the most attractive features of his theology for his admirers. It underlay *Letters to a Quaker* or *The Kingdom of Christ* (1838), which grew out of and used material from his *Letters on Baptism*, begun in 1836, but never published. In fact, the significance of baptism is much clearer in the first edition than in the much revised second edition of 1842, which is the most readily obtainable edition today.

Maurice's theology, and in particular his affirmations about the sovereignty of God and the nature of human relationships as manifested by baptism, lay at the heart of his politics. The story of his involvement in the Christian Socialist movement of 1848–54 has often been told.[19] But it is still sometimes a puzzle that such a conservative thinker should have been involved in an apparently radical movement. The explanation is that there was an almost chronic failure among the 'band of brothers' to appreciate the true import of one another's aims and intentions, and the correspondence between Maurice and Ludlow is the best indication of this. Maurice's sermons on *The Lord's Prayer*, preached in Lincoln's Inn during the spring of 1848 as the news of events in Paris came through, show how easily his real view could be misinterpreted. On 27 February he preached on 'Thy Kingdom come' and said that most people must have felt a contrast that week 'between a Kingdom which cannot be moved, and kingdoms which appeared firm one day, and have been shaken to the ground the next', referring to the French Revolution.[20] But he went on to criticize those who spoke as though the coming of God's kingdom required a change in the present order of things:

> All seem to assume that the constitution of things is evil; not that we are evil in departing from it. With strange unanimity, eager politicians, restless ecclesiastics, hopeful millenarians, seem to take it for granted that the devil is lord of the universe; only that by an improvement in the arrangements of civil life, by a stronger assertion of priestly authority, or by the final coming of the Son of Man, the evil power may be weakened or broken.[21]

A week later he returned to the same theme under the text, 'Thy will be done'. He wondered whether they were doomed to hear again the hollow phrases of sixty years before, to 'pass through another series of the same false promises, vain hopes, bitter disappointments, the same dreams of peace realized in blood, which were appointed for the last generation'. Yet to say that seemed to imply that the brotherhood of man was a fantasy or a crime.[22] Again he found his solution in God:

> We say that Christianity can bring about a true fraternity among men. But ... Christianity, as a mere system of doctrines or practices, will never make men brothers. By Christianity we must understand the reconciliation of mankind to God in Christ ... No notion, or set of notions, will bind us together; He binds us who has given his Son for us all, that we might not live for ever in separation from each other.[23]

The emphasis that Christian faith related to something God had done rather than to a set of beliefs was characteristic. So although those sermons excited, and continued to excite his hearers to forms of practical commitment and service, Maurice's own commitment remained determinedly theological. As he had put the point in the first sermon of the series:

> '*Our Father*:' there lies the expression of that fixed eternal relation which Christ's birth and death have established between the littleness of the creature and the Majesty of the Creator; the one great practical answer to the philosopher who would make heaven clear by making it cold; would assert the dignity of the Divine Essence, by emptying it of its love, and reducing it into nothingness.[24]

This was the period when Ludlow first discussed with Maurice ways in which the church might reach the masses of people who were separated from it, an issue given sudden domestic urgency by the Chartist Convention proposed for April 1848. In the event the mass demonstration planned for Kennington Common was a fiasco, but it led to the launching of *Politics for the People* by Kingsley, Ludlow and Maurice. While Ludlow looked to political change, Maurice thought that the means of averting an English political revolution might be a theological reformation.[25] A clue to his reasoning on the matter is given in a remark to another friend at that time, when in advising a course of metaphysical reading, he remarked that 'the republic of Plato is, in its highest aspect, the dream of an universal Church, in its lowest it touches closely upon French Communism'.[26]

The differences between Maurice and Ludlow on this point only gradually became clear, as the correspondence between the two men shows. Writing to Ludlow in December 1848 he said, 'I begin, where I think you [Ludlow and Carlyle] both end, in the acknowledgment of the divine sovereignty; thence I come to the Tory idea of kings reigning by the grace of God'.[27] Or again in September 1852, at the time of the controversy over a pamphlet on democracy entitled *The Duty of the Age*, written by Lord Goderich, one of the Christian Socialist group, Maurice wrote to Ludlow: 'I must begin from the Father if I am to acknowledge the Son; from the head if I am to acknowledge a body, from the one Spirit if I am to see life in the many members.[28] In 1848 he had repudiated the idea of the sovereignty of the people in any sense or form 'as at once the silliest and most blasphemous of contradictions', calling it 'the *same* contradiction of which the kings have been guilty' because 'they have reigned as if they were not in covenant with God, as if they were not governing by His grace'.[29] In his letter of 1852 to Ludlow Maurice asked a pertinent question, which is still relevant for Christian discussions of democracy:

> Those to whom you speak believe that you wish the people to govern themselves. 'Yes,' you say, 'we do. That is, we wish them to restrain themselves; that is, we wish them to submit to Christ and have Him for their king.' Well, but what I wish to know is, *do they make* Christ their king? Might they choose another if they liked? If not, your democracy is not what other people intend by it, and what they have a right to intend by it. Twist the word as you will, it must imply a right on the part of the people to choose, cashier and depose their rulers. It must

> imply that power proceeds from them, that it does not find them.[30]

Such a view was unacceptable to Maurice because he could not contemplate any situation in which the people might have the right or power to cashier God. In the same letter he wrote, 'I must have Monarchy, Aristocracy and Socialism, or rather Humanity, recognized as necessary elements and conditions of an organic Christian society.'[31] Christian Socialism for Maurice, therefore, was the assertion of God's order.

In his careful discussion of the context of this exchange, Torben Christensen noted that for Maurice democracy meant rule by self-will, whilst aristocracy referred to those who were spiritually superior – both beliefs derived from Plato.[32] It could therefore be argued that Maurice's position was essentially political rather than theological, that indeed the crucial assumptions were philosophical or epistemological, derived from Plato. But although the concepts were Plato's, what justified them in Maurice's eyes was that the ground was God. Maurice recognized in his letter of 8 September 1852 that Ludlow would find his political ideas difficult to stomach, and even acknowledged that Ludlow was more up-to-date politically than he was. But, he said, his vocation was to lay foundations on which others might build. 'I am only a digger,' he concluded.[33] Ludlow's reply was sharp. He felt that Christianity had so revolutionized the conception of man's moral and social nature that he could not take his politics or ethics from Aristotle or Plato:

> Surely the whole work of Christianity is building and not digging, – just as digging was the work, the only true work of the heathen philosopher, until the corner-stone should be laid … It does seem to me that you are liable to be carried away by Platonistic dreams about an Order, and a Kingdom, and a Beauty, self-realized in their own eternity, and which so put to shame all earthly counterparts that it becomes labour lost to attempt anything like an earthly realization of them, and all one has to do is to show them, were it only in glimpses, to

> others by tearing away the cobwebs of human systems that conceal them. I do not think this is Christianity.[34]

This criticism of the timeless, almost unhistorical nature of the theology of Maurice, derived from his Platonism, went to the heart of the matter. Hence Maurice's defence of his position, and his understanding of the calling of a theologian in general, deserves attention. His classic statement on the matter came in his reply to Ludlow's letter on 24 September:

> My business, because I am a theologian, and have no vocation except for theology, is not to build, but to dig, to show that economy and politics ... must have a ground beneath themselves, that society is not to be made anew by arrangements of ours, but is to be regenerated by finding the law and ground of its order and harmony the only secret of its existence in God. This must seem to you an unpractical and unchristian method; to me it is the only one which makes action possible, and Christianity anything more than an artificial religion for the use of believers ... To preach the Gospel of that Kingdom, the fact that it is among us, and is not to be set up at all, is my calling and business.[35]

Maurice always seems to have seen his role as that of a teacher, especially in the Socratic manner. Ludlow said of him, that 'he always went below a man's words to his real meaning, in many cases thus explaining the man to himself'[36] He certainly did not see himself as someone who was going to change society by setting up new institutions. He supported the Working Men's Associations because he saw them as a realization of God's intended way of working together. He also had high hopes of their self-educative function. His interest in working-class education did not begin with the Working Men's College, though in many ways that was his lasting memorial. Those who draw a sharp distinction between Maurice's involvement in the worker co-operatives and the Working Men's College miss the significance of the fact that Maurice, like Plato, saw all life as an education: learning and working went together.

That vision of the co-operatives as a realization of God's order was spoiled if they became human contrivances. In some ways it is remarkable that Maurice supported the Working Men's Associations as much as he did. His colleagues found his attitude surprising and unpredictable. They could not understand what he meant when he criticized the Council of Promoters of Working Men's Associations 'as hindering the gradual development of what I regard as a divine purpose, as an attempt to create a new constitution of society, when what we want is that the old constitution should exhibit its true functions and energies'.[37]

In a penetrating assessment of Maurice's Christian Socialism in 1884, Llewellyn Davies said that this letter showed that 'State Socialism of the prevalent type would have been distasteful to Maurice.' One reason was his distrust of vast machinery:

> His predisposition would have been in favour of voluntary action, implying and calling out mutual regard and consideration and the turning of hearts to hearts. And he would have hoped for no good results from compulsory redistributions, seeking to bring about by mechanical arrangements what the Maker intends to be the fruits of the awakened and enlightened spirit.[38]

Such action also tended 'to confuse the provinces of the state and the church – that is, of the law and spirit.' In August 1849 Maurice expounded the difference in this way. The state could not and should not be communist, since its nature was to uphold individual rights and possession. The church, on the other hand, was 'communist in principle'. The union of church and state thus achieved the right balance:

> Church Reformation therefore, in its highest sense, I conceive involves *theologically* the reassertion of these truths in their fullness apart from their Calvinistical and Trinitarian limitations or dilutions; *socially* the assertion on the ground of these truths of an actual living community under Christ in which no man has a right to call anything that he has his own but in

> which there is spiritual fellowship and practical co-operation; *nationally* the assertion of a union, grounded not on alliances and compromises but on the constitution of things, between this Universal Community and the State of which the principle is Personal Distinction and the symbol Property.[39]

Whilst this was a novel justification for the essential union of church and state, it was certainly not revolutionary. But Maurice and his colleagues were attacked for their alleged revolutionary views in the conservative *Quarterly Review*. In 1850 there was an attack on the staff of Queen's College, which included Maurice; and then a more substantial attack in September 1851, when Kingsley's novels, *Alton Locke* and *Yeast*, a lecture by Maurice on Co-operation, and *Politics for the People* were linked with a dozen or more literary products of the French Revolution and reviewed under the general title, 'Revolutionary Literature'. The author was J.W. Croker, who had privileged access to the *Quarterly*, and it may have been an idiosyncratic view. But it explains why the authorities at King's College were somewhat nervous about the effects of Maurice's activities on the reputation of the College.

This does not mean, however, that Maurice's dismissal over the question of eternal punishment in 1853 should be treated as a political issue masquerading as a theological one.[40] It was neither arbitrary nor coincidental that of all the issues that might have caused offence in Maurice's *Theological Essays* of 1853, eternal punishment was the one that provoked controversy. A generation later Llewellyn Davies wrote that it was 'not easy for those who are breathing the freer air of the present day to realize how imperatively, before the controversy of Mr Maurice with Dr Jelf, at least a silent acquiescence in the doctrine of a hopeless future for all who died without having turned to God was demanded by the current orthodoxy'; and in his response to Leslie Stephen in 1874 he noted that in a meeting of the London clergy to discuss Moody's proposed London mission, no one had referred to the 'hopeless doom of all who die unconverted' even though a generation before it was assumed as a commonplace.[41]

The problem as usual with Maurice was that he was fighting on two fronts at once. The *Theological Essays* were written for Unitarians, and criticized many of the theological rationalizations characteristic of that position; but they also attacked a number of the commonplaces of evangelical theology. Thus Maurice not only attacked the usual understanding of eternal punishment, but also explained the development of the doctrine as the result of the use of theology as an instrument of government. What the mediaeval church did, said Maurice, was 'to materialize the terrors of the future world, and to make those terrors the great motives to obedience'. The fatal mistake was 'the doctrine that the thing men have to dread is punishment and not sin, and that the greatest reward which the highest power in the church can hold out is deliverance from punishment, not deliverance from sin'. Luther's achievement had been to deliver us from this doctrine.[42]

Maurice's suggestion that theological development may have been due to the necessities of social control has a strikingly modern ring, and makes him appear more radical than he actually was. Some evangelical criticisms of Maurice took up this precise point. Geoffrey Rowell quotes a review of Maurice in the Wesleyan journal, *The London Quarterly Review*, and comments that there can be 'no doubting the use of hell as a sanction for maintaining the moral and social order implicit in this criticism'.[43] But although the social control argument was deployed, it does not follow that it was decisive. Torben Christensen argued convincingly that *Theological Essays* was the turning point in Maurice's reputation because it confirmed the criticisms which had been made, particularly in the *Record* from 1849, of a Coleridgean subversive tendency in theology which did include Maurice. Christensen did not think that the verdict passed on the book by contemporary scholars was on the whole unfair. 'They argued their case better and more intelligently than posterity has been wont to believe.'[44]

Maurice explained his position very clearly in his letter to Hort of November 1849. To the familiar statements about God's redemption of mankind, his choice of a family of witnesses to that redemption marked out by baptism, and the duty of those witnesses to testify that others are part of that family as well as themselves, was added a statement about the nature of the Gospel: 'the *starting-point* of the Gospel, as I read it, is the absolute Love of God; the *reward* of the Gospel is the kowledge of that love.'[45] In the end Maurice could not believe that God's love would be frustrated. Hence he was agnostic about the duration of any punishment, preferring to concentrate on the positive rather than the negative.

Maurice's arguments failed to carry the day with the Council of King's College, and at a special meeting on 27 October 1853 they resolved that the opinions set out in his essay were 'of dangerous tendency, and calculated to unsettle the minds of the theological students of King's College'. He was therefore dismissed.[46]

The later controversies of Maurice's life both involved attitudes to the Bible. He reacted violently against Mansel's Bampton Lectures of 1858 on *The Limits of Religious Thought*, and the controversy has often been regarded as generating more heat than light. Mansel summarized his argument in three propositions:

> 1. That the Absolute Nature of God is unknown to man.
> 2. That conceptions derived from human consciousness do not represent the Absolute Nature of God.
> 3. That God is revealed in scripture by means of relative conceptions, accommodated to man's faculties.[47]

Maurice objected because Mansel's argument struck at the heart of his own belief. For him what was distinctive about Christianity was precisely the fact that God had made himself known as he really was, and the scriptures revealed a God who entered into a real relationship with his creation. Mansel's theology was unacceptable because it started from the wrong end, from man instead of God. In one sense Maurice's reaction against Mansel was an example of his reaction against the Enlightenment generally.

Bishop Colenso's book on the Pentateuch in 1862 was more embarrassing to Maurice, because Colenso was a self-confessed disciple who had dedicated a book of sermons to him. Maurice reacted strongly because, as he wrote to Llewellyn Davies,

Colenso's 'idea of history is that it is a branch of arithmetic'.[48] He thought that Colenso's criticism of historicity had missed the point. In Maurice's view 'the reason knows for sure that when the Bible records a historical event, it must have taken place because it grasps the eternal truth, manifested through it'.[49] But he did not claim that the truth was independent of the facts: Maurice categorically rejected Strauss' view that the Bible could be understood as a set of myths which contained truth.[50] Thus far Maurice's view of the Bible might seem conservative: but his view that revelation was progressive, certainly in the Old Testament, made his attitude to biblical questions seem liberal. The coming of Christ was the climax of that progressive revelation, and this enabled him to reconcile a Platonic belief in eternal truths with a biblical insight into the significance of decisive events. The resulting combination left many headaches for his interpreters.

Hence his place in the nineteenth-century debate over biblical criticism is hard to assign. H.G. Wood regarded him as 'the convinced exponent of ... biblical realism'; and Michael Ramsey and Alec Vidler tended to follow suit.[51] Michael Ramsey noted that his critics said that Maurice tended to 'miss the Biblical emphasis upon those *momenta* in history in which salvation is offered and accepted' but on the whole he agreed with Wood.[52] Christensen regarded these verdicts as mistaken: 'The biblical history of revelation has a central place in Maurice's theological thinking, but it is interpreted and understood on the basis of a Platonic conception of reality.'[53]

How then should Maurice be assessed? Was he a religious rebel? In many ways he was reacting against certain characteristic emphases of Protestantism, and Christensen's analysis of his theology clearly shows his difference from the main Protestant tradition. This is one argument for his originality. The reaction against certain understandings of the atonement and the emphasis on the incarnation may also explain why Ramsey was so enthusiastic about him. There is a certain Catholic strand in his theology. This point was noted by R.H. Hutton in the last century when he wrote that

I have never been able to reconcile Maurice's profound and

> deep sense of the awful reality of sin . . . with his language as to the absolute completeness of redemption even as regards those who have not been rescued from a life of sin; nor with his language here and there – language which I believe he holds in common with the Roman Catholic Church – as to the purely negative and unreal character of sin.[54]

But if Maurice is felt to be Catholic, it is not so much the Catholicism of Aquinas as that of the neoPlatonists. Any enthusiast for Plato does well to remember the warning of Donald Mackinnon delivered at William Temple's Conference on 'The Life of the Church and the Order of Society' at Malvern in 1941, when he suggested

> that those who are striving to speak the language of a theology of crisis, perhaps possess a deeper insight into the saving truth that Christ was and is both God and man than those who make much of the 'sociological implications' of the Incarnation. For the Incarnation is not the disclosing of certain universal cosmical principles; it is the manifestation of the divine word in the harsh particularities of an individual human existence. Between that Platonism which, as Dr Inge pointed out, exercised so great an influence on English theological thought and the mystery of the Incarnation there is a great gulf.[55]

In this connection no scholar can now ignore Christensen's critique of Ramsey's assertion that Maurice presents a 'classic' doctrine of the atonement. Maurice criticized penal substitution, mainly because it made Christ's sacrifice dependent on the existence of sin, whereas he wanted to see Christ's death on the cross as the manifestation of an eternal truth. Christ was mediator before he died, not because he died.[56] Christensen's conclusion about the modern admiration for Maurice's theology was harsh. He believed that it was

> to a large extent due to the fact that it has been trimmed, as it were, to suit modern religious and theological ideas. Here his elusive arguments, his often indistinct language, and apparent

> obscurities were an advantage – it made it possible to fit him into later patterns of theological thought.[57]

Does this mean that John Kent's assessment of Maurice as responding to an incipient feeling of cultural superfluousness is correct? Obviously he was not a rationalist, and did not share the developing critique of the supernatural. But his answer was not straightforward denial. Instead he moved to a rather different position, based on Plato. In this sense he was very like Coleridge, whom John Stuart Mill described in a famous essay as 'the great awakener in this country of the spirit of philosophy, within the bounds of traditional opinions'. Similarly Mill's comparison of Bentham and Coleridge is also relevant: 'By Bentham, beyond all others, men have been led to ask themselves, in regard to any ancient or received opinion, Is it true? and by Coleridge, What is the meaning of it?'[58] Maurice relentlessly asked Coleridge's question. The effect was no less critical in nineteenth-century English theology, even if Hutton did regard him as 'essentially a spiritual knight errant'.[59] Maurice may not have been an obvious rebel, but he certainly cannot be described as orthodox. The paradox in him is well caught in Jowett's description of Maurice quoted in a letter from Benson to Lightfoot in 1866: 'All are right: – I am most right. All are wrong: – I *most* wrong.'[60]

Notes

1. O. J. Brose, *Frederick Denison Maurice: Rebellious Conformist*, Ohio University Press 1971.
2. J. Ll. Davies, 'Secularism and Mr Maurice's Theology', *Contemporary Review*, XXIV, 1874, p. 24.
3. J. H. Shorthouse, 'Frederick Denison Maurice', *The Nineteenth Century*, XV, 1884, pp. 850–51; E. S. Talbot, 'Frederick Denison Maurice', *Macmillans Magazine*, L, 1884, pp. 23, 33.
4. J. Tulloch, *Movements of Religious Thought in Britain during the Nineteenth Century* ed. A. C. Cheyne, Leicester University Press 1971, p. 261.
5. T. Christensen, *The Divine Order*, E. J. Brill 1973, p. 212; see also pp. 145–51.
6. M. C. Church, *Life and Letters of Dean Church*, Macmillan 1897,

p. 17, quoted in A.M. Ramsey, *F.D. Maurice and the Conflicts of Modern Theology*, CUP 1951, p. 18.

7. R.H. Hutton, 'Mr Maurice as Heresiarch', *Aspects of Religious and Scientific Thought*, Macmillan 1899, p. 270.
8. Ramsey, *F.D. Maurice*, p. 113.
9. J.H.S. Kent, *The End of the Line?*, SCM Press 1982, p. 31.
10. J.C. Hare, *Charges to the Clergy of the Archdeaconry of Lewes*, Macmillan 1856, x; quoted in F. Maurice, *The Life of Frederick Denison Maurice*, Macmillan 1884, i, p. 56.
11. R.H. Hutton, 'Maurice and the Unitarians', *Aspects of Religious and Scientific Thought*, p. 265.
12. Maurice, *Life*, i, pp. 106, 120, 121.
13. Ibid., i, pp. 130, 131, 132, 136–37.
14. Compare the discussion in D. Newsome, *Two Classes of Men*, John Murray 1974, pp. 112–13.
15. Maurice, *Life*, i, p. 166.
16. Ibid, i, pp. 154–55.
17. R.H. Hutton, *Essays on some of the Modern Guides of English Thought in Matters of Faith*, Macmillan 1887, p. 318.
18. Maurice, *Life*, i, p. 236.
19. For example, C.E. Raven, *Christian Socialism*, 1848–1854 Macmillan 1920: the most comprehensive account is in T. Christensen, *The Origin and History of Christian Socialism*, 1848–1854, Aarhus 1962.
20. F.D. Maurice, *The Prayer Book and the Lord's Prayer*, Macmillan 1902, p. 304.
21. Ibid., p. 311.
22. Ibid., pp. 317–18.
23. Ibid., p. 329.
24. Ibid., p. 291.
25. Maurice, *Life*, i, p. 459.
26. Ibid., i, pp. 465–66.
27. Ibid., i, p. 485.
28. Ibid., ii, p. 130.
29. Ibid., i, pp. 485–86.
30. Ibid., ii, p. 129.
31. Ibid., ii, p. 131.
32. T. Christensen, *Christian Socialism*, pp. 295ff.
33. Maurice, *Life*, ii, pp. 131–32.
34. Letter of 13 September 1852, quoted by Christensen, *Christian Socialism*, p. 306; cf. Newsome, *Two Classes of Men*, p. 113.
35. Maurice, *Life*, ii, p. 137.
36. J.M. Ludlow, 'Some of the Christian Socialists of 1848 and the following years', *Economic Review*, III, 1893, p. 493.

37. Maurice, *Life*, ii, p. 44.
38. J. Llewellyn Davies, *Social Questions from the point of view of Christian Theology*, London 1885, pp. 249, 253.
39. Maurice, *Life*, ii, pp. 8–10.
40. As suggested e.g. by F.M. McClain, Maurice: *Man and Moralist*, SPCK 1972, pp. 40–41.
41. J.Ll. Davies, 'Frederick Denison Maurice', *Contemporary Review*, XLV, 1884, p. 316; 'Secularism and Mr Maurice's Theology', *Contemporary Review*, XXIV, 1874, p. 24.
42. F.D. Maurice, *Theological Essays*, 4th edn, Macmillan 1881, pp. 386–87, 389–90.
43. G. Rowell, *Hell and the Victorians*, OUP 1974, p. 83.
44. T. Christensen, 'F.D. Maurice and the Contemporary Religious World', *Studies in Church History*, III, 1966, p. 88.
45. Maurice, *Life*, ii, pp. 16–17.
46. Ibid., ii, p. 191.
47. H.L. Mansel, *The Limits of Religious Thought Examined*, 5th edn, John Murray 1870, p. xx.
48. Maurice, *Life*, ii, p. 423.
49. Christensen, *Divine Order*, p. 157.
50. Maurice, *Life*, ii, pp. 453–55; cf. Hutton, *Modern Guides of English Thought*, pp. 320–21, 326–27.
51. H.G. Wood, *Frederick Denison Maurice*, CUP 1950, p. 35; Ramsey, *Maurice and the Conflicts of Modern Theology*, pp. 89, 97; A.R. Vidler, *F.D. Maurice and Company*, SCM Press 1966, pp. 141–42.
52. Ramsey, *Maurice and the Conflicts of Modern Theology*, p. 36.
53. Christensen, *Divine Order*, p. 158.
54. Hutton, *Modern Guides of English Thought*, pp. 318–19.
55. D.M. Mackinnon, 'Revelation and Social Justice' in *Malvern 1941*, Longmans 1941, p. 105.
56. Christensen, *Divine Order*, pp. 197–220.
57. Christensen, *Studies in Church History*, III, 1966, 87.
58. J.S. Mill, 'Coleridge', *Essays on Ethics, Religion and Society*, F.E.L. Priestley and J.M. Robson (eds), *Collected Works of John Stuart Mill*, x, Routledge 1969, p. 119.
59. Hutton, *Modern Guides of English Thought*, p. 327.
60. A.C. Benson, *The Life of Edward White Benson*, Macmillan 1900, i, 138.

8

The Power of Christian Ladyhood: Priscilla Lydia Sellon and the Creation of Anglican Sisterhoods

SEAN GILL

Neither her contemporaries nor later historians have found it easy to assess the character and achievements of Priscilla Sellon, whose creation of an Anglican religious order for women in Plymouth in 1848 provoked bitter and lengthy controversy. To the high priest of Tractarianism, Dr Pusey, 'Mother Lydia' could do no wrong, but others – including some who had been members of her community – condemned her work as part of a plot to Romanize the Church of England, and denounced her rule of the sisters as an exercise in tyrannical self-aggrandisement.[1] Writing from within the tradition of Anglo-Catholic piety, her only modern biographer, T. J. Williams, agrees with Pusey. For him Miss Sellon's was a life of selfless service lived in the face of calumny and persecution, and she is to be remembered as a rebellious innovator in the history of nineteenth-century Anglicanism, both as the restorer of the religious life for women, and as a prime mover in the Oxford Movement's concern for the poor.[2] In the standard account of the Victorian church – in which women are mainly conspicuous by their absence – Owen Chadwick is less convinced, depicting her as one of 'the indomitables of Victorian womanhood', though also pointing out the extravagance of her plans and the undue influence which she exercised over Pusey.[3] To Martha Vicinus, in her recent study of the growth of independent communities of working women in Victorian society, she appears as 'a domineering and self-righteous woman, and yet someone of considerable personality and influence';

whereas in one of the most recent discussions of the growth of female religious orders in Victorian Anglicanism, John Shelton Reed supports Williams' dismissive view of her detractors, seeing her as 'strong-minded and sometimes ill-advised', but not deserving to be called a 'petty despot'.[4]

The work of Vicinus and Reed attempts to place the growth of Anglican sisterhoods in its social context. For Vicinus, they were one of a number of attempts by single women to create for themselves worthwhile roles and self-identities within a society which regarded marriage and child-bearing as a woman's 'natural' end. This is also the view taken by Michael Hill in his study of nineteenth-century Anglican orders where he suggests that in contrast to the low church office of deaconess, the sisterhoods had 'limited but implicitly feminist goals', and that their supporters worked with 'an incipiently feminist conception of the role of women'.[5] This was so because the religious life advanced the ideal of 'celibacy as a matter of voluntary choice', and offered a form of self-government which was potentially free from male clerical control. For Hill, Pusey's unwavering support for Miss Sellon is significant as part of his more general insistence on the independence of female religious orders from parochial clerical control.[6] Reed, too, discusses Miss Sellon's work as an example of potentially subversive female independence, though he is more guarded than Hill and Vicinus in his assessment of the overall significance of the sisterhoods, arguing that the Anglo-Catholic movement embodied feminist values in such a limited way that it might best be seen as 'an alternative to feminism' rather than as a transitional stage in its development.[7] These differences of emphasis point to the more general difficulties of understanding the social significance of religion for women in Victorian England. In her overview of Victorian feminism, Philippa Levine suggests that the position of women, and the construction of masculinity and femininity, owed as much to religious values as to biological differences or to the changing needs of the economy, and sees the churches as offering women 'a role in spiritual life which at one and the same time empowered and confined them'. The implications of this contradiction have as yet been little explored by ecclesiastical historians of the period.[8]

It seems that neither the biographical approach of traditional Anglo-Catholic hagiography, nor the feminist inspired perspective of social historians make it easy to understand Priscilla Sellon's achievements. How significant a part did she really play in the establishment of the religious life for women within the Church of England? How far was she responsible for the development of an Anglo-Catholic social conscience? And in what sense, if any, should she be remembered as part of a High Church attempt to establish a more creative role for women within Victorian Anglicanism?

Certainly Miss Sellon's sisterhood of 1848 was not the first to be founded, nor was the original impulse hers. As Pusey's biographer Liddon put it, such ideas were in the air in Tractarian circles in the 1840s. In December 1839 Pusey had written to the vicar of Leeds, Dr Hook, advocating the creation of one or more sisterhoods which, he thought, would 'foster a high tone in the church', give 'holy employment to many who yearn for something', and – as a secondary advantage – would direct feminine zeal which might 'otherwise often go off in some irregular way, or go over to Rome'.[9] In 1841 Marian Hughes, the daughter of a Gloucestershire rector, dedicated herself to the religious life under Pusey's direction, but it was not until 1844 that a community for women was founded at Park Village West near Regent's Park in London. Although Miss Sellon did not visit the new sisterhood until after the beginning of her own work in Plymouth, one of the founders of the new religious community, the Reverend William Dodsworth, was a family friend.

It was in January 1848 that the Bishop of Exeter, Henry Phillpotts, issued a public appeal for help in working with the poor in the towns of Devonport, Plymouth and Stonehouse. The work, he warned, would be demanding in an environment where every third house was a beer shop, and where the children were sunk 'in absolute heathen ignorance'.[10] Miss Sellon had intended to visit Italy in the hope of recovering from the ill health which was to dog her for the rest of her life, but with encouragement from her father and Dr Pusey, she offered her services to the bishop.

From the beginning, she had a loyal helper in Miss Catherine Chambers. The work of opening schools for boys and girls in a tough sea-port proved arduous, and Miss Sellon soon broke down under the strain. This did not prevent her from privately complaining to Pusey about Miss Chambers' inadequacies. 'She is all kindness to myself,' she wrote, 'and really religious; but she has not sufficiently considered the annoyance to which she would be exposed.'[11] Like many other successful public figures, Miss Sellon relied heavily on the self-effacing drudgery of others. For the rest of her life Catherine Chambers devoted herself to dealing with the Mother Superior's private correspondence, looking after her personal needs, and overseeing the routine administration of the order. As another sister later recalled, her chief characteristic was 'self-forgetting obedience', and 'she seemed to have no will but that of her superior and her judgment'.[12] She was to be ill-rewarded for her pains, for in 1872 Miss Sellon passed her over as her successor despite the explicit provision of the statutes that the 'Mother Eldress' should become the Superior. In Miss Sellon's eyes, however, Catherine Chambers had shown herself totally unfit for the office by her growing dislike of Dr Pusey.[13]

Sister Catherine's patience and administrative abilities were much needed, for from the foundation of the Sisterhood of Mercy in October 1848, Priscilla Sellon's plans always outran the resources available to accomplish them. Within two years 'Mother Lydia' had established in and around Devonport an orphanage, a home for delinquent boys, a refuge for training girls for domestic service, an industrial school, six model lodging houses for poor families, a ragged school, a soup kitchen, and a home for old sailors, and on 5 October 1850, the foundation stone of St Dunstan's Abbey in Plymouth was laid by the Bishop of Exeter. The plans, which were never to be fully realized, were drawn up by William Butterfield who envisaged a magnificent church in the Early English style, and a large group of conventual buildings. By 1851, in consultation with Pusey, Miss Sellon was outlining an ambitious scheme to make St Dunstan's the mother house of a single united order of Anglican nuns throughout

England with herself as Superior General. According to her grandiose vision, the whole country was to be divided into triangles – symbolic of the Holy Trinity, to which her order was dedicated – with at each point of a triangle a religious house under her rule.[14] Bristol was to be the starting place in her dream of geometric empire, and in 1851 a mission centre and a convent were opened there, as well as a seaside convalescent home in Hampshire. In 1854 the activities of the Devonport sisterhood extended overseas when five of the sisters joined Florence Nightingale's party of nurses in the Crimea, an expedition which did much to familiarize the public with the usefulness of sisters of mercy in philanthropic work.[15]

Having absorbed the older Park Village West community at the end of the Crimean War, further work was undertaken in the East End of London, and expansion continued without regard to cost. In 1862 Pusey gave a large part of his deceased mother's estate to purchase land and build a priory and hospital at Ascot, whilst in 1864 three sisters were sent as missionaries to Honolulu. By this time the society had been elaborately organized by Miss Sellon into three orders. The first was that of the sisters of mercy and was devoted to social work; the second order was enclosed and contemplative; the third consisted of sisters of charity who might live either in community or at home, and who undertook works of philanthropy under a renewable engagement of two years rather than making the life-long commitment required of the first two orders. But as Williams admits, much that was undertaken in the first flush of enthusiasm had to be abandoned, and even then much of the work was carried out by paid helpers, there being too few sisters. At the time of her death in 1876, the financial affairs of the sisterhood were in considerable disarray.

One of the most important aims behind so much frantic activity was Miss Sellon's desire to help the poor. Indeed within the mythology of an Anglo-Catholic historiography in which the slum priest has become the symbol of Tractarian social concern, she has been awarded a place of honour:

> From the time when Priscilla Sellon, blessed and encouraged

> by Dr Pusey, commenced her work in the stews of Devonport, up to the present day, the Catholic Movement has always been discovered among the poor and outcaste.[16]

Among perhaps, but not of, for just as the Anglo-Catholic priest was expected to be a gentleman, so the sister of mercy was to be a lady. Far from being considered as an obstacle to the work, the gulf of social class separating the sister from the poor was considered essential both as a means of innoculating her against the contagion of working-class vice, and as a way of providing suitable examples of moral and spiritual elevation, particularly in work amongst fallen women. As a former sister, Miss Goodman, recalled:

> It was Miss Sellon's impression, judging from the whole tone and spirit of the training of the sisters, that very little could be done towards elevating the working classes by persons whose tastes, habits, and general cultivation of mind were very little above those they would raise; and she sought most carefully to keep up in her sisters a taste for the beautiful, and altogether to retain amongst them a refinement of mind.[17]

In so far as charitable work made it necessary to bridge the gap between rich and poor, condescension was a useful help, Miss Sellon making it a rule amongst the sisters 'to suppose that the tastes of the working classes to be much the same as those of the higher, unless we had direct evidence to the contrary'.[18]

The daughter of a naval officer, and of independent means, she herself always remained acutely aware of social distinctions. When government inspectors attempted to visit her schools to assess their efficiency, she wrote indignantly to the future Lord Halifax that her schools in Plymouth could not fail to be at least as good as those elsewhere as they were run by 'singularly highly accomplished ladies'; as for the inspectors, they 'were quite young men and apparently not gentlemen, at least one does not know who they are'.[19] Such social distinctions were also incorporated into the life of the sisterhood, use being made of an order of serving sisters. As the rule of the orphan's home at Devonport made clear, they were to be treated kindly, 'mindful that although these be servants in outward circumstances, they are still daughters of God'.[20]

In their dealings with the poor, class differences were often reinforced in the early sisterhoods, if subtly transmuted in tone, by one of their most notable features: a pervasive archaisizing mediaevalism. This was of course evident in the architectural and liturgical styles of Tractarian spirituality, and it contributed to an air of unreality in the religious life of the sisterhoods which was in sharp contrast to the harsh world of the streets. At St Dunstan's, Miss Sellon adopted the panoply of a mediaeval abbess, whilst all the rooms were given suitable names: the 'sheepfold' for the community room, 'rest' for the Mother Superior's sitting room, 'houses of hope' for the lodging houses, 'houses of peace' for the refuges for orphaned girls. Miss Sellon believed that a withdrawal from the grim and arduous work on the streets into the haven of conventual life was a necessity for the sisters, but a sense of romantic mediaevalism also helped to sustain the work, and to create a sense of *noblesse oblige*. Not untypical was the approach of sister Katherine Warburton, the first superior of St Mary's Priory in the East End of London, who worked with Priscilla Sellon during the cholera epidemic of 1866. Brought up on a heady educational brew of Arthurian legend, lives of the mediaeval saints, and the history of the Stuarts – 'whose charm, and unworthiness, and romance alike appealed to her' – her biographer rather improbably likens her work in London to a mediaeval crusade in which she was to be found 'serving her Prynce, and following Him to the East in far away Haggerston'.[21] The social vision of Anglican sisterhoods which was nourished on a spirituality such as this was not surprisingly a conservative one: a belief in a deferential organic social order in which the poor had needs and the rich the duty of relieving them, but which was incapable of contemplating fundamental political or economic change.

Miss Sellon fully shared this outlook, seeing social problems largely in terms of individual moral responsibility and direct personal influence. Writing to Lord Halifax in 1870, she regretted the distress caused by cholera 'amongst the respectable poor', but felt that even a life's work could only hope 'to make some few better people'.[22] At the beginning of her work in Devonport in 1848 the need to make 'better people' had been particularly pressing in the wake of Chartist demands for the vote, and revolution in Europe. 'Startled by the want of deference of manner which one always meets with in agricultural districts,' she embarked upon a vigorous educational campaign the significance of which was not lost on Pusey. Writing to a friend at Eton in December 1848 in praise of her work, he described her efforts as 'a romance of religious life', and thought that the boys whom she taught were either 'the materials of earnest and good citizens or of Socialists and Chartists'. Happily all was well: Miss Sellon's boys were soon singing the national anthem – 'a substitute for some Chartist song of wickedness'.[23] F.D. Maurice was equally fulsome in his praise of her influence on the young poor of Devonport. Writing either in support of sisterhoods or in opposition to them – as always it is hard to be sure with Maurice – he enthused:

> No more conspicuous instance of the power of Christian Ladyhood upon the roughest male natures, is to be found in recent records. What could any man's voice or man's teaching have done to awake the chivalry which was latent in those little ragamuffins, and which came forth in response to female grace and gentleness?[24]

Yet for all the tireless devotion and bravery of Miss Sellon and her sisters, nowhere more evident than in the cholera epidemics of 1849 and 1866, it is not hard to see why the social work of the sisterhoods, like that of the Anglo-Catholic movement in general, failed to win over the poor to the church. However self-sacrificially it was offered, help *de haut en bas* was not enough and was often resented. In 1860, for example, Miss Sellon's scheme to send unemployed weavers from the East End of London to the north of England where work existed foundered on the refusal of the would-be beneficiaries to move.[25]

Such demanding work amongst the needy could not be undertaken without considerable commitment and discipline. This indeed was part of its attraction to single women seeking meaningful employment outside the respectable but constricting confines of the Victorian middle-class home. In establishing her sisterhood, Priscilla Sellon therefore ran the danger of offending against contemporary ideas of appropriate middle-class female behaviour. As one of her bitterest critics complained, 'having all the menial work to do for themselves, it was no uncommon thing for these young ladies, brought up in all the refinements of polite life, to be carrying at half-past five o'clock in the morning a large dust barrel to the top of the Court, – a feat requiring their utmost strength'.[26] But the degree of hardship faced by the sisters was controversial for other reasons, too. For one thing the formulation of an appropriate rule was a considerable problem for the early Protestant sisterhoods. In discussing their creation, the Anglican Newman of 1840 believed even more strongly than Pusey that they were 'the only means of saving some of our best members from turning Roman Catholics', but that they could only be formed on the basis of inward principle, and could not be made externally.[27] Yet this was bound to be the case with Anglican religious orders which could only draw upon Roman Catholic experience at second-hand. But the establishment of a suitable way of life for female religious was made much harder by Pusey's morbid passion for self-denial and the mortification of the flesh. His enthusiasm for prolonged fasting and the use of both hair shirts and 'the Discipline' (a thin whip cord with five knots), helped to create a situation at the Park Villge community which resulted in the death of one of the sisters.[28] Another of the Park Village sisters who had been sent to help Miss Sellon during the outbreak of cholera in Plymouth in 1849 turned out to be too weak to leave her bed, having kept a fast 'suggestive of the monks of the Egyptian Desert', partly in imitation of Dr Pusey's practice.[29] But Miss Sellon herself was not averse to harsh measures. In 1849 it was claimed that one of the sisters had been made to lie on the floor and make the sign of the cross with her tongue to atone for a misdemeanour. In reply, she defended the practice if carried out in private.[30]

Low Church critics continued to make sweeping charges against her, claiming that she expected to be obeyed as Christ himself. In the feverish atmosphere of a Victorian anti-Catholicism inflamed by the restoration of the Roman hierarchy in 1850, much of this might be put down to the hysterical Protestant belief that those who entered a convent must inevitably sacrifice both reason and conscience. Indeed one critic went so far as to suggest that she used her 'singular skill in the mesmeric art' to maintain her control over the unfortunate sisterhood.[31] However, even less hostile sources were critical of her methods. For example, Dr Neale, who founded the Anglican sisterhood at East Grinstead, abhorred what he called 'the pseudo-ascetism' of Miss Sellon's order, and regarded her as a woman 'one hardly can make common cause with'.[32] Those who left the order disillusioned by her rule claimed later that she imposed an austerity on others which she did not always practice herself, and that the formal statutes of the society became progressively more severe as time went on. Her authority seems, however, to have been based more on the force of her personality than upon the formal statutes of the community. Despite her increasing physical infirmity, she was a charismatic figure remembered by Sister Katherine Warburton during the cholera outbreak of 1866 as 'a most striking person with commanding gestures, and a peculiarly imperative wave of a very well shaped hand'.[33] Nowhere was this exercise of personal authority more evident than in the elaborate procedures for advancement within the order. New recruits came first as novices, and were then admitted to the appropriately named order of 'child', a state they could remain in for many years depending upon the will of the Mother Superior. As Pusey's future biographer Maria Trench realized, 'there were no Chapters, no elections of novices; *every thing* depended on the Superior's *dictum*'. The oldest sister at Ascot Priory put it more succinctly: 'We are a despotic monarchy without a Parliament'.[34]

Miss Sellon's biographer attributes her love of command to a sense of military discipline which she inherited from her naval father, but otherwise says little about her personal qualities. Some of these are evident from her role as a controversialist. She was, she claimed – in the midst of a bitter pamphlet war over the ordering of her community – 'ignorant of controversy', and had little knowledge of the divisions within the church.[35] This was to say the least disingenuous. In 1850 she entered into a sharp exchange of letters with Lord Campbell, insisting that he withdraw his financial support for her society as she held him responsible for the Gorham Judgment which seemed to question the High Church belief in baptismal regeneration, and she was annoyed when he chose to publish their correspondence in full.[36] Perhaps her reticence is understandable, as theology was a study women were not encouraged to pursue – it was, warned Ruskin at his most oracular, the 'one dangerous science for women' which should not form part of their education.[37] Not surprisingly, most Victorian Anglican women who contributed to theological discussion did so obliquely as hymn writers, novelists, or social reformers.

As both she and her opponents were well aware, the founding of Anglican sisterhoods, in which she played such a public role, was part of a Tractarian attempt to alter radically the life and theology of the Church of England. Partly for this reason, from its inception in 1848, the Devonport sisterhood aroused local opposition. Claims that the sisters had set up an oratory where Pusey administered communion, and even worse that they wore crosses and recited Roman Catholic offices, led the Bishop of Exeter to conduct a public enquiry. Miss Sellon's defence was a theatrical *tour de force* which exploited male sensibilities to the full. Rising from her sick-bed, she rejected charges of attempting to introduce the Roman conventual system into England; and as for the suggestion that the sisters wore crosses, what, she asked, would be thought of anyone who enquired of an attendant what an English woman wore beneath her dress or laid upon her pillow? Dr Phillpotts' gallantry was aroused. Miss Sellon, he concluded, was a good, 'he had almost said "angelic", woman', and whilst the use of flowers and a crucifix in the oratory was regrettable, 'ladies were ladies'.[38] But inspite of the bishop's chivalrous judgment, Protestant fears were not so easily allayed, and the festivities for the laying of the foundation stone of St Dunstan's Abbey in 1850 were disrupted by a mob which pelted the sisters and clergy with potatoes and plates.[39] Further accusations against Miss Sellon were not without effect, and in 1852 Dr Phillpotts resigned as visitor to the community unhappy at what he called 'the extravagance of the Superior's claim on the obedience of the Sisterhood'.[40] The question of obedience, and in particular the taking of lifelong vows, aroused episcopal concern whenever the question of granting official recognition to sisterhoods was raised; and Miss Sellon's methods provided opponents with ready ammunition to such an extent that the Bishop of Llandaff cited her as an example of the evils of the system in the convocation debate on the subject in 1862.[41]

But Miss Sellon's notoriety as a leading protagonist of the High Church cause derived not only from her creation of an Anglican nunnery, but also from her close association with Pusey. From the beginning of her work in 1848, when she led him into public controversy over the use of High Church ritual at Devonport, until her later years, when he made use of Ascot Priory as a summer retreat, she received his unwavering emotional and financial support. Margaret Cusack, who left the order to become a Roman Catholic nun, claimed that Dr Pusey 'had an infatuation for Miss Sellon which was very little short of mania. The woman had laid a spell on him ... and held him in thrall to the bitter end.'[42] Another former sister held the same jaundiced view suggesting that any sister who appealed to Pusey against Miss Sellon's rule did so in vain as 'he treated all remonstrance with regard to the life as murmurings and a falling away from grace'.[43] Others were quick to draw conclusions about the nature of their relationship, which forced her brother to write to *The Times* to contradict a previous account of his sister's supposed marriage to Pusey – might not the offspring of their alliance be called 'the Pusey Miscellany' asked one Oxford wit?[44] As their correspondence was destroyed 'from a fear of the use which unscrupulous controversialists might have made of facts perfectly innocent in themselves', it is hard to assess the nature of their relationship, but Pusey's unbounded confidence in Priscilla Sellon's judgment, and his refusal to entertain the slightest criticism of her, suggest that Miss Cusack, though a hostile witness, did not exaggerate.[45] In 1863 the rector of Blickling, Dr Meyrick, whose daughter had been a member of the Devonport community, wrote bluntly to Pusey 'that no man, woman, or thing in England has so turned away Christian sympathy from the Church cause and the Church party as Miss Sellon'. Pusey's unwavering support of her had, he felt, 'alienated many who would otherwise have been ready to be led by him'.[46] But Pusey's confidence in the sisterhood remained unshaken: it was, he told Miss Trench a decade later, admirably governed and the sisters were very happy.[47]

Following Miss Sellon's death in November 1876, Pusey could not fail to be aware that whereas other sisterhoods continued to grow, Devonport could not attract novices even though there was ample room for them. 'Rabbits will come and tenant an empty hole; Novices will not come because there are cells made for them,' he lamented.[48] Apart from the dissimilarity in habits between rabbits and novices, he blamed the lack of recruits on the unjustified prejudice of spiritual directors against Miss Sellon, and a general falling away on the part of young women from the austere spiritual standards of the past. As for a solution, he could only suggest planting trees on the drive of Ascot Priory in the hope of making it more attractive to novices.[49] When Miss Trench attempted to face him with the truth, he was moved too deeply to listen:

> Once I tried to say to him, when he was lamenting the want of fresh blood in the Society, that of course I knew nothing of the life – that I could only judge of the minds of those outside, and that I could not help knowing that without some modification to the constitution, English girls would not join it, I shall never forget the deeply pained but steadfastly determined expression of his face as he answered more sternly than I ever heard him speak, '*Then it must die*'.[50]

Margaret Goodman claimed that it was because of Pusey's infatuation for Miss Sellon, 'and the fact that she did not in a general way get on with the clergy,' that he argued in favour of the independence of sisterhoods from parochial clerical control.[51] For Pusey, however, this was a matter of principle not of personalities. Even where he could be sure of clerical support for the High Church cause, he was insistent on the need for independence. This involved him in 1864 in an acrimonious correspondence with the Revd Arthur Stanton, whom he was asking to work at St Saviour's Leeds with the help of Miss Sellon's sisters. Overriding Stanton's objections, he repeatedly denied that the clergy had 'any right to interference or check or wish to control any work which religious women wish to set about in their parish'.[52] But in arguing in this way, to what extent was Pusey proposing an 'incipiently feminist' conception of the role of women in the church with Miss Sellon as its chief exemplar?

It is true that one of the commonest objections to sisterhoods was that they lured young single women away from parental authority and domestic duties. As Charles Kingsley put the matter in typically pugnacious style in his novel *Yeast*, published in 1851, one of the chief attractions of sisterhoods for young women was the hope of entering 'a higher place in heaven than the relations whom they had left behind them', whilst in the meantime life could be carried on 'unshackled by the interference of parents, and other such merely fleshly relationships'.[53] In the light of such fears, one of the most damaging charges brought against Miss Sellon was that she had persuaded a young woman to join her order without parental consent, and had attacked one of the central shibboleths of Victorian society by arguing that 'the love of home is also another idol, – a very sweet and honourable one, but one which, alas, comes often between us and high duties to our church, the poor, and our Lord himself'.[54] Another critic claimed that the undermining of patriarchal authority on specious religious grounds by 'the Sellon System' threatened the entire social fabric.[55] That the desire to lead an independent single life might be one of the attractions of convent life was also recognized by the Bishop of Oxford speaking at the Church Congress held in Dublin in 1868. It was, he warned, a great evil for young women to embark on such a course because marriage was the primary obligation for young women 'distinctly laid down for us by the Holy ghost, through the pen of the apostle Paul', though he regretted that in the present 'highly artificial state of society' there were many women who for demographic reasons could not marry.[56] Another worried observer of the growth of Anglican sisterhoods agreed, claiming that young women 'vainly expect to find within the walls of the convent a sanctity not attainable in the fulfilment of domestic duties, and are thus allured to quit the path marked out by Providence, for a Via Sacra of their own choice'.[57] For this author, it was not only the escape from parental ties, but also the resulting self-government and freedom from male clerical control that was a potential source of anxiety. This was made possible by the flow of donations which would give the sisterhoods financial independence, and also by the kind of recruits the orders would attract:

> I regret the necessity of thus hinting that communities of pious ladies may ever become otherwise than perfectly submissive to authority and perfectly manageable; but the stern firmness of purpose which has placed so many members of the 'Holmes' within their walls, naturally creates some misgiving on the subject.[58]

Advocates of sisterhoods were well aware of these charges and were careful not to deny the overriding claims of family duty upon young women. In supporting their creation, the Bishop of Brechin began by emphasizing that 'to marry, to guide the house, to bear children, to educate them in the fear and love of God, is the customary lot and duty of woman'.[59] Speaking in favour of sisterhoods at the Church Congress in Oxford in 1862, the Revd T.T. Carter also tried to reaffirm traditional Victorian family values by stressing that 'Home is the source of all pure relations, the nurse of all holy discipline, the seed-plot of all the virtues,' though this sat uneasily with his reminder that 'the gospel is wider than the home,' and that it 'includes separation from the world, and from all natural ties, as one form of life within its sphere'.[60]

In fact nothing in the Anglo-Catholic support of sisterhoods was intended to challenge the prevailing belief in the complementary but different qualities of men and women, and the corresponding division of social roles which this entailed. Indeed it did much to reinforce it. At the 1862 Church Congress, Pusey was quite explicit about this. The role of the sister was to be that of 'the pioneer for the parish priest' coming to the poor as 'an angel from heaven' in circumstances where he might not be welcome. It was, he argued, the sister's specifically feminine attributes which made this possible:

> The longing for the religious life is deeply and widely spread amid our Christian ladies. Women are guided not by controversial arguments but by instinctive feeling. Controversy they leave to us.[61]

Not unnaturally, this view did not find favour with Maria Trench who felt that Pusey ignored her literary aspirations. 'Dr Pusey', she complained, 'certainly always seemed to me to understand and to try to satisfy, any amount of devotional and spiritual craving in women, but to have neither understanding of or sympathy for the most moderate intellectual craving on their part.' He believed, she concluded, in 'the antithesis between bonnets and brains'.[62]

Drawing as it did upon the richly misogynist tradition of the Fathers, and committed to upholding the authority of an exclusively male priesthood, the Oxford Movement, of which sisterhoods were a part, could lead nowhere in terms of creating responsible roles for women within the Church of England if these were to be based on any belief in the equality of the sexes.[63] The point was not lost upon *The Athenaeum* in 1861. Reviewing together Miss Goodman's accusations against Miss Sellon, and Caroline Dall's plea for female suffrage in America, the writer concluded that whatever mistakes Miss Sellon had made, her way of 'self-abnegation and devotedness' was infinitely preferable for women to that advocated by Caroline Dall.[64]

For those who believed that gender-based differences were God-given, and who saw an antithesis between masculine intellect and toughness on the one hand, and the more feminine qualities of compassion and self-sacrifice on the other, the aims and organization of a sisterhood were ideally suited to make full use of the latter. It might be true that obedience and self-denial were essential parts of the religious life for both men and women, but as the Revd T. T. Carter pointed out to the sisters at Clewer, this was true in a special sense in their case. In contemplating the holy angels – into whose nature Carter seems to have had privileged insight – one could see that they exhibited two 'special characteristics of woman's true vocation', especially in her relation to man: 'unselfish love and submissiveness of will'.[65] Miss

Sellon herself put this distinction between the sexes, and its consequences for the religious life, as clearly as anyone:

> ... it may be for men to argue for truth, to reason with the learned of the nineteenth century, to preach to the refined sensualist or the intellectual philosopher as the noble penitent of old from the hill of Mars: but for us, Mary Magdalene of blessed memory has taught us our place; we are to lie at the foot of our Lord in silence; in tears, in love.[66]

Of course Priscilla Sellon's opponents may well have wondered how this applied in her case. The truth was that there was a wide discrepancy between the social myths about women generated by Anglican theology and the reality of their existence within the church. In such a situation ironies and contradictions abounded. For example, the Oxford Congress of 1862, which met partly to praise the usefulness of women's work within the church, began by deciding that ladies could not be admitted as members. Fortunately, however, the physical geography of the Sheldonian Theatre allowed them to be admitted without impropriety as spectators in the upper galleries.[67]

Aspiring to a role of leadership within the church, Priscilla Sellon's position was more than usually contradictory. Far from being the restorer of Anglican religious life, as her biographer claims, she came closer than anyone else to wrecking Tractarian efforts to gain acceptance for sisterhoods. Nor did her work amongst the poor do much to alleviate their lot or win their allegiance to the Church of England. Yet like Florence Nightingale, whom she resembled to such an extent that they could hardly have co-existed in the Crimea, she succeeded in exercising power more by manipulating than by deferring to Victorian theological and social prescriptions for correct female behaviour.[68] As a result, neither the image of the benignly comforting lady of the lamp in Miss Nightingale's case, nor Maurice's panegyric on 'female grace and gentleness' in Miss Sellon's had much, if any, substance in reality. But despite her many shortcomings, she successfully overcame some of the formidable difficulties facing any woman who aspired to a position of influence within a male-dominated church. The extent of her success was not lost upon the evangelical *Christian Observer*. Included in its lengthy catalogue of her faults was 'the gross assumption by one of their sex of rights and powers which the language and still more the spirit of the Holy Scriptures seems to deny to the female sex'.[69] In that sense, Priscilla Sellon was more of a religious rebel than Pusey could have understood and she would have cared to admit.

Notes

1. For criticisms by disaffected former sisters see Margaret Cusack, *The Story of my Life*, London 1891; and Margaret Goodman, *Experiences of an English Sister of Mercy*, London 1861, and *Sisterhoods in the Church of England*, London 1863. In Margaret Cusack's view, 'like all bullies, she was a coward at heart, and could have been easily subdued if she had found any one who was capable of coping with her', op.cit., p.71.
2. Thomas Jay Williams, *Priscilla Lydia Sellon. The Restorer After Three Centuries Of The Religious Life In The English Church*, SPCK, revd edn 1965. Williams regards his book as 'the vindication of Miss Sellon's true greatness and nobility of character from the aspersions of her traducers', p.xxii.
3. Owen Chadwick, *The Victorian Church*, Part I, 3rd edn, A. & C. Black 1971; reissued SCM Press 1987, pp.507–8.
4. M. Vicinus, *Independent Women. Work And Community For Single Women 1850–1920*, Virago. 1985, pp.69–71; and John Shelton Reed, 'A Female Movement: The Feminization of Nineteenth-Century Anglo-Catholicism', *Anglican And Episcopal History*, vol.57, 1988, pp.199–238.
5. M. Hill, *The Religious Order. A study of virtuoso religion and its legitimation in the nineteenth-century Church of England*, Heinemann 1973, pp.271–2.
6. A. Deacon and M. Hill, 'The Problem of Surplus Women' in the Nineteenth Century: Secular and Religious Alternatives' in *A Sociological Yearbook of Religion in Britain* 5, SCM Press 1972, pp.96–7.
7. Reed, op. cit., p.238.
8. Philippa Levine, *Victorian Feminism 1850–1900*, Hutchinson 1987, pp.11–12. In *Evangelicalism in Modern Britain. A History From The 1730s to The 1980s*, Unwin Hyman 1989, p.129, David Bebbington argues that despite its emphasis on the domestic role of women,

evangelical piety did much to satisfy their aspirations and was more important in this respect than organized feminism. This fails to take into account the role of evangelical theology in the construction and reinforcement of limiting gender stereotypes for both men and women. Gail Malmgreen suggests the need for a more sensitive approach which keeps alive 'the complex tension between religion as opiate and as an embodiment of ideological and institutional sexism, and religion as transcendent and liberating force', in Gail Malmgreen (ed.), *Religion in the Lives of English Women, 1760–1930*, Croom Helm 1986, pp. 6–7.

9. H.P. Liddon, *The Life Of Edward Bouverie Pusey*, London 1894, vol. 3, p. 6.
10. Williams, op. cit., p. 11.
11. Ibid., p. 14.
12. Anecdotes of Sister Clara, copy, Pusey House Papers, Oxford. I am grateful to Mr Peter Mayhead, and to Father Peter Cobb, for help with sources.
13. Williams, op. cit., p. 281.
14. Ibid., p. 90.
15. Anne Summers, *Angels And Citizens. British Women as Military Nurses 1854–1914*, Routledge 1988, puts the work of the sisters in a wider context.
16. E. G. Peck, *The Social Implications of the Oxford Movement*, Scribners 1933, p. 80. Two attempts to challenge this tradition by stressing the middle-class and élitist nature of Anglo-Catholicism are J. E. B. Munson, 'The Oxford Movement by the end of the Nineteenth Century: The Anglo-Catholic Clergy', in *Church History*, 1975, pp. 382–395, and D. Hilliard, 'Unenglish and Unmanly: Anglo-Catholicism and Homosexuality', in *Victorian Studies*, 1982, pp. 181–210.
17. M. Goodman, *Sisterhoods*, p. 147.
18. Ibid., p. 141.
19. Sellon to Halifax, undated letter, Pusey House Papers, Oxford.
20. E.K. Browne, *Annals of the Tractarian Movement from 1842 to 1860*, 3rd edn, London 1861, p. 171. Bridget Hill observes that 'Sisterhoods no more challenged the class distinctions within society than they concerned themselves with the problems of women generally'. See B. Hill, 'A Refuge From Men: The Idea Of A Protestant Nunnery', *Past and Present*, no. 117, November 1987, which analyses the arguments put forward in favour of female Protestant orders from the Reformation to the early nineteenth century.
21. *Memories of Mother Kate*, London 1925, pp. 25–6.
22. Sellon to Halifax, 31 January 1870, Pusey House Papers, Oxford.
23. Dr Pusey, Sketch of the Devonport Sisterhood, copy, Pusey House Papers, Oxford.

24. F.D. Maurice, 'On Sisterhoods', *The Victoria Magazine*, 1863, p.296.
25. Williams, op. cit., p.204.
26. The Revd James Spurrell, *Miss Sellon And 'The Sisters Of Mercy'*, London 1852, p.29.
27. Liddon, op. cit., p.6.
28. K. Dennison, 'Dr Pusey as Confessor and Spiritual Director' in P. Butler (ed.), *Pusey Rediscovered*, SPCK 1983, pp.220–222.
29. Williams, op. cit., p.51.
30. Lydia Sellon, *Reply to a Tract by the Revd J. Spurrell, Vicar of Great Shelford, containing certain charges concerning the Society of the Sisters of Mary of Devonport and Plymouth*, 3rd edn, London 1852, pp.4–5.
31. The Revd W.G. Cookesley, *A Letter To His Grace The Archbishop Of Dublin On The Nature, Government, And Tendency Of Miss Sellon's Establishment At Devonport, Called 'The Sisters Of Mercy'*, 3rd edn, London 1853, p.9. Cookesley attempted to disarm sceptics by claiming that 'the power of mesmerism can only be properly appreciated by those who have had opportunities of witnessing its effects, on young females of ardent and vivid imaginations, but of feeble and ductile will'.
32. *Letters Of John Mason Neale*, London 1910, pp.234, 237.
33. K. Warburton, *Memories of a Sister of St Saviour's Priory*, London 1903, p.85.
34. Reminiscences of Maria Trench, Pusey House Papers, Oxford.
35. Sellon, op. cit., p.27.
36. Browne, op. cit., pp.276–281, prints the letters in full.
37. John Ruskin, *Sesame and Lilies*, London 1905 edn, p.127. While Ruskin did not object to women studying subjects other than theology, their educational aims and methods should differ from those of men, he thought, since 'a man ought to know any language or science he learns thoroughly – while a woman ought to know the same language or science, only so far as may enable her to sympathize in her husbands's pleasures, and in those of his best friends' (ibid, p.128).
38. Williams, op. cit., pp.38–41.
39. Ibid., p.80.
40. Ibid., p.101.
41. *The Guardian*, 19 February 1862, p.183.
42. Cusack, op. cit, p.67.
43. Goodman, *Sisterhoods*, p.70.
44. *The Times*, 8 January 1859.
45. A.M. Allchin, *The Silent Rebellion. Anglican Religious Communities 1845–1900*, SCM Press 1958, pp.127–136 discusses the nature of their relationship and offers this explanation for the destruction of their correspondence.

46. Meyrick Papers, MEY 2/1/1, Pusey House, Oxford.
47. Pusey to Miss Trench, 24 August 1874, Pusey House Papers, Oxford.
48. Pusey to Miss Trench, 27 December 1877, Pusey House Papers, Oxford, quoted in Allchin, op. cit.
49. Miss Trench, Reminiscences, Pusey House Papers, Oxford.
50. Ibid quoted in Allchin,. op. cit.
51. Goodman, *Sisterhoods*. pp.40–41.
52. G.W.E. Russell, *Arthur Stanton*, London 1917, p.60.
53. C. Kingsley, *Yeast: A Problem*, 4th edn, London 1879, p.153.
54. J. Spurrell, op. cit., p.4.
55. The Revd W. Coles, *Sisters Of Mercy, Sisters Of Misery: Or Miss Sellon In The Family*, 2nd edn, London 1852, p.17.
56. *Authorized Report Of The Church Congress, Held At Dublin*, Dublin, 1868, pp.210–211.
57. Anon, '*Sisterhoods Considered. With Remarks Upon The Bishop of Brechin's Plea For Sisterhoods*', London 1850, p.5.
58. Ibid., p.16. Little work has been done to try and analyse the social backgrounds and motivations of nineteenth-century female religious, partly because the surviving evidence is scanty and often inaccessible. A recent discussion of a number of Roman Catholic orders is Susan O'Brien, 'Lay-sisters and Good Mothers: Working-class Women in English Convents, 1840–1910' in W.J. Shiels and D. Wood (eds), *Women In The Church. Studies In Church History*, vol.27, Oxford 1990, pp.453–465. In an earlier article she discussed both the extent and the limits of female independence from male clerical control within nineteenth-century English Roman Catholic nunneries. See Susan O'Brien, '*Terra Incognita*: The Nun In Nineteenth-Century England', in *Past and Present*, no.121, November 1988, pp.110–140. I understand that S.D. Mumm of the University of Sussex is currently carrying out research on the development of Anglican sisterhoods in Victorian England.
59. A.P. Forbes, *A Plea For Sisterhoods*, London 1849, pp.11–12.
60. T.T. Carter, 'On Sisterhoods', *Report Of The Proceedings Of The Church Congress Of 1862*, Oxford 1862, pp.128–135.
61. Ibid., p.143. Quoted in Hill,. op. cit., p.259.
62. Maria Trench, Reminiscences, Pusey House Papers, Oxford.
63. Benedicta Ward observes of the Oxford Movement's leaders that 'all the Christian writings they proposed to their fellow Christians came from the milieu of monasticism'. She does not, however, pursue the implications of this from a feminist point of view, in a volume published to celebrate the 150th anniversary of the beginnings of the movement. Simply to observe that 'these men proposed religious consecration specifically as a parallel to their own consecration through their ordina-

tion to the priesthood' begs a number of questions relating to power and gender within the church. See Benedicta Ward, 'A Tractarian Inheritance: The religious life in a patristic perspective' in G. Rowell (ed.), *Tradition Renewed. The Oxford Movement Conference Papers*, Darton, Longman & Todd 1986. It is an indication of the decline of Anglo-Catholicism that the publisher's claim that the book was 'the major academic contribution' to the anniversary was true almost by default.

64. *The Athenaeum*, December 1861, pp.873–4, reviewing Margaret Goodman's *Experiences of an English Sister of Mercy*, London 1861, and Caroline Dall's *Women's Rights under the Law*, Boston 1861.
65. T.T. Carter, *Spiritual Instructions*, London 1879, p.152.
66. L. Sellon, *A few words to some women of the Church of God in England*, 3rd edn, London 1850, p.23.
67. *Proceedings*, op. cit., pp.vii–viii.
68. For Florence Nightingale, see F.B. Smith, *Florence Nightingale. Reputation and Power*, Croom Helm 1982, who attempts to expose the 'fallacy ... that doers of good deeds must necessarily be good in themselves' – a point which is often lost on denominationally minded historians.
69. *The Christian Observer*, London 1852, p.392.

9

Edward McGlynn: A Rebel Against the Archbishop of New York

HUGH MCLEOD

I

The 1886 election for Mayor of New York was unique in the city's history. For the first and only time a Labor candidate mounted an effective challenge to the established parties, and in the event finished ahead of the Republican and close behind the victorious Democrat. The Labor candidate was Henry George, author of *Progress and Poverty* and advocate of the Single Tax on the ownership of land. His best known supporter was Fr Edward McGlynn, pastor of St Stephen's Roman Catholic parish on the Middle East Side of Manhattan.[1] McGlynn made only one speech during the campaign, but it was remembered for many years afterwards – both for what he said, and for what followed as a result of the speech. At a McGlynn Memorial Dinner in the 1920s, one of his admirers recalled the scene:

> By standing on tiptoe where I stood in the upper gallery jammed against the wall, I could see the magnificent head and big body of Reverend Dr McGlynn as he walked to the center of the stage and held up his hand for silence. He began: 'Our Father Who art in Heaven, hallowed be Thy name. Thy kingdom come, Thy will be done *on earth*, as it is in heaven.' Then his voice was drowned in tumultuous applause which shook the walls and lasted, it seemed to me, for more than ten minutes before the preacher could proceed ... When his voice could again be heard, he continued: 'That is why I, a frocked priest, stand tonight upon a political platform to urge the

election of Henry George as Mayor of New York, because the triumph of his ideas means the bringing about of conditions under which it will be possible to do God's will on earth as it is done in heaven.'[2]

The Archbishop of New York, Michael Corrigan, had already told McGlynn to keep out of George's campaign. The day after McGlynn's speech, Corrigan suspended him from his priestly functions for two weeks. Thus was launched the 'McGlynn Affair', which dominated the history of the Catholic Church in New York for the next eight years, and continued to divide American Catholics long after the dispute was finally resolved in a way that fully satisfied neither of the main protagonists.

The main stages in the controversy can be summarized very briefly. After the election, Corrigan issued a Pastoral Letter condemning George's ideas, and asserting that the right to private ownership of land was an essential part of the church's teaching. When McGlynn, in a newspaper interview, re-affirmed his support for George, he was suspended again, and in January 1887 Corrigan removed him from the pastorate of St Stephen's. Meanwhile, Cardinal Simeoni, Prefect of Propaganda, had summoned McGlynn to Rome to explain his teaching on the land question. He refused to go, and in May Pope Leo XIII gave him forty days to comply. McGlynn still refused, and in July he was ex-communicated. As soon as the dispute became public knowledge, a widespread movement in support of McGlynn developed.

When he was removed from his pastorate, his parishioners revolted, and life was made impossible for his successor, Mgr Donnelly, who soon had to make way for the more subtle and tactful Fr Charles Colton, one of McGlynn's former assistants. Gradually Colton gained control of the situation within the parish, though at the cost of some defections. Meanwhile McGlynn's more committed supporters joined him in the Anti-Poverty Society, founded in April 1887, which held meetings every Sunday evening, the centrepiece being an address by the exiled pastor. These addresses combined two genres – the sermon and the political speech – in a way that appealed strongly to many

New Yorkers and, at least in the early months, audiences of between two and three thousand were common. The meetings were a source of growing concern to Corrigan, who eventually prohibited Catholics from attending them. This became the cause of various *causes célèbres*, notably the case of John McGuire, who died at an Anti-Poverty meeting and was refused Catholic burial. Shortly before McGlynn's ex-communication, an estimated 75,000 people had marched to Union Square to attend a rally in his support. But the massive backing provided by lay Catholics, together with the more discreet support of fellow New York priests, could do nothing to save McGlynn. When succour arrived, it came from outside New York – from more liberal American bishops, and from Rome.

Corrigan as leader of the conservative wing of the hierarchy had been in constant conflict with such colleagues as Cardinal Gibbons and Archbishop Ireland who, among many other points of disagreement with the Archbishop of New York, believed that his doctrinaire political conservatism threatened to alienate working-class Catholics from the church. At Rome, Corrigan had the support of Propaganda, but was distrusted by the Secretary of State, Cardinal Rampolla. In 1892, the balance of power in Rome favoured Rampolla, and when Archbishop Satolli was sent to the United States as Papal Ablegate, one of the tasks entrusted to him was that of ending the dispute between Corrigan and McGlynn. The latter was asked to prepare a statement of his teaching on the land question. Having satisfied himself of McGlynn's orthodoxy, Satolli restored him to the church just before Christmas 1892. It was to be another two years, however, before Corrigan offered him a parish, and then it was not anywhere in New York City, but in the small upstate town of Newburgh. There McGlynn continued as pastor until his death in 1900, still preaching the same doctrines that had led to his suspension, but now bereft of much of his former influence.

II

As Robert Emmett Curran points out,[3] the McGlynn affair evoked immense interest among American Catholics, not only because of the drama of the events and the personalities involved, but because it brought into focus so many of the issues that were dividing the church in the 1880s and 1890s. Most obviously, the dispute was about the relationship between the church and the Labor movement, but Corrigan and McGlynn also differed over the schooling of Catholic children, relations between Catholics and the Protestant majority in American society, and, of course, the rights of Catholic priests and laypeople *vis-à-vis* their bishops. Moreover, Corrigan suspected McGlynn of a degree of theological liberalism that amounted to heresy.

In background the two antagonists had much in common. McGlynn was born in New York City in 1837, the son of Irish immigrants, and he was to inherit a considerable sum of money as a result of his father's success as a builder. Corrigan was born in Newark in 1839 of Irish parentage, and in due course inherited considerable property accumulated by his father during his career as a wholesale grocer and liquor dealer. Both showed sufficient early promise to be sent to study in Rome, where their later roles were reversed, for McGlynn, who was regarded as a star student, was prefect of Corrigan's class. He apparently regarded the future archbishop as 'narrow-minded' and 'girlish'.[4] After their return to America, however, their careers diverged. McGlynn became an assistant in a New York City parish in 1861, and remained for the rest of his life primarily a pastor and preacher. Corrigan quickly established himself as an administrator: he never held a position in a parish, but rose from being head of a seminary to Vicar-General of the Newark diocese, Bishop of Newark in 1873, co-adjutor to the Archbishop of New York in 1880, and Archbishop of New York from 1885 until his death in 1902.

In the 1860s and 1870s, McGlynn had doubled the role of *enfant terrible* with that of *Wunderkind*. After being appointed pastor of St Stephen's at the early age of twenty-nine, he quickly established his church in East 28th Street as one of the best known in the city. In 1872 a guide to New York picked out St Stephen's for special mention. The author noted that the church seated nearly 4000 people and was 'usually crowded'. McGlynn was in demand as a preacher on special occasions, such as the dedication of new churches, and seems to have been held in high regard by Cardinal McCloskey, Archbishop of New York from 1864 to 1885. Perhaps the most revealing comment on this phase of McGlynn's career was made by Cardinal Gibbons, just at the point when his fame was turning to notoriety. In January 1887, McGlynn's closest ally among the New York clergy, Richard Burtsell, had dinner with the Cardinal, who praised McGlynn as 'a typical American priest, to whom he introduced in preference any personal friends who asked for letters of introduction to a priest in New York'.[5] By this time McGlynn was well established as a rebel. But he was a rebel of an unusual kind, one who was widely regarded as one of the church's showpieces, but was inexorably led to disaster by his refusal to be bounded by any of the written or unwritten rules that governed the life of a Catholic priest in the later nineteenth century.

So long as McCloskey remained Archbishop, McGlynn was shielded from the attacks that came from some his colleagues in the archdiocese, from other bishops, and later from Rome. McGlynn was never far from controversy, but the attacks had reached a first climax in 1882, following his conversion to Henry George's Single Tax, and his vocal support for the Irish Land League. Other major issues included McGlynn's support for public schools and consequent refusal to build a parish school; his opposition to any form of public support for religious institutions; his friendly relations with Protestant ministers; and his membership of a clerical discussion group notorious for wide-ranging questioning of existing Catholic orthodoxies. Corrigan thus regarded the speech at Chickering Hall on 1 October 1886 as the final straw. He disapproved of his predecessor's cautious style of leadership, and believed that bishops were meant to 'rule' their dioceses. From Corrigan's perspective, McGlynn was an incorrigible trouble-maker: when he refused to accept various private warnings, a public example had to be made of him.

III

McGlynn was a man of commanding presence, who evoked strong reactions – of admiration, and even love from some, and of hatred from others. Six feet two inches tall, thickly built, with dark hair (receding somewhat by 1886), pale eyes, and a prominent jaw, which could give him an air of truculence, he often wore an expression of boyish innocence, adding no doubt to the charm which he held for many people. McGlynn's popularity was indeed a part of his undoing, for he always had a tendency to play to the gallery. When speaking to an audience, he usually did without notes, and this may partly explain his penchant for colourful, but ill-considered, pieces of improvisation, such as his reference to Pope Leo XIII as a 'bag of bones'. However, he wrote in much the same style as he talked. For instance in criticizing schools and charitable institutions run by religious orders, he alleged that monks, priests and nuns 'denounce our schools and other public institutions, in language at times brutal, if not obscene, while indulging in pharasaic glorification of their own institutions and themselves'. He went on to claim that if there were no public schools, there would be few parochial schools either.[6] In a church thick with taboos, McGlynn simply said and did as he liked. This was what made him such a refreshing figure for many of his contemporaries, but it also explains why his superiors and many of his colleagues found him so threatening. This habit of breaking taboos arose partly from the lack of any tactical sense. Where Burtsell combined an independent mind and considerable courage with an acute sense of prudence, McGlynn was a bull in a china shop. Where Burtsell counselled his assistants to behave with discretion, McGlynn encouraged his to flaunt their loyalty to him in ways that were bound to get them into trouble. In the early stages of the conflict with Corrigan, Burtsell continually warned McGlynn of the dangers of risking suspension, whereas McGlynn was blithely confident that he could ride any storms that came his way.[7]

In a characteristic diatribe against current trends in the American church, launched shortly after his ex-communication, McGlynn ridiculed the taste of many bishops for dressing in purple and being addressed as 'Your Grace', and their requirement that priests wear the 'Roman collar'. He quoted a fellow-priest who remarked that the collars ought to carry the name of the wearer's bishop.[8] This was typical of the style of sardonic humour that made up much of the conversation of priests with other priests. Burtsell's diary, which records many such conversations, reflects a cynical view of the hierarchy and often of other priests in the archdiocese. Archbishop Hughes was suspected of having paid a girl to kiss a troublesome priest in the street in order to 'ruin him'. McCloskey was accused of suppressing any evidence of the 'leakage' of Catholics in his arch-diocese and of being mainly motivated by vanity. Farley, Corrigan's successor, was 'a sneak'.[9] Gossip about the sexual and drinking habits of their colleagues seems to have been of consuming interest to many priests, and the diary provides details of many such rumours.[10] But there was a world of difference between what a man like Burtsell said to his colleagues and what he said in public. A bitter complaint against McGlynn was that he failed to recognize this distinction and thus insisted on 'washing the church's dirty linen in public'.[11] Most Catholics had experienced too much bigotry and malice to engage readily in any heart-searching in the presence of outsiders. The public face of the church was thus one of extreme touchiness, and Catholics who broke ranks were seen by many as traitors.

McGlynn's habit of breaking ranks was partly due to a highly developed sense of the rights of individual conscience. He was, as Roohan puts it,[12] 'awash with an exuberant, optimistic and truculent Americanism', which inevitably conflicted with his role in the middle ranks of a tightly-disciplined hierarchical organization, led from the top. This Americanism seems to be the key to much of McGlynn's thinking. Curran suggests that the Civil War was the great formative experience for many of McGlynn's circle.[13] Like, Burtsell, and like Farrell, his first pastor, he was a fervent abolitionist and identified himself strongly with the Union cause. He believed that the United States was a land of destiny: 'in the providence of God our Father, it is marked out to be the leading nation of the world, in the very vanguard of political power and progress and everything that leads to the highest civilization.' He regarded the Founding Fathers as religious men, propounding great religious truths. 'The immortal preamble of the Declaration of Independence' represented 'the politics of the Lord's Prayer' in that it pronounced that 'all men are equal, and that they are endowed by their Creator with certain inalienable rights'. And what was good for America was good for the Catholic Church. He condemned the undemocratic methods of appointing bishops, without any reference to the wishes of clergy or people. He looked forward to the day when a 'democratic pope' would walk down Broadway in a stove-pipe hat 'with an umbrella under his arm'. His enthusiastic support for the public schools arose from his concern for national unity and for inculcating the younger generation with American ideals. Parochial schools posed a double threat as strongholds of unAmerican values and unAmerican languages. He dreamt of 'one magnificent American nationality, covering a whole continent, speaking one language, enjoying equal laws, its members living together in perfect peace and fraternity, and accomplishing for humanity greater wonders of civilization than the world has yet ventured to hope for'.[14]

In certain respects, McGlynn would have been at home in one of the major Protestant denominations – as a Congregationalist, for instance. It is symptomatic of the essentially 'Protestant' quality of his political outlook that he had a great influence on Walter Rauschenbusch who, at the time of the 'affair', was a young Baptist pastor in New York. McGlynn's catch-phrase, 'Thy will be done *on earth*', gave Rauschenbusch the key to his new understanding of Christianity, as he moved from individualistic pietism to the social gospel.[15] Rauschenbusch would broaden and sharpen McGlynn's critique of contemporary American society by moving beyond the latter's preoccupation with the evils arising from private ownership of land. He was also more cautious about looking into the future. But they would have agreed about the direction in which things were moving. Excusably carried away by his enthusiasm for the centenary of Washington's inauguration as first American president, McGlynn predicted that in a hundred years time (in 1987, to be precise), 'the doctrine of the equal rights of all men to all natural opportunities will have become a commonplace' and 'the prophecy of Isaiah will have been made good' as 'men shall learn war no more and man, governed no longer by despots, shall be governed by himself in the Parliament of Man'.[16]

It was this utopianism which set McGlynn apart from most of his Catholic contemporaries. For example, he saw Henry George as 'a man sent from God'. It is hard to imagine one of the many Tammany-voting priests using this kind of language about his favourite politicians. The alliance between the church and Tammany Hall was essentially instrumental, and recognized as such by both sides. McCloskey, Corrigan and others saw the relationship as being in the church's best interests, and thus in the interest of the souls of Catholics. But the church was under no illusion as to the character of many Tammany politicians, and no one believed that voting Democrat would advance the coming of the kingdom of God on earth. This pragmatism fitted in well with the pessimistic assessment of human nature, and the tendency to stress the judgment rather than the love of God, that characterized much of the Catholic teaching of the time.[17] This overriding consciousness of human frailty provided a justification for the authoritarian style of leadership practised by many priests of this generation. No doubt they would have seen McGlynn's view of God and human nature as sentimental and unrealistic. Indeed, his critics accused him of excessive leniency in his practice as a pastor because he encouraged people to go to communion every day, and did not require them to go to confession first, unless they were aware of having committed a grievious sin. They also objected to the fact that people were in the habit of kneeling at the altar rail in McGlynn's church while carrying tin cans and bundles.[18]

IV

Nineteenth-century New Yorkers liked to fill their walls with portraits of their heroes. On the Sunday following McGlynn's removal from St Stephen's, it was said that a shopkeeper who stocked portraits of prominent priests quickly sold out of pictures of McGlynn, but that an old woman bought a portrait of

Corrigan, in order to tear it up and stamp on the pieces. Eighteen months later, a priest in a neighbouring East Side parish was refusing the sacraments to the members of one household until they burnt a portrait of McGlynn that was hanging on their wall.[19] These conflicts over images reflect an important fact about the dispute between Corrigan and McGlynn. For the battle was not only between two men, but between two conflicting concepts of holiness, of which the two chief protagonists were symbols. Each was invested by his admirers and detractors with all sorts of qualities that may have borne little relation to reality. At least in the case of McGlynn, we know much more about the McGlynn legend than about the man himself, and the sources do not always permit us to judge with any great confidence how close the legend was to the living man.

The battle was fought at two levels. At the more obvious level, it was a battle about politics. To one side, McGlynn was 'the people's priest'; to the other, he was a 'socialistic agitator'. But this debate merely polarized the Catholic community along class lines, and the result was a stalemate. The Corriganites could certainly win a paper victory, for they controlled the positions of power and influence.[20] But the McGlynnites had the numbers. The Corriganites could not win the hearts and minds of the Catholic masses by simply denouncing McGlynn's politics, any more than arguing the merits of the Single Tax could persuade the Archbishop and the Catholic élite that McGlynn should be reinstated. So the debate rapidly moved to a second level, where each side tried to persuade the other by appealing to shared values.

To his followers, McGlynn was a holy man. They especially liked to dwell on his work as a confessor. A former assistant claimed that McGlynn had 'almost lived' in the confessional, and at an early stage in the conflict Burtsell told Corrigan that 'during all this agitation I had heard the doctor make only one complaint and that was that he could no longer hear confessions'. By contrast, McGlynn's successor, Donnelly, discredited himself in the eyes of many St Stephen's people by marching into the church, a policeman at his side, while confessions were being heard, ordering everybody out, and tearing down McGlynn's name from his box. Later, a group of women tried to turn McGlynn's confessional into a shrine.[21] There also were many stories of McGlynn's generosity. A typical tale was of the consternation caused when a man was found dead in the Hudson, and could only be identified by the fact that his clothes were marked 'Dr Edward McGlynn': he turned out to be a tramp to whom McGlynn had given his clothes. Moral support, as well as material, was always available to those in need. According to a former assistant: 'It was sufficient for any priest to be in trouble to secure for him a home in Dr McGlynn's house, and comfort and courage in his counsel.'[22]

Thus the McGlynn legend presented him as an outstanding exemplar both of general Christian charity and of more specifically priestly qualities. St Stephen's parish was famous not only for its extensive network of charitable institutions, but also for the lavish decoration of the church and the fine music.[23] There were two ways of looking at this. The Vicar-General pointed to the large parish debt, and claimed that McGlynn was incompetent to be a pastor. His admirers saw these as further evidence both of his warm heart and of his love of the house of God. And indeed McGlynn always insisted that the priest and the social reformer were integrally related, rather than being divergent and indeed conflicting aspects of his personality, as his critics tended to assume. (For instance, a history of St Stephen's parish published in the 1890s referred to McGlynn as a good priest who 'unfortunately' got mixed up in politics.)[24] McGlynn claimed that his conversion to the doctrines of Henry George arose directly out of his experience as a priest – his desire to alleviate the sufferings of the poor, with whom he was in continuous contact, and for whom individual charity could do so little, and his wish to vindicate God, by showing that he had provided the means for a decent life for all, and that human misery was the product of human greed and ignorance rather than divine malevolence. It was a constant theme of McGlynn's that men and women were rejecting God because of the church's neglect, its identification with the rich, or its preaching of doctrines that gave the poor little hope that their lot on earth could ever be improved. Nor was this just a debating point, thought up in the heat of his quarrel with

Corrigan: as early as 1865, Burtsell and McGlynn had been concerned about the alienation of many poor Catholics from the church and the insufficient zeal shown by the archdiocesan authorities in tackling the problem.[25]

McGlynn's admirers liked to refer to him as the type of the *soggarth aroon* – a Gaelic term for 'the good priest'.[26] It was this image that the Corriganites had to smash. The task was a difficult one, for at the beginning of the 'affair' the picture of McGlynn as a model priest seems to have been largely accepted even by Bishop McQuaid of Rochester, who loathed his politics and liberal theological tendencies.[27] The Corriganites were willing to use any argument, however implausible, to discredit the pastor of St Stephen's, and a fair amount of barrel-scraping went on. However, they had two main lines of attack. The first was the time-honoured tactic of discrediting a clerical opponent by trying to prove that he was involved with a woman. For Irish-American Catholics this was the deadliest accusation that could be made against a priest. It compromised irrevocably his claims to be a holy man set apart for the service of God. It is perhaps significant that Corrigan made special efforts to trump the McGlynnites' ace, the *soggarth aroon*'s renowned love of the confessional. He now offered a new explanation of why McGlynn spent so much time there – he was using it to extract sexual favours from his female parishioners. From January 1887, the Corriganites began spreading rumours about McGlynn's sex-life, and some of these were reported in the press. The evidence convinced Corrigan, though even some of his supporters were doubtful, and there is no sign that any McGlynnites were persuaded. They, in any case, were busy spreading rumours about the sex-lives of Corrigan and his Vicar-General.[28]

However, the second line of attack was more effective. This was the charge that McGlynn was a disobedient and disloyal priest whose egocentric arrogance had led him to betray the Pope, his archbishop and the whole Catholic community. The Corriganites countered the image of the *soggarth aroon* with a rival ideal of holiness, and one that McGlynn had no prospect of living up to. This was the ideal of the humble and devoted Catholic, whose holiness was reflected in willing submission to ecclesiastical superiors – even when their commands were least welcome – and on identification with the church so complete that any merely individual opinion, identity or ambition was superfluous. A group of German priests, who were the first in the archdiocese to declare their support for Corrigan, resorted to military metaphors in order to explain their disgust with McGlynn: 'A good Catholic will obey his pastor, a good priest will obey his commander, the Bishop, and all will obey the Commander-in-Chief, the Holy Father, in matters of faith and morality.'[29] Nuns were generally held to be the supreme embodiment of this ideal of humility and self-abnegation. To call in question the reality of their vocation or the value of their work was akin to criticizing one's own mother: it was to break the strongest of the taboos with which American Catholics were surrounded. When, therefore, Corrigan's close ally, Bishop McQuaid, read McGlynn's article of August 1887, which included some criticism of religious orders, he was beside himself with anger. He launched into a personal attack from his cathedral pulpit, accusing McGlynn of unmanliness, 'gross coarseness', and conduct that 'no Catholic worthy of the name' could tolerate.[30]

It was perhaps fortunate for McGlynn that few Catholics read the *North American Review*, in which his article appeared. However, everyone was aware that he had refused to go to Rome when summoned, and had thus broken the second most powerful taboo, that which protected the person of the Pope from any direct criticism. The late nineteenth century was a period when emphasis on the internal cohesion of the church and separate identity of Catholics reached unprecedented heights, and this sense of identity was focussed above all on the Pope.[31] Like McGlynn, Leo XIII looked down on his followers from the walls of many a tenement flat, and McGlynn himself, after his excommunication was lifted, referred to the Pope in terms almost as sycophantic as those which he had once ridiculed.[32] Many of his closest allies urged him to go to Rome, and when he refused, some abandoned him. Their case was put most clearly by Patrick Ford, editor of the widely-read radical paper, *The Irish World*, which had strongly supported McGlynn in the early days of the 'affair':

> Whilst he confined himself to the discussion of that question [the land] I was with him, but when he went beyond that – when he began to traduce the church and insult and defy the Pope amid the applause of scoffing infidels and avowed enemies of the entire Christian system – then I halted and drew the line.[33]

V

At the beginning of the 'affair', Burtsell warned McGlynn that 'a suspension would take away from him the confidence of our people: he would be looked upon with suspicion'. A more sanguine McGlynn supporter declared, however: 'I think they will have to excommunicate one or two besides Dr McGlynn; they will have to excommunicate some millions of American Catholics.'[34] In the event, Catholics were more divided in their response than either of these prophecies might suggest. There were those who opposed McGlynn from the start, notably most members of the Catholic élite, those Catholics who had close links with the Democratic Party, and most priests of German background. There were a great many (perhaps the largest group) who initially sympathized with McGlynn, but drew back as he became ever more deeply embroiled in conflict with the church authorities. There also were considerable numbers of New York Catholics who remained loyal to McGlynn through thick and thin, as is indicated by Corrigan's long-running attempts to stop Catholics attending Anti-Poverty meetings. And there were some Catholics who broke away from the church altogether.[35] The latter group must have been relatively small, in view of the fact that surveys in the early 1900s found that around 90% of Irish-born New Yorkers claimed to be Catholics, and around 90% of Irish-born Catholics claimed membership of a specific parish.[36] However, there is some evidence that the church's social base was narrowing in the period following the McGlynn affair, and that some sections of the New York Irish were becoming more conspicuously identified with the church than others.

In 1901 St Stephen's published a list of contributors to parish funds. Of 282 persons listed, 142 could be identified in the schedules of the 1900 Federal Census.[37] The overwhelming majority were Irish-born or of Irish parentage. 43% of the heads of contributing households were in middle-class jobs, and only 22% were in semi-skilled or unskilled manual jobs; however, in a random sample of households in the parish with members of Irish stock, only 25% of heads were in middle-class jobs, and 50% were semi-skilled and unskilled manual workers.[38] When particular areas of work are separated out, a concentration of active parishioners in public employment becomes apparent. 13% of the heads of contributing households worked in the police, the fire department, the post office, the courts or other city offices, as against 1% of the heads in the random sample. A contributors' list for 1904 from St Paul's on the Middle West Side shows the same tendencies, though in less pronounced form – an over-representation of the upper middle class and of public employees (especially policemen), and an under-representation of unskilled workers. It may well be objected that any contributors' list is biased towards those with large, or at least regular incomes. However, it is worth noting that a list from Sacred Heart on the Middle West Side in 1882 had shown that a lot of very poor people *were* contributing regularly to parish funds, and that contributors made up a remarkably well-balanced cross-section of the local population of Irish stock: 23% of heads of contributing households had been in middle-class jobs, and 51% in semi-skilled or unskilled manual jobs, as against 18% and 48% respectively in a random sample.[39]

In 1886 a newspaper article suggested that McGlynn had alienated most of his richer parishioners, and that they had left to join the neighbouring St Leo's church, leaving McGlynn 'with the poor he loves so well'. This was an oversimplification, for many of McGlynn's strongest supporters were drawn from the lower middle class.[40] They also included a considerable number of middle-class women.[41] (It may be relevant that McGlynn was one of the very few Catholic priests of his time who supported the enfranchisement of women.)[42] However, it would appear that under McGlynn's successor, Fr Colton, precisely the reverse process was taking place: the poor were leaving, while the rich were coming back, together with those sections of the working and lower middle classes whose area of employment put a premium on connections with Tammany Hall. And while the statistical evidence concerning the changes at St Stephen's is rather fragmentary, there is no doubt as to the ways in which the kind of Catholicism taught at St Stephen's changed under Colton.

The top priorities were now the founding of a parish school and getting rid of the parish debt. The former was set up almost at once, and by 1900 had 1000 pupils. The elimination of the debt, which required the cancellation of many of McGlynn's charitable schemes, was completed by 1894. Devotions to Mary, the Sacred Heart, St Anne and St Anthony – themes which do not figure prominently in surviving records of McGlynn's ministry – now became central features of parish life.[43] Under Colton, St Stephen's became a stronghold of the kind of Catholicism, dominant in turn-of-the-century New York, which saw Christian living in terms of adherence to a complex set of formal rules, which only the clergy were qualified to interpret.[44] Sometimes this took the form of what Messbarger terms 'spiritual numerology based on precise units of grace-giving words and deeds'.[45] It also led to a preoccupation with individual sanctification that largely excluded the social gospel preached by those like McGlynn. Colton's *Church Bulletin* offers a striking example, which indicates how far St Stephen's had travelled since January 1887. The 'Parish Notes and Suggestions' column for November 1900, after urging better attendance at special services and devotions, and in particular the taking of Communion on First Fridays, went on to claim that: 'Our Lord promised that those receiving consecutively on nine first Fridays of the month would achieve the salvation of their souls.'

Notes

1. The standard hagiography is S. Bell, *Rebel, Priest and Prophet: A Biography of Dr Edward McGlynn*, New York 1937. S. Malone, *Dr Edward McGlynn*, New York 1918, is a useful compilation of reminiscences and excerpts from his speeches. R. E. Curran, *Michael Augustine*

Corrigan and the Shaping of Conservative Catholicism in America, Arno Press, New York 1978, supersedes all previous accounts of the 'McGlynn Affair'. It also has a useful guide to sources.

2. Bell, op.cit., pp.37–38.
3. Curran, op.cit., pp.254–255.
4. Ibid., p.36.
5. J.D. McCabe, *Lights and Shadows of New York Life*, New York 1872, p.495; J.G. Shea, *The Catholic Churches of New York City*, New York 1880, pp.200, 206–208, 237, 384, 641; R.E. Curran, 'Prelude to Americanism: The New York Accademia and Clerical Radicalism in the late Nineteenth Century', *Church History*, XLVII, 1978, p.57; Richard Burtsell, Diary (Archives of the Archdiocese of New York), 29 January 1887.
6. E. McGlynn, 'The New Know-Nothingism and the Old,' *North American Review*, August 1887, pp.200–201.
7. Burtsell, Diary, 29 September and 7 October 1886, 5 May 1887.
8. McGlynn, op.cit., p.198.
9. Burtsell, Diary, 14 June 1865, 8 April 1865, 9 February 1887.
10. Ibid., 18 June 1865, 26 January 1889, March 1889.
11. Reported in ibid., 26 September 1887.
12. J.E. Roohan, *American Catholics and the Social Question 1865–1900*, Arno Press, New York 1976, p.371.
13. Curran, 'Prelude to Americanism,' p.51.
14. Malone, op.cit., p.81; E. McGlynn, 'The Vatican and the United States,' *Forum*, September 1893, pp.10–13; Bell, op.cit., p.89; McGlynn, 'The New Know-Nothingism,' p.203.
15. K.-J. Jaehn, *Rauschenbusch: The Formative Years*, Judson Press, Valley Forge 1976, pp.14–15.
16. Malone, op.cit., p.81.
17. For examples of contemporary sermons, see Shea, op. cit., e.g. pp.303, 501. See also J.P. Dolan, *The American Catholic Experience*, Doubleday, New York 1985, pp.221–236. For the political approach of New York priests, see H.J. Browne, *One Stop above Hell's Kitchen: Sacred Heart Parish in Clinton*, New York 1977, pp.60–71. See also the wide-ranging discussion in D.N. Doyle, 'Catholicism, politics and Irish America since 1890', *The Irish in America: Emigration, Assimilation and Impact* ed. P.J. Drudy, CUP 1985, pp.191–230.
18. Burtsell, Diary, 3 December 1886, 15 February 1887.
19. Bell, op.cit., p.49; Burtsell, Diary, 5 August 1888.
20. For Corrigan's links with the Catholic lay elite see Curran, *Corrigan*, pp.197–199, 313–315 and passim.
21. Malone, op. cit., p.111; Burtsell, Diary, 10 January 1887; H. George Jr,

The Life of Henry George, London 1900, pp. 489–490; Curran, *Corrigan*, p. 227.

22. Bell, op.cit., pp. 18–19; Malone, op.cit., p. 111. Further examples reported in *New York Times*, 12 December 1886.
23. Curran, *Corrigan*, p. 171; Shea, op.cit., pp. 664–666.
24. C. M. Moore, *The Church of St Stephen's 1849–1894*, New York n.d..
25. Bell, op.cit., pp. 20–24; Malone, op.cit., pp. 25–26; Burtsell, Diary, 25 May 1865 and passim.
26. See for instance a poem 'Soggarth Aroon' in Malone, op.cit., p. 129.
27. F. J. Zwierlein, *The Life and Letters of Bishop McQuaid*, 3 vols, Rochester, NY 1925–7, III, p. 15.
28. Curran, *Corrigan*, pp. 276–286; M. F. Egan, *Recollections of a Happy Life*, London 1924, pp. 137–139; Burtsell, Diary, 4 April 1888.
29. Zwierlein, op.cit., III, pp. 32–33.
30. Ibid., pp. 46–47.
31. H. McLeod, 'Building the Catholic Ghetto: Catholic Organizations 1870–1914', *Voluntary Religion* ed. W. J. Sheils and D. Wood, Blackwell 1986, p. 428.
32. See the description of a 'typical' tenement flat in E. Herzfeld, *Family Monographs*, New York 1905, pp. 44–46; McGlynn, 'The Vatican,' pp. 20–22.
33. *Irish World*, 29 October 1887. See also J. P. Rodechko, *Patrick Ford and his Search for America*, Arno Press, New York 1976, pp. 168–169.
34. Burtsell, Diary, 29 September 1886; R. E. Curran, 'The McGlynn Affair and the Shaping of the New Conservatism in American Catholicism, 1886–1894', *Catholic Historical Review*, LXVI, 1980, p. 184. Curran's article is the best short account of the 'affair'.
35. T. Sugrue, *A Catholic speaks his Mind*, New York 1952, p. 44; E. G. Flynn, *The Rebel Girl*, 2nd edn, International Publishers, New York 1973, pp. 42–43.
36. H.McLeod, 'Catholicism and the New York Irish 1880–1910', *Disciplines of Faith* ed. J. Obelkevich and others, Routledge and Kegan Paul 1987, p. 338.
37. *Church Bulletin* of St Stephen's Church, February 1901 (in New York Public Library). 16 contributors were anonymous or gave no address; 25 were scattered across the city; of the 241 contributors giving addresses in the area round the church 59% were identified.
38. The occupational classification is taken from: S. Thernstrom, *The Other Bostonians*, Harvard University Press 1973, pp. 290–292.
39. *Calendar* of the Church of St Paul the Apostle, February 1904 (at St Paul's rectory); Church Collectors' Book (at Sacred Heart rectory).
40. *New York Times*, 12 December 1886; Bell, op.cit., lists the members of the deputation of McGlynn's parishioners sent to plead his case before

Corrigan, and I have identified fourteen of them in *Trow's New York City Directory* 1887–8.

41. Curran, *Corrigan*, p. 389. Ten of the thirty-five parishioners who went to see Corrigan were women. *Irish World*, 12 February 1887, identified Miss Munier, leader of the choir, and Miss Sarah McCaffery as leaders of the more militant faction among them.
42. J.J. Kenneally, 'Catholicism and Woman Suffrage in Massachussets', *Catholic Historical Review*, LIII, 1967–8, p. 47.
43. Moore, op.cit., pp. 16–24; *Church Bulletin*, 1900–1902, passim.
44. See, for instance, P.J. Murnion, 'Towards Theopolitan Ministry: The Changing Structure of the Pastoral Ministry, New York 1920–1970', Columbia University Ph.D. thesis 1972, p. 130.
45. P. Messbarger, *Fiction with a Parochial Purpose*, Boston University Press 1971, p. 141.

10

True to Stereotype? Vivian and Dorothy Pomeroy and the Rebels in Lumb Lane

CLYDE BINFIELD

Of all Evangelical Nonconformists, Congregationalists were most frequently found announcing rebellion at Evangelicalism's liberalmost bounds. Trends already clear by 1860 were commonplace by 1920. How might a Congregational church arrive in such pastures?

To begin with an Oxford college magazine. It contains not so much a story, more an aperçu: 'Paul Lerith – a Modern Chronicle'. Its author is anonymous beyond the initials DTP. It is Sunday night and a parson, Paul Lerith, is relaxing with his wife. She bursts out: 'There are Fraternals and there are Sewing Meetings, but we are of the immortal gods for whom Monday was made to be a day of bliss under the sky – we hear the earth sing! Very pleasant it is to be emancipated, O my open necked Paul!'

As for all parsons and their wives the weekday round of meeting and visiting follows blissful Monday. And then it 'is Friday and Sunday looms horribly' (here it should be understood that DTP is the parson's wife – 'I had a dream of being great, a fear is upon me that I shall only be known for a certain *pleasantness* and the ability to talk at PME!'). 'I sit in my den, pen in hand. A complicated sentence about common kitchens and efficient communal management is evolving.' Paul charges in. It is sermon-writing time and inspiration has fled. 'You learn French, but do you translate Bergson for me? No, you read wretched novels to "aid your human research". You learn German, but do you render the mighty Eucken intelligible to me? ... Why did you never learn Hebrew, you wretched Suffragette?' He explodes. 'I won't be a piffler ... I *won't*.' And he hurtles back to finish his sermon.

'It was a good sermon, *real*, one of Paul's inspirations. I was moved.' But, sermon over, there was the gauntlet of the Vestibule Committee to be run: four of them, each true to a type.

> A queer revulsion of feeling welled up within me ... the pathos of existence, the committee, everybody: Paul and I in particular ... so eager – so alive, so lacking the denominational sense: us two with our background of hopes and our muddled aspirations running a Church! ... It seemed suddenly grotesque.

How young and Oxford and advanced. How apt for 1914 this parson's wife, so much her husband's equal. None of it is what it seems. It may be Oxford but it is not Anglican. The magazine is that of Mansfield College which trained Congregational ministers.[1] Paul Lerith, therefore, was a Congregational minister. Hence the teamwork of husband and wife, soon to be non-fictionally reflected in Claud and Constance Coltman, the Mansfield-trained husband-and-wife team, she the first ordained English Congregational woman minister.[2] The Leriths are not the Coltmans. This is 1914 and the Coltmans' day came in 1917. So who are they, and where their church?

To the magazine add a souvenir and a manual. They concern the same community. The souvenir lists 455 members and 509 adherents. Many names resonate. One, Delius, positively chimes. The manual also resonates. It describes an 'Educational Institute': four departments, forty teachers, three hundred pupils, celebrating 'The Institution of the Dear Love of Comrades'. That love unfolds from the Buds and Blossoms, children 'in the early morning of life', past the Voyagers 'who, like little ships, are just venturing from port and setting sail on the stormy ocean of the world', through the Crusaders 'zealously striving to overcome evil', to the Experimenders, of all ages, for whom the conventional wisdom of make-do-and-mend has been replaced by the kindly adventure of experiment and mend.

The relationship between school and church was a constitutional minefield. This school was self-governing and separately financed though it was hoped that 'mutual knowledge and close sympathy' were ensured by the parent church's committee structure: a council of thirty (seven of them women) elected by ballot and fed by sub-committees. It was a large operation, packaged in a building which would be full if each child, adherent and member arrived together. The operation's managing director, its representative in the eyes of the world, was the minister. This one was new and his stipend had dropped accordingly. His tone is clear from this wartime message to his church:

> ... conventional Christianity is morally bankrupt. The world is waiting for a better leadership. It will surely find what it seeks in the authentic message and divinely human spirit of Jesus. My ministry is firmly shaping as an endeavour to present and press the gospel of equal comradeship in the consciousness of the One Creative Life.

His church's tone colours its yearbook cover: a swastika at each top corner and two daffodils above the centre. Such self-consciousness as might merit a Paul Lerith.

The church is Greenfield, Bradford.[3] It existed from 1852 to 1938. It flourished from 1888 to 1923. In 1914 its minister was Vivian Tawse Pomeroy, Wadham and Mansfield Colleges Oxford. He was Paul Lerith and his wife, Dorothy Tremayne Pomeroy, whom he married in Mansfield's chapel, was DTP. Here nuance is folded in nuance. Greenfield was Congregational but many Congregationalists found it hard to take. Pomeroy was its eighth minister. The first had been a Wesleyan, the seventh a Welsh Calvinistic Methodist. Pomeroy himself was born Wesleyan and died Unitarian while a friend who became a Catholic priest insisted that Dorothy Pomeroy had the Catholic essence within her.[4] So it is with many gathered city churches, a reminder of the deceptiveness of the chapel stereotype which springs most easily to educated minds.

Only Greenfield's life-span fits that stereotype, meeting the classic mould of a suburban church – ninety years divided equally into growth, prime and decline though Greenfield's variant was thirty-five years uncertain growth and fifteen of swift decline. Little else typified this notorious church. Its building was second rate: large, towerless, spireless, chapel Italianate of 1876 replacing small, towerless, spireless, chapel gothic (just a bell-less bell-turret at one gable end) of 1852.[5] It had none of the force of the great preaching centres. The setting matched the building: Lumb Lane, off-centre for Manningham, soon to be on the slide.

> There is more Lumb than lane about it now. There are some nice houses, my church, three fried fish shops, a mill and the Infirmary ... You can tell it is interesting ...[6]

Here was a suburb shifting before its first residents could take breath. To succeed a Congregational church must be at a social confluence, well-placed for mission while easily placed for the villas of those who paid the bills, took the sittings and guaranteed the stipend. So quicksilver was Greenfield's social confluence that it would test the strongest vocation to keep the cause going while the villas slipped downmarket and the gardens were built over and the city centre chapels leap-frogged out.

It was thirty-five years before such leadership was found.[7] Until then Greenfield marked time; sixty-six members in 1858, one hundred and six in 1870. The church bickered. It could not keep its ministers. Its stipend – £140 in the 1850s, £150 in the 1880s – was a deterrent. Its survival may be attributed to four factors: an injection of lay leadership in the late 1880s; an almost simultaneous injection of ministerial leadership; a change of theological direction by that leadership; and sufficient willingness all round to allow change to play its part in growth rather than division.

Victorian Bradford was believed to be a Nonconformist and Liberal power. Here was the 'Nonconformist Conscience' translated into municipal life, but with a doctrinaire side to its politics which was disastrous for Bradford's Liberalism and none too good for its Nonconformity. Bradford Labour was the result. The story has been amply documented.[8] It may be suggested as follows: in 1885 there were forty-three Liberal and sixteen Tory councillors; in 1913 there were twenty-nine Liberals, thirty-four Tories, one Independent and twenty Labour. These figures hide considerable drama. In 1913, 27.2% voted Liberal, 29.7% voted Tory and 43.1% Labour.[9] That period, 1885–1913, coincides with Greenfield's prime; and much of Greenfield's notoriety lay in the conviction that, while not Labour at prayer, it was where Bradford's Labour leaders could pray if that were how the mood took them.

The infusion of key leadership indirectly reflects that urban expansion which otherwise passed Greenfield by. In 1877 Airedale College was grandly reopened on Manningham's furthermost edge. While chapels attached to theological colleges seldom flourished they attracted thoughtfully prosperous congregations because colleges were often in good areas and careful preaching was assured. For nine years some thoughtfully prosperous Bradfordians worshipped at Airedale. They formed a church. They called a minister. When he went they turned to Greenfield, also vacant and supposedly in low water.[10]

This revived the future which ended with Greenfield's first decade. Nonconformist colleges attract two myths. One, that of the Dissenting Academy, is heroic. The other, fostered autobiographically by ministerial failures, is depressing. Yet they provided an intellectual focus for the aspiring but under-educated young. Arguably a cultural force in their community, they were certainly an energizing force for their denomination. Bradford had Airedale, housed from 1834 four-square and elegant at Undercliffe where an immediate (and thoughtfully prosperous) consequence was College Chapel.[11] Bradford's other Congregational churches also benefitted, among them Greenfield.

By 1863 Greenfield's members (twenty-six men, seventy-six women)[12] included a nucleus of civic and collegiate intelligence. The senior deacon was H.B. Byles, the stationer-bookseller brother of William Byles of *The Bradford Observer*.[13] The members included two Airedale tutors, R.G. Hartley and H.B. Creak.[14] The minister was their brother-in-law, Thomas Gasquoine, fresh from the Manchester lectures of that 'Nestor of heretics', A.J. Scott.[15] They typify Congregationalism's teaching families: high minds, narrow means and far horizons. But Greenfield was only their almost forcing house. Gasquoine left for Oswestry in February 1863 and Hartley for Madagascar in June. Creak died in 1864 and in 1866 the Byleses crossed into Lancashire. It was twenty years before Greenfield was again so ministerially connected. By then Byles' minister son was a decade away from Unitarianism; Creak's son was a Cambridge wrangler; and Gasquoine had assisted in the Leicester Conference of 1877 which gave Congregationalism the thrill of controversy without the pain of division and opened up the role which Greenfield made its own.[16] By then Airedale had deserted Undercliffe classical and its secure College Chapel for Emm Lane Gothic and its fitful College Hall. Now was Greenfield's hour. Greenfield and College Hall merged. The immediate impact was organizational.

Practically speaking a Congregational church was two interrelated meetings. Its policy was determined by church meeting (all members meeting with equal voting and speaking rights) and directed by the deacons' meeting, up to a dozen men (women came later) elected sometimes for life, increasingly for much less, by church meeting to whom they were answerable. The minister, whose call was issued by church meeting, chaired both. Since Congregational churches bred activity they also bred committees but these were not integral to the church's polity. Greenfield, however, inserted an intermediate tier. Church members still met. So did deacons. But the management of daily affairs lay with a committee elected by church and congregation. The deacons sat on it *ex officio* but the rest need not all be church members. They met monthly, ultimately responsible to the Greenfield electorate but in effect sovereign, fed by the complex of subcommittees which moderated church life. This system, frequently refined as to details, prevailed for the rest of Greenfield's existence. Thus a wide slice of life was swept into Greenfield's Christian polity. There was a price to be paid. Church meetings became options for the older-fashioned or the spiritually minded. Church membership turned into a useful sort of badge. On the other hand Greenfield's church life like Bradford's Liberal politics engaged the energies of a network of activists. It was dubious churchmanship but it was fine stewardship.[17]

That network, uniform neither in character nor outlook, announced Greenfield to the world and coloured its rebel reputation. In 1893 as in 1863 it included two Airedale tutors: Elkanah Armitage, a Cambridge first with an assured background in cotton and cousinhood and a Newnham wife specializing in Norman castles; Archibald Duff, a Canadian Scot, McGill, Andover, Halle and Göttingen to Armitage's Manchester, Stuttgart and Cambridge, whose wife became a JP, and whose daughter was a Labour activist.[18] They were a formidable study in contrasts, Armitage torn between Keswick and Hegel agonizing at his pupils' secularity, Duff wedded to Higher Criticism championing their boldness, both in love with Germany, happy in their Liberalism, Armitage conciliatory, Duff unpredictable. Armitage's diaries, the abbreviated jottings of a busy man under discipline, communicate the excitements of Bradford Congregationalism in the 1890s.[19]

Duff had come from College Hall. So had Rudolf Delius, that essence of Bradford's commercial cosmopolitanism, a Bielefeld-born wool and yarn merchant whose firm in Arundel Street should not be confused with that of his fourth cousin, Julius, the composer's father, in East Parade. Rudolf was Vice-Consul for Norway and Sweden. His wife was from Moscow. He was easily typecast:[20]

> Mr Delius was a German and almost worshipped at the shrine of Bismarck ... We had nothing in common there ...
>
> I remember preaching one Sunday on 'The earth is the Lord's', in spite of which we had made it the landlord's, and protesting against the injustices of our land system, and pleading for a more just distribution of material wealth. He told me he did not like the sermon. Why did I preach about such things? 'What can I do, Mr Delius, when these things stare me in the face, and I see their results in the poverty of so many?'
>
> 'Pass them over in silence', he said ... This was his social philosophy. He was most generous in charity, a case of poverty got his quick sympathy. If I wanted money help for some one in need I could always get it from him ... Yet if you began to argue

> with him the rights of the workers to a higher status he was adamant ...[21]

Delius was a church member. The larger local commerce's representative face was found in a seatholder, Briggs Priestley, stuff manufacturer, brother, son and son-in-law of Liberal MPs and one himself from 1906. His background was Baptist, his wife's was Congregationalist. They were a couple of clout and bottom:[22]

> He and his wife had been most kind to me always. Once when I needed a change and rest they sent me a cheque for £60 to go to Switzerland. Other people in their circle often chipped them about their supporting a New Theologian and a Socialist parson. Why did they go to Greenfield? They had withstood for years the pressure of influential people. After my appearance on the ILP platform, the pressure was renewed, and they left the church. They were the richest members of my congregation.[23]

Three other names extend the clout and cosmopolitanism. Of these William Claridge sat least easily in Greenfield's pews. He was an accountant, with Trinity Cambridge and a dozen years' teaching at Bradford Grammar School behind him. In 1902, that key year for so political an accolade, he was Chairman of Bradford School Board. His minister's radicalism discounted that received Nonconformist wisdom about public education which was Claridge's passion.[24]

George Beaumont was another College Hall man, a Bradford alderman's son, educated in Europe, partner in Simon Israel and Co., shipping merchants, founder of 'United Foreign Circles', an 'institution devoted to the encouragement of study and conversation in foreign languages'.[25] At Greenfield foreign but living languages united higher criticism and higher commerce. Higher conscience came into it too. In 1890 General Booth hit Bradford. One consequence was described by Greenfield's minister:

> I said it was a fine opportunity for secularists who denounced

the belief in a future world to do something for this one. If this life was the only one, would they come forward generously and help their unfortunate fellows to get something out of it? General Booth had said jocularly that anyone was at liberty to criticize the scheme if he would subscribe £5 for the privilege. I received a letter signed 'A secularist', protesting against my remarks about secularists, and enclosing £5 ... The letter bore a stamp photograph of the writer ...

... Some time afterwards we had a conference in our schoolroom ... We had them frequently on theological and social questions.

I saw two men sitting together, one of whom I recognized by the stamp photograph. 'Here is my secularist' ... I thought.

... So began my acquaintance with Mr Percy Lund ...

Lund was, as his minister described him, 'an unusual type of man'.

In diet a vegetarian, in former days an English and Swiss mountain climber, a great Nature lover, artistic in temperament, steeped in Wordsworth and other poets, in religion distinctly eclectic ... For over twenty years he has studied the Bible according to some allegorical standard which has made it for him a very rich book ... I have not been able to follow his investigations ... [26]

That was as well since this man so 'steel true and blade-straight' combined Congregationalism with Theosophy, retranslating 'the first chapters of Genesis, endeavouring to show that the personal and place names in that book represented eternal principles rather than mere people and places on the map' and developing a 'line of thought whose purpose was to discover the deeper spiritual meaning of our fairy stories, our folk lore, and the stories of Greek mythology'.[27]

Lund was a fortunate businessman for in him hobby and occupation merged. His hobby was photography. His profession was printing. His name and quality survive in Lund, Humphries, the London architectural publishers. In Lund's day his firm did

Greenfield's printing, hence the mystic motifs of swastika and daffodils.

These were characters enough for any church, their personalities converting the day-to-day Bradford facts of earning and living from stereotype to prototype. The agent in this was Greenfield's minister for over twenty years, T. Rhondda Williams.

Rhondda Williams is so representative an Edwardian minister as to be far larger than life: Welsh speaking but not very Welsh accented; self-taught; a Calvinistic Methodist turned Congregationalist; a miner's son who by his own choice left school at nine for the mines; who in his 'teens joined Ebenezer, Tonypandy and in his twenties left the Welsh speaking ministry for the English, Dowlais with its 700 members for Neath's 120. And so to England itself: Greenfield where he quadrupled his stipend, doubled his membership and changed, as he put it, from the coal and steel world of Williams and Evans to the wool and textile one of 'Ramsbottom, Higgenbottom, Hagenback, Wolfenden, Ollerenshaw, Murgatroyd', (or, as at Percy Lund's funeral, Longbottom, Horsfall and Pighill); 'different industrial processes contributing to a different *temper* and outlook'.[28]

To stoke that temper Williams brought youth, passion and orthodoxy. Youth passed, passion remained. Much later a frustrated young Anglican was spellbound by this pulpit giant who yet face-to-face was 'quite an ordinary personality' with little small talk – or none for the young.[29] The orthodoxy was upended. Williams had left eternal punishment behind in Wales. Now, buffeted by higher critical fellow ministers, the rest followed, 'leaving me with a devastating sense of desolation in some cold and arid desert whose icy winds drove frost to my soul'.[30] The result was a New Theology (he used the phrase, so he liked to insist, before it became popular), broad, undisciplined, refusing to call itself Evangelical: 'it is for the Catholic aspects of religion I care. I hate to see the sectarian flag hoisted over a continent of truth.' It was a Social Gospel; 'nothing is merely secular, for, the moment man touches it, it is in contact with spirit, and the latter is affected by it. All so-called secular questions are therefore soul-questions.'[31]

There were bold consequences. Local ministers who fell doctrinally foul of their churches were championed. When Ryan Street ejected William Rosling, with wife and five children, 'on the charge that his preaching is not orthodox', Greenfield took up the cudgels:

> We are obliged ... to enter our most solemn protest ... and we assure Mr Rosling of our admiration of his fearless stand for conviction, and trust that the cross he so bravely bears may be transfigured for him, by the Master's presence, into a crown of rejoicing.[32]

Rosling became a Unitarian.

By now Greenfield had Bradford's largest Congregational membership and Yorkshire's third largest. This, with the visits from General Booth and to Seebohm Rowntree; the sharing of feminist platforms with Adela and Christabel Pankhurst and of Labour platforms with Fred Jowett, institutionalized its rebellious reputation.[33]

Then, in 1909, Williams left Bradford for Brighton and northern soot for such glare that at first he had to wear dark glasses.[34]

Williams was inimitable but what followed was an extraordinarily apt combination of contrasts and continuities. From Rhondda Williams to Vivian Pomeroy was from the late forties to the late twenties; South Wales to London Cornwall; a miner's home to a city draper's; a very elementary school, self-help and Carmarthen College to City of London School, Wadham and Mansfield College; a slightly Welsh accent to a decidedly Oxford one. What they shared was evangelical passion modernized into Labour politics, women's rights and a dislike for expected formulae. Paul Lerith lacked 'the denominational sense'. Rhondda Williams' 'ecclesiastical bump seems missing'. [35] For Pomeroy church membership was 'equal comradeship in the consciousness of the One Creative Life'.[36] For Williams it was 'the fundamental belief that we are experiencing Spiritual Reality'.[37]

Pomeroy's formation was Wesleyan. His father, Ambrose Pomeroy, was a supporter of the West London Mission, active in Progressive politics and chairman of London County Council's

Parks Committee. Vivian was intended for the Wesleyan ministry, had stayed a while at Cliff College but fell under the spell of that prematurely grey, preternaturally appealing, pulpit Prince Charming of theological liberalism, R.J. Campbell. Hence Mansfield and the Congregational ministry. Greenfield was his first pastorate.[38]

Pomeroy's Bradford years might be summarized as an ecclesiastical politicizing of Rhondda Williamsism. When the 'New Theology' hit the headlines Williams secured L.P. Jacks the Unitarian, Claude Montefiore the Liberal Jew and R.J. Campbell to lecture in St. George's Hall and Greenfield moved into Campbell's camp.[39] With Pomeroy the visiting celebrities were W.E. Orchard, Maude Royden and Margaret Macmillan. Then came gowns for the choir and pieces in *Christian Commonwealth*, the house journal for those socialistically catholicizing (and sometimes theosophizing) Congregationalists who felt as Orchard did. The weeknight tradition of usefully unlikely speakers was maintained. In Williams' day that might be Miss Jones the sanitary inspector; in Pomeroy's it was a London lecturer on anthroposophy, for now was Lund's hour.[40] The Armitages and Priestleys had gone. Delius and Beaumont were dead. Only Duff enthused erratically on. In 1912, however, a choice spirit was admitted to membership: J. Arthur Hill, 'a confirmed invalid who was known to but a few people at Greenfield, but ... who took considerable interest in religious questions and was moreover a man of culture, being corresponding secretary for Sir Oliver Lodge'. That autumn Hill gave a paper to a church meeting which his health required another to deliver. Its theme? 'The Faith of a Reverent Agnostic'.[41]

Now that such waywardness was denominationally commonplace Greenfield moved paradoxically to the denominational periphery, a fellowship of defensively blithe spirits fascinating to the clever young. Airedale's ordinands liked to see Greenfield as forbidden land since that added to the attractions of its worship (though with a college tutor in the pews and a college governor in the pulpit any such prohibition was notional).[42] And there were still persecuted ministers to be publicly championed. Hence church meeting's solemn

> protest in the name of our Great Lord and Saviour and in the name of our sacred Nonconformity and Free Church principles against the attempt now being made to eject the Revd Percy W. Jones of Doncaster from the Yorkshire Congregational Union ...[43]

Like Ryan Street's William Rosling, Doncaster's Percy Jones became a Unitarian minister.[44]

There was a steady – purists would urge, an inevitable – weakening of churchmanship. Attendance at church meeting had been an embarrassment in Williams' hey-day: thirty-two in February 1906 (the year of maximum membership – 514), thirty-nine in March, 'very few' in May. The August after Miss Jowett, ever one for bright ideas, urged that church meetings become 'more enthusiastic and helpful' with tea perhaps and a general get-together, ten got together. From November 1909 to January 1911 no church meetings were held. The reason was simple: the management committee functioned well and with Greenfield between pastors there was insufficient churchly business to warrant a church meeting.[45] That was sensible but it was a betrayal of the Congregational ideal however much its pragmatism was in line with the Congregational way of doing things. Pomeroy used his first church meeting to speak on 'the vital importance of the monthly church meeting in the life of the church'. There is evidence that attendance improved but that evidence is suggestively patchy. No church meetings were recorded for 1913, only one in 1914 and again in 1915; none from November 1915 to 1920.[46] Then come accounts of two meetings, each characteristically Greenfield. In 1920 Pomeroy spoke on 'The Spirit of our Church Life':

> ... The Communion Service was not the centrepoint of our Religion. Rather was it a token of our Fellowship with our Master and with one another and the Church Meeting should be the centre point. We met, not round an Altar, but at a round table. There we learnt Love, through Service and self-sacrifice. He spoke of the differences between us and other sects, and sketched the Constitution of our Church ...[47]

The following year Pomeroy turned to 'The Basis of our Fellowship':

> We seek a truth that makes beautiful all the manifold relationships of our lives. In the supreme excellence of Jesus we find our peace and the Star that leads us onward into the more perfect life. We find the Divine Spirit in all truth, our ritual in human service, and the basis of our life in Divine love.

Dorothy Pomeroy followed that with 'Women's place in the Church'. She was 'very inspiring' but the most suggestive part of the meeting focussed again on communion 'and the advisability of endeavouring to get the whole congregation to stay to it. It was thought by some that it tended to keep some of the Congregation away.'[48]

Such precious rebels are easily criticized, but that is to miss the genius which held Greenfield together before its diffusion into other Bradford churches where elderly Greenfielders may still be picked out. The clue to that genius lies in the Educational Institute.

Greenfield's institute, all flowers and festivity, myth and pilgrimage, was shaped by the Pomeroys and Lund though it was neither their creation nor their peculiarity. It was part of a surprisingly wide movement.[49] Nonetheless the master's touch was needed, Greenfield's buds blossoming into voyagers, voyagers disembarking as crusaders, set to experiment and mend until ready at the last for the Pilgrim Path, led by Percy Lund 'the dear Philosopher' and fired by that extraordinary, childless couple, the Pomeroys, who painted their furniture in primary colours and liked to eat on the floor and wrote stories and held extreme views. Dorothy, 'tall and slim and very elegant, always very elegantly dressed', was 'very keen Labour'; so keen that in 1920 she stood for the council as an ILP candidate. And Vivian, 'Pom', was a man whose power lay in words with the young in mind.[50]

He still lives through those words for though their accent has gone and their surviving style is of a different cut from current fashion and the idiom has changed, the originality remains. His prayers are still used, swift insights and sudden shafts of sense.[51] There is the sermon preached at Greenfield on *Sex-Education and Religion.* Its text was New Testament. Its opening was Greek myth: Theseus slaying the Minotaur in the Labyrinth, who then 'by the help of the thread found his way out to the sunlight and the fair face of his Beloved'. Inevitably Browning is quoted, but Elizabeth not Robert:

> When our two souls stand up erect and strong;
> Face to face; silent; drawing nigh and nigher,
> Until the lengthening wings break into fire
> At either curved point.

There is the attack on secrecy: 'Keeping things dark helps to make them dirty'. There is personal reminiscence:

> I can still see myself, as a boy, sitting in the pew of a Wesleyan Church and appearing to be a most devout lover of the Bible, because I was searching the Old Testament for hints upon strange matters, upon which no better information was given me by parents and friends.

And there is affirmation: 'I insist that we have no longer any business to talk about purity unless we have yielded allegiance to two truths: 1 *Sex is not shameful;* 2 *Every human being has a right to knowledge at an appropriate age.*'[52]

How full was Greenfield on that evening, 7 March 1920? Enough stir was made for the management committee to get Lund, Humphries to print it. Or was it that the sermon coincided with the preacher's first attempt to press his resignation on an unready people?[53]

A minister who preaches sex in early spring; a minister's wife who stands for Labour in early autumn; a management committee which countenances whist drives and dances and only falters at a young men's dancing class because of supervisory problems, not principle (they were right: soon the choir 'referred to the difficulty experienced in holding the choir rehearsals owing to a dancing class being held in the room above'):[54] surely quickstepping rebels have become bunny-hugging revolutionaries. The minister's stories must settle that perspective.

Pomeroy published several collections of stories.[55] Two appeared while he was at Greenfield: *The Merry Monopedes* and *Legends of Lumb Lane*, 'fairy stories', thought one admirer, 'which were so ridiculously simple and which, spoken in any other than Mr Pomeroy's musical voice would have been simply ridiculous'.[56] Perhaps. The stories are often arch and almost contrived. Their present charm rests on glimpses of vanished social habits and things once taken for granted: furnishings and slang and casts of mind. But they are better than that. A redeemingly affectionate sharpness drains the sugar. And since any preacher knows that it is children's addresses which stay in the mind, it is to be noticed how adroitly Pomeroy tailors his message to children *and* their parents. The Disney morality world of Mary Poppins is never far away but the method stays in the mind as it touches the heart. As, for example, the beginning and end of 'The Other Side of Things', 'Spoken to the children at the Civic Service, attended by the Lord Mayor and Corporation of Bradford':

> Every Thursday he comes to our house, walks round the weedy, winding garden, through the old yard gates and past the kitchen window. He wears a very, very old battered hat, and he is always most helpful about things I don't know what to do with – things like a retired top-hat or buttoned boots with patent toe-caps. He always says: 'My missus'll fix em up. He has come to us for years. We think a lot of him. I don't know what we should do without him. He is also a friend of the family. He is our dustman ...
>
> ....
>
> Soon everything grew misty, and I knew I had to go. I cried to the Prince: 'Oh, let me see your face before I go.' He leaned over me, and I saw the loveliest face, quite strange, yet known ... it was the face of our dustman. 'How did you get here?' I whispered. 'How did you grow to care? How did you learn to do all this for the Unwanted?' He smiled, and I saw his eyes stray back to the city of things as we see them, beyond the

darkening mist. 'I had good practice with the unwanted things over yonder,' he answered; and he pushed me gently back ... into my yellow chair, into Bradford as it is.[57]

The end is soon told. Greenfield was Pomeroy's only English as it was his only Congregational pastorate. In August 1923 he sailed for New York to lecture on the League of Nations and to take stock.[58] He was quickly invited to become minister of First Parish, Milton, Massachusetts. That was his only American as it was his only Unitarian pastorate. Dorothy Pomeroy died in 1942, Vivian Pomeroy in 1961, Rhondda Williams in 1945.

Greenfield died in 1938. When the Pomeroys left it was Bradford's second largest and Yorkshire's sixteenth largest Congregational church, with 305 members.[59] The spirit, though not the membership, remained unquenched. In January 1928 the church adopted a covenant, a gesture to orthodox Congregationalism couched in purest modernism and impeccably printed by Percy Lund:

> We believe that all the religions of the world have been but efforts of mankind to express the Spirit of God, each faith being suited to its own time and place.
>
> We believe that the religion of Jesus most perfectly expresses the essentials of the faiths of the world.
>
> We believe that the function of the Church is to declare the whole mind of Christ with a view to its application to the entire field of individual and social life ...[60]

Greenfield's last church meeting was one of its best attended. On 13 April 1938 ninety-two members accepted from the Christian Scientists an offer of £2,200. They dissolved the church and dispersed. Moralists will see modernism as the solvent and poetic justice in the purchase. It seems more sensible to see rapid local social change as explanation and Greenfield's decision as a last, realistic rebelliousness.[61]

The final word like the first should rest with Dorothy Pomeroy. She thought it quite likely that they 'would be in prison before very long, for America was the most reactionary country in the world just now – (laughter) – but, in prison or out, they would know that the first seeds were sown at Greenfield (laughter and hear, hear)'.[62]

Notes

1. DTP, 'Paul Lerith – A Modern Chronicle', *Mansfield College Magazine*, Vol. IX, No. 1, March 1914, pp. 6–9.
2. Elaine Kaye, 'Constance Coltman – A Forgotten Pioneer', *Journal United Reformed Church History Society*, Vol. 4, No. 2, May 1988.
3. Greenfield Congregational Church, Bradford, *'A Souvenir' of the Jubilee Celebration Services ... 1902*, Percy Lund, Humphries and Co., 1902; *The Educational Institute of Greenfield Church, Carlisle Road Lumb Lane Bradford* (Bradford n.d.) pp. 1–11; *Church Manual* 1915.
4. Thus W.E. Orchard in January 1942. I am indebted to Miss Elaine Kaye for this information.
5. Cost over £5,000; architects Hope and Jardine. Greenfield Congregational Church, 'New Chapel Committee Minute Book', Bradford City Archives, 53D 80/2/5/a.
6. V.T. Pomeroy, 'The Stone Dog', *The Legends of Lumb Lane*, Percy Lund, Humphries and Co., n.d., p. 37.
7. *'A Souvenir'*, pp. 9–14; 'Church Meetings Minute Book 1853–77', 53D 80/2/2/a.
8. J.A. Jowitt and R.K. S. Taylor (eds), *Nineteenth Century Bradford Elections*, University of Leeds, Bradford Centre Occasional Papers, No. 1, 1979; *Bradford 1890–1914: The Cradle of the Independent Labour Party*, No. 2, 1980; Rosemary Joynes, 'The Bradford Independent Labour Party and Trade Unionism c.1890–1914', typescript, 1982: J. Reynolds, *The Great Paternalist, Titus Salt and the growth of Nineteenth-Century Bradford*, Maurice Temple Smith 1983; D.G. Wright, 'Politics and Opinion in Nineteenth-Century Bradford 1832–1880', Unpublished University of Leeds Ph.D. thesis, 1966.
9. Joynes, op.cit., pp. 16, 17–18, 25–29, esp.p. 27. I owe this reference to Professor Keith Laybourn.
10. *Congregational Year Books*, 1880–7, passim; K.W. Wadsworth, *Yorkshire United Independent College*, Independent Press 1954, pp. 130–1; *'A Souvenir'*, p. 14.
11. J.G. Miall, *Congregationalism in Yorkshire*, John Snow and Co. 1868, pp. 237–8.
12. 28 December 1862, 'Minute Book 1853–77', 53D 80/2/2/a.
13. Henry Beuzeville Byles, 1810–1888; see (F.G. Byles), *William Byles by*

his Youngest Son, private, Weymouth 1932.

14. Hartley, 1836–1870, see J. Sibree, *A Register of Missionaries, Deputations etc. From 1796–1923*, London Missionary Society, 4th edn 1923 p.80; Creak, 1821–1864, see *Congregational Year Book*, 1865, pp.230–2.
15. J.P. Newell, 'A Nestor of Nonconformist Heretics: A.J. Scott (1805–66)', *Journal United Reformed Church History Society*, Vol.3, No.1, May 1983 pp.16–24.
16. Revd John Byles, 1839–1901 (A. Mearns, *London Congregational Directory*, 1889, p.118): he became a Unitarian in 1898; Thomas Gasquoine Creak, 1860–1922, J.A. Venn, *Alumni Cantabrigienses*, part II, Vol.II, p.173; Mark D. Johnson, 'Thomas Gasquoine and the Origins of the Leicester Conference', *JURCHS*, Vol.2, No.10, October 1982,p.345 ff
17. '*A Souvenir*', pp.90–6; T. Rhondda Williams, *How I Found my Faith*, Cassell and Co. 1938, pp.42–3.
18. For Armitage, 1844–1929, see *Congregational Year Book*, 1931 pp.222–3; for Duff, 1845–1934, see ibid., 1935, pp.273–4.
19. I have been indebted to the late Revd H.A. Wilson for access to these diaries.
20. For Rudolph Delius 1846–1903 see W.H. Smith and W.T. Pike, *West Riding of Yorkshire at the Opening of the Twentieth Century: Contemporary Biographies*, Brighton 1902, p.281; I am also indebted to Mr R. Delius and Mrs E. Lovibond.
21. Williams, op. cit, p.138.
22. For Priestley (1859–1932) see M. Stenton and S. Lees (eds), *Who's Who of British Members of Parliament*, Vol.II 1886–1918, The Harvester Press, p.292.
23. Williams, op. cit., p.124.
24. For Claridge b.1856, see *Christian World*, General Election Supplement, 4 January 1906. He contributed 'The Movement for Civic Control in Education' to W. Evans and W. Claridge, *James Hirst Hollowell and The Movement for Civic Control in Education*, Northern Counties Education League 1911, pp.169–311.
25. For Beaumont, 1849–1908, see Pike, op. cit., p.259.
26. Williams, op. cit., pp.128–9.
27. For Lund, 1863–1943, see *Bradford Telegraph and Argus*, 15 and 17 February 1943. I am indebted to Mr and Mrs D. Steele for this and other information.
28. Williams, op. cit., p.41 and passim.
29. I am indebted to Mr N. Jenner and Mr N. Webb for personal recollections of Williams.
30. Williams, op. cit., p.48.

31. Ibid., pp.76, 102.
32. 31 January 1906, 'Church Meetings Minute Book 1903–1938', 53D 80/2/2C.
33. *Congregational Year Book*, 1907, pp.317–328; Williams, op. cit., 127, 105, 130, 110.
34. Ibid., p.149.
35. Ibid., p.76
36. *Church Manual*, 1915, p.2.
37. Williams, op. cit., p.162
38. 'Our Special Commissioner', *The Free Churches of Bradford. Written for the Christian Globe*, c.1912: in Bradford Central Library. I owe this reference to Revd Dr Leonard Smith; I am also much indebted for information to Mrs G. Pomeroy.
39. 'Management Committee Minute Book, 1901–1908', passim, esp. 8 July 1907, 53D 80/2/4a.
40. 'Council Minute Book 1916–1923'; passim, 53D 80/2/4d
41. 'Church Meetings Minute Book 1903–1938', 2 May, 3 October 1912, 53D 80/2/2C.
42. Revd Dr J. Marsh to author, 6 February 1984.
43. 'Church Meetings Minute Book 1903–1938', March 1911.
44. Jones (b.1871), had been an African missionary, Sibree op. cit., p.134.
45. 'Church Meetings Minute Book 1903–1938'.
46. Ibid. Pomeroy's first church meeting was 1 November 1911.
47. Ibid., 29 April 1920. 70 were present.
48. Ibid., 23 March 1921. 50–60 were present.
49. See C. Binfield, 'Freedom through Discipline: The Concept of Little Church', *Monks, Hermits and the Ascetic Tradition*, Studies in Church History, Vol.22 (ed. W.J. Sheils), Blackwell 1985, pp.405–419.
50. I am indebted to Mr and Mrs D. Steele, the late Mrs M. Jenkinson, Miss E.M. Wilmott of Bradford Central Library for this information.
51. 'Classics of Unitarian Prayer', thus T.D. Wintle, *Unitarian Prayers. The Unitarian Universalist Christian*, Spring/Summer 1984, Vol.39, Nos.1–2 p.3, esp. pp.60, 66, 67.
52. V.T. Pomeroy, *Sex-Education and Religion*, Percy Lund, Humphries and Co. 1920.
53. 'Council Minute Book 1916–1923', 53D 80/2/4d, 8 March 1920.
54. Ibid., 3 February, 8 December 1919.
55. *The Merry Monopedes and Other Stories for Little Children*, James Clarke c.1917; *The Legends of Lumb Lane*, Percy Lund, Humphries and Co. Ltd., n.d; *The Enchanted Children. Twenty Five-Minute Tales*, Lindsey Press 1938. *Another Story, Please!*, Boston, Mass. 1947.
56. Cutting dated 27 June 1923 in 53D 80/2/4d.
57. *Legends of Lumb Lane*, pp.53, 56.

58. Cutting dated 27 June 1923, art. cit.
59. *Congregational Year Book* 1924, pp. 247–258.
60. Inserted in 'Church Meetings Minute Book 1903–1938'.
61. Ibid, 13 April 1938; see also M.H. and A.D.F., *Little Lane and Greenfield*, Bradford 1948, esp. pp. 30–1.
62. Cutting dated 27 June 1923. Pomeroy's papers, covering his Bradford and Milton ministries, are now in the Andover-Harvard Theological Library, Harvard Divinity School; I am indebted to Dr A. Seaburg, Curator of MSS, for information about this deposit.

11

Against the Simple Gospel: John Day Thompson and the New Evangelism in Primitive Methodism

STUART MEWS

The Primitive Methodism into which John Kent was born in 1923 had come a long way from the fervent evangelistic sect of a hundred years before.'[1] In the 1920s, the Prims were licking their wounds as they tried to overcome the spiritual demoralization of the First World War which only accelerated the decline in membership which they would have experienced anyway through the movement of population from country to town, the secularization of the Trade Unions, the increased sophistication which despised anything which proclaimed itself 'primitive', and the death in 1925 of their astonishingly generous financial benefactor, Sir William P. Hartley. Primitive Methodists did attempt to come to terms with the new post-war world, but in ways which sometimes alienated their only available potential allies if they were not to wander alone in the inter-war desert. One instance of the attempt to equip themselves for the new age was the revision of their doctrinal statement by the conference of 1921. This made the momentous decision to remove all reference to the name of John Wesley. Coming only one year after the setting up of a committee with the Wesleyans and United Methodists to explore the possibilities of union, this might have seemed a deliberately provocative act.[2] For that committee had specifically *included* Wesley's name in its doctrinal statement. However the PM conference decision of 1921 was not so much a move in the protracted chess game which was to lead to Methodist union in 1932, so much as the culmination of thinking which went back to the 1890s, back to the Connexion's one case of heresy, back to the courageous ministry of John Day Thompson. For in the career of Thompson and reactions to him, can be found clear signs of the social, political, and cultural tensions which were particularly acute in Primitive Methodism in the last quarter of the nineteenth century.

Primitive Methodism was unusual in being an evangelical religious movement in which power was dispersed amongst its members instead of being concentrated in a spiritual élite. From a relatively early stage in its history, it was receptive to the popular radicalism of those deprived groups of country labourers, miners and fishermen from which its congregations were drawn. There was also a degree of intellectual openness. Sharing the anguish of the hungry, ill-clothed and poor did not mean unreflective credulity. The Primitive Methodists of Banbury might accept the teaching of an Anglican clergyman in 1851 that the cry of a child during its baptism was a sign of the devil departing, but their new young minister, George Warner, an untrained Warwickshire farmer's son, robustly warned them against such nonsense.[3] Though Warner was dismissive of Tractarian views of baptismal regeneration he did, however, believe profoundly in the in-filling of the spirit. This doctrine of entire sanctification seemed to many Methodists to be a logical extension of Wesley's teaching about perfection. It was being promoted by revivalists from America like James Caughey on his evangelistic tours of England in the 1840s.[4] Among the Primitives, one of Caughey's earliest disciples was Parkinson Milson, who had heard him at Hull in 1845, and obtained the blessing in the following year: 'I seemed as if electrified from the crown of my head to the soles of my feet! ... I found myself repeating .... "This is heaven! This is heaven!"'[5]

George Warner had no doubt that entire sanctification was 'distinctly a second blessing instantaneously received by faith'.[6] He moved in that wider evangelical subculture which crossed denominational boundaries and was to surface at holiness conventions in Oxford, Mildmay, and later, Keswick. In those circles he came into contact with American teachers like Asa Mahan, chief exponent of Oberlin 'perfectionism', with whom he shared the platform at conventions in 1874 at Sutton, Guildford, and

South Hackney. In the same year, he also clashed with W.E. Boardman, the American advocate of the 'Higher Life', with whom he disagreed about the control of dreams.[7] 1874 was also the year in which he was pulled out of circuit ministry to become, despite opposition, the Connexion's first travelling evangelist and holiness teacher. An elderly layman, Theodore Jones, had become convinced that the failure of the denomination to grow – decreases were reported in 1871 and 1873 – was due to a decline in spiritual fervour, and with others offered £100 if a suitable man could be found to tour the country leading evangelistic and holiness meetings.[8]

Warner's appointment was a significant moment in the consolidation of Primitive Methodism. It marked what W.R. Ward has called 'the watershed between revival and revivalism'.[9] In the early years of enthusiastic growth, every minister was expected to be able to reap a harvest of souls, but in the 1870s, the conditions which nurtured spontaneous revival had largely gone. 'We don't hear much of extensive revivals', complained the denomination's magazine in 1877.[10] They could still sometimes flare up, but were now usually restricted to off-the-beaten track places like the traditional fishing community, which in 1878 lived ghetto-like in the fashionable spa town of Scarborough. Parkinson Milson had moved to the town in the previous year and set about raising the expectations of the circuit. In January 1878 he held special services where 'entire sanctification' was 'preached with earnestness'. Overcome by emotion, a local preacher fell to the floor, 'under the Divine influence', suggested Milson. 'Great concern was felt for the brother's state, but I regarded it as a "sign" of a special work'. With expectations so dramatically aroused, only the catalyst was now needed to ignite the fires of revival. Within weeks, a young fisherman died tragically after being crushed between his ship and the pier. His teenage friends were powerfully affected by the funeral, and a revival in which two hundred were converted soon got underway.[11]

Young, unskilled fishermen belonged, however, to the Connexion's past, not its future. Moreover there were signs that something of a polarization was occuring between those who saw the future of the denomination in increased piety and those who embraced political activism. Primitive Methodists provided much of the leadership for the 'revolt of the field' and in the political awakening of the Durham and Derbyshire miners.[12] The modest rise in their social status and the extension of the franchise, particularly in the 1885 Reform Act, opened new avenues for political involvement, a development which disturbed some older and better-off sympathizers. Mr Jones might have provided money because he wanted to recall Primitive Methodism to its spiritual roots but also, perhaps, to delay the political awakening. Such hopes had little chance of success. In 1880 even the other-worldly Parkinson Milson, still in Scarborough, addressed a missionary meeting 'with a yellow favour in my coat'. He had never before made such a public demonstration of his commitment. 'At first I felt as if I must take it off, but I considered that our Connexion owes many of its privileges to Liberalism, and also how Toryism, tyranny and beer, work together'.[13] In 1884 John Day Thompson, writing in the denominational magazine on 'Modern Socialism and Christianity', could argue that 'the social question is indisputably the great question of the times'. He held that Christians 'can never consistently hold themselves aloof from movements of social reform. They *must* have something to say upon them.'[14] In 1886 Mr Jones withdrew all financial support in a display of disgust at the denominational newspaper's enthusiasm for Gladstone's Irish home rule policy.[15]

In its robust partisanship, the paper was only reflecting the nearly unanimous views of the Connexional leadership. The day after the close of the annual conference at Derby in 1886, a public meeting in support of Gladstone's Irish policy was held in the town attended by that year's President, John Atkinson, and most of the leading officials. Earlier in the week, a deputation from the Connexion had only been prevented by the size of the crowd from presenting an address to the GOM when his train passed through Derby station.[16]

George Warner had begun his ministry in remote country circuits at the tail-end of the heroic phase of Primitive Methodism, when he had often preached in the open air. In the 1870s and 1880s, he was more likely to be found in urban chapels. His appeal now, however, was directed towards securing more costly levels of personal renunciation, commitment and behaviour, or what could be seen as 'respectability'. At Hull, an elderly, long-serving local preacher, who had long been a slave to his pipe, was 'lifted into the higher life', and gave up tobacco. 'He never felt the least desire for it after.'[17] At a time when the conversion of outsiders was becoming a rare phenomenon, leading the next generation to the penitent form and inducing the second blessing in longer-standing members gave the impression of progress, even though the total number of members was only marginally increasing, and allowing for the increases in the population, actually falling as a percentage. At Newbury in 1878, the same year as the Scarborough revival, Warner was booked to preach in a newly-built chapel ('they do not appear to have had much consecration in it') and amongst the converts 'were several intelligent youths, who had passed their examinations for the civil service'.[18] Preaching to budding civil servants was a far cry from the denomination's original clientele, and some of the more far-sighted regional leaders were eager to respond to the new situation and equip their ministry better for more critical congregations.

It was a twenty-year struggle to persuade the Connexion that it would benefit from training its ministers. For many years, the devoted but humourless James Macpherson gave tuition to probationers in the Manchester district in basic skills with some theology. When the decision was taken to open a Theological Institute in Manchester in 1876, he was appointed first Principal, perhaps to reassure traditionalists. He was also, with James Travis, appointed joint secretary of the committee responsible for raising money for the project. A gifted linguist with considerable learning but little imagination, he had a simple trust in divine providence. In 1878, while the revival was in full swing in Scarborough, a woman left £50 in gold coins with Parkinson Milson for the college fund. To Macpherson, this was a clear sign of divine intervention:

> Mark the Providence. On Monday a gentleman in London promised me £100, providing I got £400 in hundreds or fifties;

and before the challenge was made known, here comes your cheque for £50.[19]

Ministers now went to college for twelve months, but the standard of teaching was considered by A. S. Peake, a minister's son who had been elected to a fellowship at Merton College, Oxford, to be in 1891 'disgraceful': 'Our people have failed to keep pace with the advance of the nation in education and general culture'.[20] An outstanding biblical scholar, Peake has been credited with saving the Free churches in Britain from anything like America's destructive fundamentalist controversy. His first publication on 'The Synoptic Problem' was based on a talk given to ministers and appeared in the *Primitive Methodist Quarterly Review* in 1891, but the first article in the *Review* sympathetic to the new critical approach to the Bible had come three years before, in 1888 from the pen of John Day Thompson.[21]

Thompson belonged to the new generation. Articled in his teens to a firm of analytical chemists, his frame of mind was always searching and critical. His grandfather, John Day, had been a leading minister (he was briefly Book Steward); his father, Alexander Thompson, was a prominent lay official in South Shields, where he had moved in 1841. For over forty years, the father was employed at the Jarrow chemical works, beginning as a labourer and ending as a manager. As well as his work for chapel and circuit, an important indicator of his outlook was his membership of the local committee for university extension classes.[22]

It was as a Prim of the third generation, with a scientific training, that John Day Thompson attempted to lead his denomination to face the challenge of the day. The Prims had reached South Shields in 1821. Their first chapel was a converted sail-loft, opened by William Clowes, who recorded, 'The congregation seemed to be all on the move.'[23] But ten years later, after rapid growth, membership plummeted 'owing to the disturbances and movings in the collieries'.[24] Described as 'one of the most aggressive of the northern circuits',[25] it gradually recovered under the leadership of some of the Connexion's outstanding ministers, who included six Presidents. In 1878 Thompson, having entered the ministry in 1868, returned to his hometown as circuit minister. In October, George Warner arrived to conduct a mission for a week. At first, he encountered some hostility: 'the ministers and people generally had little faith in the doctrine of holiness, as taught by Wesley and others.' Gradually his preaching won them round, and as a result of the services over a hundred claimed salvation. According to Warner himself, 'the best phase of the work done was the sanctifying power in the church – the way the subject of heart-purity took hold of leaders and preachers'. Two of the three circuit ministers were evidently won round to the new doctrine.[26] But one remained in doubt, and though no names are given, the likelihood is that the sceptic about Wesley and his teaching was John Day Thompson. Certainly it was the case that in January 1878, he was preaching on the parable of the talents and stressing the necessity for active use in this world of God-given gifts.[27] It must have been disturbing when three years later, his own father, Alexander, now sixty, at special services, 'received an extraordinary baptism of sanctifying power'.[28]

Six years after Thompson left South Shields, the circuit received its most outstanding minister, Arthur T. Guttery, who was later to be a colleague at Holborn Hall, the Connexional headquarters. If in George Warner South Shields encountered pietism, in Guttery it found the social gospel. Brought up in Canada where his father was in the 1870s the leading Primitive Methodist minister in Toronto, Guttery flung himself into Liberal Party propaganda. 'Politics were part of his religion.'[29] And he put his considerable oratorical gifts at the service of his party, so much so that in 1885 his father reminded him that his chief work was to preach the gospel. In January, he had become a recognized lecturer for the Liberal Party and toured the north speaking from political platforms. For about a month, he was criticized in the local press, but he claimed that his own people supported him. When his father became anxious about the focus of his energies, he protested that political activity did not detract from spiritual growth: 'We are having conversions and, at the end of the year, shall have I believe, a respectable increase.' 'This quiet growth is my preference,' he wrote, somewhat defensively, expressing a view which would have astounded the early pioneers. 'Churches as well as plants that grow very fast usually die as quickly.'[30]

In 1880, three American Methodist ministers, J.S. Inskip, W. McDonald and J.A. Wood, had been invited by Primitive Methodists to hold holiness meetings in Hull and Grimsby. George Warner had been holding a mission at Beverley, which was in the Hull I circuit, and picked up the vibrations. He recorded that one of the circuit ministers, Benjamin Fell, 'got wondrously blessed at their services, and now wonders how he dared to preach at all before, seeing, as he now does, how greatly he needed the inward annointing so necessary as an equipment for the work of the ministry.'[31] Twenty-five years later, Fell could still look back back to 1880 'as a time of divine visitation'.[32] Yet these ideas cannot have been new to him. He had previously been Parkinson Milson's colleague in Scarborough and shared with him in gathering in the fruits of the revival. Possibly one difference between the English and American versions of holiness preaching may have been a difference of tone. Milson was so much more solemn and serious, as he himself hinted: 'Have heard the Americans ... Very good and sweet. Said many things I have been saying for years ... These men can shout and pray and smile and lift up hands.' They were also less constrained by convention. 'They believe in public seeking of it, not going into private rooms, and in public confession of it.'[33]

A significant feature of the Hull meetings had been the number of Primitive Methodist ministers who had made 'the act of full surrender'. It was not surprising that so many were dissatisfied with their spiritual condition. Many of them were just as worried about their future material prospects. Before 1874 the Connexion had no superannuation scheme, 'hence many preachers were anxious'.[34] Even when the Superannuated Ministers, Widows and Orphans Fund was established, its allowances soon had to be reduced. 'This is not to the credit of our church,' commented the *Magazine* in 1877.[35] In the same year, it was announced that the Missionary Fund for both home and overseas missions 'is in an embarrassed condition'.[36] Debts on the current account were allowed to accumulate until in March 1880 they had reached over £5,000. 'There was no panic but there was uneasiness.'[37] Firm action retrieved the situation, but at the cost of withdrawing missionaries, rejecting promising openings, and reducing grants to needy circuits.[38] Meanwhile agricultural depression and a slump in trade in the early 1880s following a period of extensive chapel building placed many chapel trusts in difficulties and caused them to be 'almost paralysed for aggressive work'.[39] Adding to these pressing worries was the bouyant enthusiasm of the Salvation Army, as it challenged the Prims their own ground in the late 1870s and early 1880s.[40] Against on a background of financial uncertainty and some spiritual demoralization, it was not surprising that many ministers eagerly sought a second blessing as promised by the American visitors.

Moreover if Pentecostal life and power could be reintroduced into the societies, both spiritual and financial deficiencies could be remedied together. At the 1881 Primitive Methodist conference, many of those who had been led by the Americans to spiritual renewal met together to consider setting up their own group, but concerned that hostility might be aroused by what could be seen as forming 'a separate order', they delayed until 1889.[41]

Meanwhile a group of more traditionalist ministers, who included Parkinson Milson and James Macpherson, met in Manchester in 1883 to plan a new paper, *The Primitive Methodist World*.[42]

In 1892 John Day Thompson was sent by the Conference to Adelaide in South Australia as successor to the fervent poet-prophet Hugh Gilmour.[43] The church in Wellington Square was then at the height of its influence in what Douglas Pike has called 'the paradise of dissent'.[44] Like Thompson, Gilmour had spent most of his ministry in County Durham, and in the 1880s had, like Guttery, joyfully baptized the political struggle. 'Not in isolation and meditation do we serve God', he declared in 1884, in defiance of Primitive pietists, 'but in the service of men.'[45] In Preston, Lancashire, he had been President of the Liberal Association and denounced the high rents charged working families. In Adelaide, he supported the dockers in their strike in 1890 and called for the state ownership of the shipping industry. Convinced by Henry George, he became President of the Adelaide branch of the Single Tax League. Gilmour's gospel was one of divine immanence indwelling in all human beings and finding practical expression in a Christian welfare society. Formal belief did not have a high priority. 'Don't say you believe what you do not believe. Believe what you can, if ever so little.'[46]

As Gilmour's successor, Thompson soon found spheres in which he could exercise influence. He enthusiastically supported the federation movement, and wrote and spoke for it. He became active in the campaign which won votes for women in South Australia in 1894. Winning the trust of the Labour movement, he was presented with an illuminated scroll, signed amongst others by Catherine Helen Spence, 'Australia's first feminist', who was one of his regular Sunday night congregation.[47] At first, he had found his new surroundings uncongenial. 'I wish I were back among you all again,' he wrote to A.S. Peake. 'We are doing excellently well, but oh! it is not England. I feel shut off from literary circles altogether. I have none like-minded.'[48] He was writing primarily to arrange for the correction of proofs of an article for the *Review* on Deuteronomy 'advocating the new view'. He hoped later to write on Job and Daniel: 'In a few years I trust we shall have sane views of the OT prevalent among us'. In Adelaide, despite his initial misgivings, he found the atmosphere congenial to the growth of liberal thought, and in his large Bible class, he expounded the critical approach to the Bible. Though attacked in Adelaide by the Wesleyans for his acceptance of Darwin's theory of evolution,[49] Thompson's ministry turned his church into 'the Mecca of the casual churchgoer'. A newspaper profile in 1894 referred to his 'subtle magnetism' and his world-affirming attitudes. 'He enjoys a laugh does Day Thompson'; he could not keep still, but was 'as mercurial as a parched pea on a hotplate'.[50]

It was when Thompson began to apply the historical method, not only to the Old Testament, but to the New as well, that trouble was aroused. The flashpoint was the delivery and publication of an address on 'The Simple Gospel' in 1894 in which he attacked the view that it was the duty of ministers to proclaim 'the simple Gospel' and leave on one side critical questions and what came to be called 'the social Gospel'.[51] Opinion within Primitive

Methodism was by 1894 beginning to move his way. A cultural revolution was taking place in the Theological Institute after the appointment in 1893 of John Watson and Arthur S. Peake. Peake was gently leading his students through a re-assessment of the scriptures. Dr John Watson, who had been Thompson's predecessor but one in Adelaide was, according to Peake, 'very open to new ideas'.[52] In 1892 he had differentiated between' the new evangelism', which was appearing in the form of 'social Christianity' and the individualism which had characterized the old. 'The church may from time to time receive new light from the Holy Spirit on the import of Christ's saving purpose,' he suggested. 'The new evangelism confronts a condition of things, and is called to solve practical problems ... Our paralysis, as an evangelistic body, is due, in our opinion to the fact that we do not as yet fully understand, and are unable to adapt ourselves to, these new conditions.'[53]

Thompson's address in Adelaide outraged the old guard, whose rallying point was the *Primitive Methodist World*. Unfortunately, neither Thompson's address nor the numbers of the *Primitive Methodist World* in which his critics launched their attack have survived. However, it is possible from other Primitive Methodist sources to establish in general terms the course of events. It seems that Thompson's address on 'The Simple Gospel' was printed, and that a copy fell into the hands of James Macpherson, the elderly ex-principal of the Theological Institute. Years later, Thompson described his old adversary as 'hard as nails': 'he had a certain dourness ... and a certain uncompromisingness'.[54] In the *Primitive Methodist World* Macpherson attacked Thompson for deviating from Methodist doctrine. A protracted and vicious controversy then opened in the correspondence columns. Not satisfied with Thompson's response, Macpherson and his successor as principal, Joseph Wood, together with others, tried to lodge a formal charge of heretical teaching, and requested the Conference to deliver the verdict. The Edinburgh Conference refused to consider Macpherson's memorial because 'it is irregular and unconstitutional'.[55] His only remedy was to begin again, start from the bottom, and try to convince the North Adelaide circuit to condemn its minister, no easy task for a

Scotsman living thousands of miles away. Not surprisingly, the circuit refused. Macpherson tried again at the South Australia district meeting, which 'virtually acquitted Thompson' though conceding that he had 'exposed himself to be misunderstood and misjudged'.[56] Now the Conference could be invoked as the final court of appeal. So in 1896 at Burnley, 'for the first time in our history', the Primitive Methodist Conference 'had a serious heresy case before it'.[57] The Committee of Complaints and Appeals proposed the appointment of a sub-committee to make recommendations, but this was challenged from the floor of the Conference. W. Jones Davies, who sympathized with Thompson, and as principal of the Theological Institute from 1908 was to scorn those who demanded of their minister, 'Why does he not give us the simple gospel?'[58] moved an amendment urging the need to settle the matter there and then. Moreover, the Conference composed as it was of two-thirds laymen was in his opinion better suited to deal with the matter than a committee of theological experts. Another minister, George Fawcett, Governor of Elmfield school, the Connexion's boarding school for boys, seconded, but the secretary of the General Committee, William Goodman, who was responsible for ensuring that the Conference ran smoothly, felt that there really was insufficient time; in any case, Macpherson's allegations had yet to be published. It was a layman, William Beckwith, a magistrate from Leeds, who lifted the discussion to a higher plane. He felt that they should address the issue forthwith, and urged them to endorse the decisions of the lower courts. They should remember the transitional nature of theological thought: 'not one of them stood just where he stood twenty years ago (cheers and cries of "Yes")'. They should remember the spirit and genius of their constitution which was the spirit of liberty and elasticity. He reminded them that in their eighty-six years' existence, they had not had a single controversy over doctrine. Surely they should accept Thompson's assurance that he believed Methodist doctrine?

The evident support for these views stung Macpherson into the sour observation that Mr Beckwith did not know anything at all about the issues at stake. The Connexional historian, Bickerstaffe Kendall, now weighed in with a plea that they should look to the spirit rather than the letter of their laws. 'To a man who was manifestly loyal to Christ, he would give some little latitude.' Moreover, if these ashes were raked over, were they so sure that no one would be burned? In his view, controversies grew when they were resuscitated, and, with a side-swipe at the Church of England, he warned that with sacerdotalism on the increase, they could not afford a divisive wrangle. Dr John Watson, Principal of the Theological Institute, rose to support Thompson, his successor but one in Adelaide, and in doing so demonstrated that they now had a man of enlightened views in the Principal's chair. Indeed it may have been partly their sense of outrage at the direction in which the college was being taken that lay behind the chagrin of its first two Principals. After Watson's speech 'a scene of confusion' ensued. Perhaps sensing that opinion was moving against them, the traditionalists gave vent to a series of outbursts that were 'hectoring, protesting and it must be said threatening'.[59] John Smith was one of their pioneer missionaries in Southern Africa where he had built up the mission at Aliwal North. There he had been relieved by John Watson, whom he in turn succeeded when he returned to Aliwal for a second stint. Smith was now the Connexion's missionary secretary and maintained the same uncomplicated beliefs which had sustained him in Africa, and which he was to display in his fierce opposition to Hugh Price Hughes' support for Chamberlain's war against the Boers.[60] With some desperation, he dangled before the delegates the spectre of dwindling missionary resources. Australia was associated in many minds with missionary work and Smith warned that they were losing collectors and subscribers because members were being asked to support teaching with which they could not agree. This allegation provoked cries of 'Evidence?' to which Smith responded that 'that was not the place for evidence. (A voice, "Then let's not have the statement", and cheers). He claimed that he was within his rights ("No, no," and uproar)'.[61] Incensed by the antagonism which greeted his unsubstantiated assertions, Smith's speech descended from indignation to bathos. To the hilarity of delegates, he announced that there had been seven hundred different theories of the higher criticism during the last fifty years, and six hundred of them had already disappeared. His former colleague, John Watson, now intervened and saved him from further ridicule by curtly reminding him that it was not higher criticism which was on trial. The amendment when eventually put was lost by two votes.

With considerable presence of mind, Beckwith then moved a second amendment, that no further action be taken. He reminded them of the length of time which had elapsed, the affirmation by Thompson of his loyalty to Methodist doctrine, and the dismissal of charges by his circuit and district meetings. Statements from Australia were now read. A delegate from Harrogate testified that when Thompson had been their minister he had inspired many to more active service. John Watson sketched in something of the background and stated that Thompson's position was only intelligible to those who knew the people and the situation he was addressing. Thompson, he assured them, had the confidence of his congregation: 'they loved him and felt that he was instructing them as few men had done in the word of God'. If he had a fault, it was his over-eagerness to reconcile Methodist doctrine with science and modern thought. This portrayal of Thompson as a figure deserving their sympathy was too much for James Macpherson, who tetchily tried to retrieve the situation in a speech which, the Connexional newspaper reported, 'gave rise to much confusion, not to say heat', and produced the unedifying sight of an indignant riposte from 'a very youthful delegate'. In defiant mood, Macpherson declared that he would not change his view 'even if the whole conference voted against him'. He still insisted that there were statements in Thompson's address which were 'flat contradictions of Methodist doctrine' and which should be retracted. But the majority were in no mood for a heresy hunt, and Beckwith's amendment was carried by an overwhelming majority.

In 1898 Thompson was forced by his wife's poor health to return to England. He was appointed to the Liverpool Vth circuit, Aintree, which brought under his pastoral care the most influential layman in the Connexion, the jam manufacturer William P. Hartley. In 1903 the confidence of his colleagues was demonstrated when Thompson was elected as Secretary of that year's Conference. After his next circuit, Blackpool, the poacher turned gamekeeper when he was elected in 1909 to the most influential position in his church, that of Secretary of the General Committee. In 1915, he was elected President without any opposition. As Secretary, he proved himself to be, in A. S. Peake's estimation, 'a brilliant administrator' with 'a tactful but masterful handling of difficult situations'.[62] As the leading national official, it fell to him to oversee the concluding year of the Primitive Methodist centenary celebrations, and then to sum up their significance. This he did in a little book, *The Church That Found Herself*. The title was borrowed from a story by Rudyard Kipling about a ship which made her maiden voyage across the Atlantic. The Primitive Methodist Church had now found itself, Thompson concluded. 'But what is the self that we are, and that we have found? ... It does not reside in our christening, our mere name ... Our differentia can no more be found, as some have thought it could, in our earlier lack of culture and a certain conceit of ignorance which, truth to say, was not always out of evidence in days gone by ... We are of the genus of Evangelicalism, we are of the species of Methodism, but our differentia is our spirit of flexibility.'[63] It was to free that flexibility from archaic restraints that Thompson now used his by now considerable influence to press for a revision of the doctrinal formularies of his church. 'We have made one great sweep in cutting out the reference to John Wesley's sermons and Notes on the New Testament,' he reported in 1916. He admitted that some would have preferred to leave well alone, but among the younger ministers there was intense desire for a revised statement 'which did no violence to the modern intellect'. He went on to claim that an advantage of the revision 'will make it very much less easy to raise theological storms about a man's teaching than it was a generation ago'. There was, he maintained, 'much less desire for heresy-hunting now'.[64] That was partly due to an increase in tolerance, but was also a result of a decline in doctrinal preaching. There had been a shift of emphasis to the human side of things, the moral, social, and humanitarian implications and obligations. Thompson was now President of the Primitive Methodist Church. He was also superintendent of the Cambridge circuit, where his assistant, Herbert G. Marsh, remembers that he still 'believed in shock tactics in proclaiming the truth'.[65] As President, with the First World War creating new challenges, Thompson was anxious to prevent liberal theology from being discredited by its association with German thought.[66]

The revision of the doctrinal clause in the Primitive Methodist Deed Poll took longer than Thompson expected. The proposals which went to the Conference in 1916 evoked a counter-statement from A.S. Peake, and a decision was delayed by the understanding that no controversial measures should be passed by a shortened wartime Conference. As editor of the *Holborn Review*, Thompson initiated a symposium on Creed revision. In it Lewis Humphries, a Tutor at Hartley College, as the theological institution in Manchester was now called, made short work of the existing doctrinal statement: 'The living Christ is more to us than the dead Wesley.'[67] Eventually agreement was reached in 1921, but sadly Thompson did not live to see this culmination of his life's endeavours. He died in 1919.

Looking back on Thompson's career and the controversies he provoked, A.S. Peake speculated on his responsibility for them, and the light they threw on his personality. 'There was in him a combative strain, which was a valuable asset, but occasionally made his utterances intentionally provocative.' Peake also detected 'a rather impish delight in shocking people'. There was, he claimed, 'an occasional flippancy of expression in dealing with sacred things which jarred on the sensitive'.[68] Herbert Marsh recalled that having grown up in Cambridge, and then returning as minister, at Thompson's 'special invitation', he was in a good position to assess his work. 'He was a man much loved by the people for his character and pastoral work, but although it was tolerated, his message was not well received.' Marsh recalled an old saint telling him, 'I like Mr Thompson, but I wish he would not say the things he says in his preaching.' Further enquiry revealed that the offending sermon had been on the book of Daniel. 'His introduction was something like this: The book of Daniel, it is a fairy story like Jack the Giant Killer!'[69] To Bickerstaffe Kendall. He was 'the bold thinker, the sworn foe of traditionalism, possessed to the finger-tips with the scientific spirit, and yet with all this, as in the case of Dr R.F. Horton – whom in many respects he so closely resembles – the spiritual mystic side of his nature will not be repressed but successfully asserts its rights'.[70] 'He was always a child of the light,' concluded Peake. He did valuable work as a pioneer helping to keep his church in touch with new currents of thought, and troubling the waters which left to themselves were only too apt to become stagnant.'[71]

Notes

1. For a helpful outline of the development of Primitive Methodism from revivalist sect to denomination, see John Munsey Turner, *Conflict and Reconciliation. Studies in Methodism and Ecumenicalism in England 1740–1982*, Epworth Press 1966, pp. 20–43.
2. On the doctrinal difficulties of Methodist union, see John Kent, *The Age of Disunity*, Epworth Press 1966, pp. 20–43.
3. J. Stephenson, *The Man of Faith and Fire, or, the Life and Work of the Rev. G. Warner*, Robert Bryant 1902, p. 19.
4. John Kent, *Holding the Fort: Studies in Victorian Revivalism*, Epworth Press 1973, p. 295; Richard Carwardine, *Trans-Atlantic Revivalism: Popular Evangelicalism in Britain and America, 1790–1865*, Greenwood 1978, pp. 102f.
5. George Shaw, *Life of Rev. Parkinson Milson (Primitive Methodist Minister)*, Simpkin, Marshall, Hamilton, Kent & Co. 1893, p. 32.
6. Shaw, op. cit., p. 14.
7. Stephenson, op. cit., p. 143, D.W. Bebbington, *Evangelicalism in Modern Britain. A History from the 1730s, to the 1980s*, Unwin Hyman 1989, p. 164f.
8. Stephenson, op. cit., p. 142, *The Primitive Methodist*, 26 February 1874.
9. W.R. Ward, *Religion and English Society 1790–1850*, Batsford 1972, p. 287.
10. *Primitive Methodist Magazine* 1877 p. 569.
11. Shaw, op. cit., pp. 302–8.
12. Nigel Scotland, *Methodism and the Revolt of the Field: A Study of the Methodist Contribution to Agricultural Trades Unions in East Anglia 1872–96*, Allen Sutton 1981; Pamela Horn, 'Methodism and Agricultural Trade Unionism in Oxfordshire: The 1870s', *Proceedings of the Wesley Historical Society*, XXXVII, pp. 69–71; Robert Moore, *Pitmen, Preachers & Politics: The Effects of Methodism in a Durham Mining Community*, CUP 1974.
13. Shaw, op. cit. p. 321.

14. *Primitive Methodist Quarterly Review* 1884, pp. 625, 629.
15. Stephenson, op. cit., p. 249.
16. *The Primitive Methodist*, 24 June 1886.
17. Stephenson, op. cit., pp. 161f.
18. Ibid., p. 176.
19. James Macpherson – Parkinson Milson, 5 December 1878; Shaw, op. cit., p. 315.
20. Arthur S. Peake – Samuel Peake, 24 June 1891; John T. Wilkinson, *Arthur Samuel Peake, A Biography*, Epworth Press 1971, p. 48.
21. John Day Thompson, 'Scripture Interpretation: Old and New Methods', *Primitive Methodist Quarterly Review* 1888, pp. 18–35.
22. *Primitive Methodist Magazine* 1886, pp. 689–692.
23. H. Bickerstaffe Kendall, *History of the Primitive Methodist Church* vol. II, Edwin Dalton 1909, p. 166.
24. *Primitive Methodist Magazine* 1833, pp. 376–7; Julia Stewart Werner, *The Primitive Methodist Connexion: Its Background and Early History*, University of Wisconsin Press 1984, p. 171.
25. J. G. Bowran, *The Life of Arthur Thomas Guttery, D. D.*, London n.d., p. 57.
26. Stephenson, op. cit., p. 178.
27. Ralph Hayson, Notebook entry 13 January 1878; Robert Moore, op. cit., p. 98.
28. *Primitive Methodist Quarterly Magazine* 1886, p. 692.
29. Bowran, op. cit., p. 100.
30. Ibid., p. 41f.
31. Stephenson, op. cit., p. 195.
32. *Aldersgats Primitive Methodist Magazine* 1905, p. 507f.
33. Shaw, op. cit., p. 349.
34. *Seventy-Five Years. The Life and Work of James Travis as seen by himself and judged by others* ed. John Day Thompson, W. A. Hammond 1914, p. 66.
35. *Primitive Methodist Magazine* 1877, p. 472.
36. Ibid., p. 699.
37. Thompson, op. cit., p. 77.
38. Ibid., p. 80.
39. Ibid., p. 82.
40. Stuart Mews, 'The General and the Bishops: Alternative Responses to Dechristianisation', *Later Victorian Britain 1867–1900* eds T. R. Gourvish and Alan O'Day, Macmillan 1988, p. 213.
41. Matthew P. Davison, 'The Holiness Association', *Primitive Methodist Quarterly Review* 1898, p. 295.
42. Shaw, op cit., pp. 345f.
43. Thompson assessed his predecessor in 'Hugh Gilmour', *Primitive*

Methodist Quarterly Review 1892, pp.385–401. See also Arnold D. Hunt, *A Tall Cedar in our Lebanon: Hugh Gilmour and Primitive Methodism*, Lutheran Publishing House, Adelaide 1985.

44. John Day Thompson, 'Australian Side-Lights on Free Church Principles: 1 The History of Religious Freedom in New South Wales', *Aldersgate Primitive Methodist Magazine* 1901, pp.54–6. See also John Watson, 'Primitive Methodism in South Australia', *Primitive Methodist Magazine* 1886, pp.677–78. For an excellent modern history see Arnold D. Hunt, *This Side of Heaven*, Lutheran Publishing House, Adelaide 1985. I am indebted to Dr Hunt for sharing with me his expert knowledge of Methodism in Adelaide.
45. Hunt, *A Tall Cedar*, p.17
46. Hugh Gilmour, *Sermons*, Adelaide 1892, p.59, quoted in Hunt, *A Tall Cedar*, p.24.
47. Susan Eade, 'Catherine Helen Spence', *Australian Dictionary of Biography* vol. 6, 1851–90, University of Melbourne Press 1976, p.168.
48. Methodist Church Archives, Manchester: Peake MS pk IV 1718, John Day Thompson – A.S. Peake, 9 January 1893.
49. *Christian Weekly*, 23 October 1896; Hunt, *This Side of Heaven*, p.141.
50. *The Quiz and the Lantern*, 1 November 1894.
51. *Christian Commonwealth*, 11 October 1916, *The Primitive Methodist*, 25 June 1896.
52. A.S. Peake, 'Dr. John Watson', *Aldersgate Primitive Methodist Magazine* 1913, p.368.
53. John Watson, 'Evangelism, Old and New', *Primitive Methodist Quarterly Review* 1892, pp.688, 694. See also his Hartley Lecture for 1898, *The Fatherhood of God*, Thomas Mitchell 1899.
54. J.D. Thompson, 'Some Theologians and Philosophers of the Century', *Aldersgate Primitive Methodist Magazine* 1919, p.22.
55. Methodist Church Archives, Manchester: Conference Manuscript Journal 1895, p.325.
56. *The Primitive Methodist*, 25 June 1896 p.437.
57. Ibid.
58. W. Jones Davies, *The Minister at Work*, Charles H. Kelly 1910, p.55.
59. *The Primitive Methodist*, 25 June 1896 p.437.
60. John Kent, 'Hugh Price Hughes and the Nonconformist Conscience', *Essays in Modern English Church History* ed. G.V. Bennett & J.D. Walsh, A. & C. Black 1966, p.201.
61. *The Primitive Methodist*, 25 June 1896, p.426.
62. A.S. Peake, 'In Memoriam: H.B. Kendall and J.D. Thompson', *Holborn Review* 1919, pp.381f.
63. J.D. Thompson, *The Church That Found Herself*, London 1912 pp.87f.

64. *Christian Commonwealth*, 11 October 1916.
65. Letter from the Revd Dr Herbert G. Marsh to author, 22 December 1975.
66. See his critical review of the off-balanced attack on German liberal theology launched by P.T. Forsyth's *The Christian Ethic of War*, Longmans, Green, and Co. 1916, in the *Holborn Review* 1916, p.593. See also Stuart Mews, 'Neo-orthodoxy, Liberalism and War: Karl Barth, P.T. Forsyth and John Oman 1914–18', *Renaissance and Renewal in Christian History* ed. Derek Baker, Blackwell 1977, p.371.
67. A. Lewis Humphries, 'Creed Revision', *Holborn Review* 1917, p.245.
68. A.S. Peake, 'In Memoriam', pp.381f.
69. Dr H.G. Marsh to author, 22 December 1975.
70. H. Bickerstaffe Kendall, *History of the Primitive Methodist Church* vol. II, p.433.
71. Peake, art. cit., p.382.

12

C. F. Andrews and the Failure of the Modern Missionary Movement

JEFFREY COX

C. F. Andrews was a religious rebel in twentieth-century India, a rebel against British rule as well as a rebel against the missionary movement. After serving as an Anglican missionary with the Cambridge Mission to Delhi between 1904 and 1914, he left the missionary world to become a close friend and associate of Gandhi, an important publicist for the Indian national movement, President of the Indian Trades Union Congress, Rabindranath Tagore's literary agent in England, and the person who has been credited with securing the abolition of indentured service in the British Empire. One of the few missionaries who managed to get the sympathetic attention of the Indian national movement and subsequently of some nationalist historians, he has been the subject of two major recent British academic studies.[1] On the centenary of his birth in 1971 the Government of India honoured him with a special postage stamp.

Andrews condemned the missionary movement to India as a failure. His critique is far more persuasive than those of most nationalist or secular Western historians, who usually dismiss missionaries as little more than the religious agents of global imperialism. Andrews not only had an intimate knowledge of what he rejected, he spent most of his life after 1914 attempting to find an alternative way to be a witness for Christ as an Englishman in India. He remained by his own lights a kind of missionary while criticizing wholesale the missionary presence in India, and deserves to be treated as a missionary theorist of considerable stature. He cannot be understood at all without reference to his theology.[2]

The purpose of this essay is to examine the reasons for Andrews' critical judgment, and to consider its relevance for a broader re-interpretation of the missionary movement in India and elsewhere.[3] Andrews developed his ideas about the missionary movement while a member of the Cambridge Mission to Delhi. Even after rejecting the missionary movement, he retained a certain amount of wistful sympathy for his own mission and remained on friendly terms with some of his ex-colleagues. But his view of the nature of the missionary movement was naturally shaped by his experience within a particular mission, and criticism of the missionary presence in India often meant in practice criticism of the Anglican presence in Delhi.

The Cambridge Mission to Delhi was founded in the 1870s under the influence of B.F. Westcott, then Regius Professor of Divinity at Cambridge (and later Bishop of Durham), and Thomas Valpy French, a veteran Anglican missionary to north-west India (and later first Bishop of Lahore). They encouraged Cambridge undergraduates, both individually and in well-attended public addresses, to think in terms of a special mission to India from Cambridge. Westcott held up as a model the Alexandrian school of the second and third centuries, where Clement and Origen brought the culture of the Greeks to bear on Christian truth.[4]

The Alexandrian school was notable, according to Westcott, for its recognition of truth in non-Christian philosophies. Clement believed that the Greek philosophers had possessed a genuine but incomplete truth which found its fulfillment in Christ. Thus, God's revelation of truth had not been limited to the Jews, but had been partially revealed to others in preparation for the full revelation in Christ.

Throughout the early and mid-nineteenth century, Protestant missionaries in India had conducted a frontal assault on Hinduism and Islam. Regarding both as systems riddled with error, polluted and defiled from the beginning, they had hoped to demonstrate the complete truth of Christianity by contrasting it with the complete falsehood of Hinduism and Islam. The Alexandrian model provided another way forward. To Westcott, Hinduism was the Hellenism of nineteenth-century India. Instead of focussing on error, missionaries should look for truth in Hinduism and identify ways in which the lesser truth pointed to the greater truth in Christ. Both Westcott and French believed that missionaries should clothe Christian truth in Hindu and Islamic cultural forms. Just as Christianity and Hellenic culture mingled in the apologetics of second and third-century Alexandria, Christianity and Hindu culture would mingle in late nineteenth-century India. 'And is it too much to hope,' Westcott asked, 'that we may yet see on the Indus, or the Ganges, some new Alexandria?'[5] From this centre 'Hindu-Christian' Indian theologians, of the stature of the 'Greek-Christian' theologians Clement and Origen, would eventually lead India and ultimately all of Asia to Christ.

In 1878 the first two Cambridge graduates, dedicated to a common life of celibacy, service, and thought, sailed for Delhi to work in connection with a small mission previously established by the Society for the Propagation of the Gospel (SPG).[6] The next year they were joined by S. S. Allnutt and G. A. Lefroy, who died within a year of each other forty years later after a lifetime of service to the Anglican church in India.[7] Together Allnutt and Lefroy did more to shape the Cambridge Mission than anyone else. They created a moderately High Church and celibate 'Brotherhood' which became the nucleus of a much larger Anglican missionary establishment in Delhi. The size of the Brotherhood varied from four to six men, but they always provided leadership to a larger Delhi Anglican SPG mission which grew to thirty-seven missionaries by 1914 and included teachers, a community of celibate English women, and some Indian clergymen and teachers.[8]

Like other theories of mission, Westcott's vision of a new Alexandria provided little practical guidance to a missionary facing immediate decisions. Lefroy, Allnutt, and the other Cambridge Brothers sincerely wished to engage in dialogue between East and West, and develop a new Indian form of Christianity. But exactly how does one go about discovering a new Clement or a new Origen? While the Cambridge brothers pondered this question in the early 1880s, the government of India began to take a role in shaping their mission. Allnutt and

Lefroy received a letter from the government, accompanied by an offer of money, requesting the Cambridge Mission to open a college for students of all religions. In this mutually beneficial relationship, the government would contribute to a relatively inexpensive extension of Western education for Indians while the mission would have an opportunity to influence the upper classes of Delhi. Perhaps they would find an Origen in the classroom.

Allnutt and Lefroy and the other Cambridge Brothers established St Stephen's College in the 1880s, an activity which provided welcome relief from another major and very unwelcome task. Soon after their arrival, the Cambridge Brothers found thrust upon them the care and discipline of several hundred Christian converts who came from an outcast 'untouchable' community of leatherworkers, the Chamars.[9] The Chamars had no place in Westcott's theory of missions, and certainly not in the expectations of High Church Cambridge graduates in search of a young Origen. Lefroy complained bitterly of '... the tremendous adverse influence which our connection with these despised Chamars exercises on all our attempts at contact with the higher classes'.[10]

The Chamars converted to Anglicanism for good reasons of their own. There is certainly no evidence that they acted with greater hypocrisy or more impure motives than the missionaries who stood in judgment over them. But Lefroy labelled them 'Christians in nothing but name', the evidence for this rather summary pronouncement being the continuation of ties between Christian Chamars and other Chamars, including the 'sharing of feasts, idolatrous and otherwise'.[11] Determined to prevent Chamar slackness from discrediting Christianity in Delhi, Lefroy plunged into the task of parochial care with a programme which featured discipline and excommunication for backsliders and cheap rental housing for the pious. By 1890 he had reduced the Christian Chamar community to a few families who were tenants of the mission.

Having disposed of the Chamar problem, the Cambridge Brothers were free to behave like the majority of nineteenth-century Anglican clergymen everywhere in the world, including England. Their practical approach to church expansion was one of institutional expansion. Clergymen, including missionaries, created and presided over Christian institutions. Christian values radiated from these institutions, converting some, influencing others in more subtle ways, and improving the moral tone of the surrounding society. A clergyman carried out his professional responsibilities primarily by acting as an influential person in the community and by encouraging other influential persons to set good moral examples for their inferiors, to attend church if possible, and to contribute money to philanthropies, including the church.

Between 1880 and 1914 the Cambridge Mission and SPG expanded the SPG's small High School, and created St Stephen's College, St Stephen's High School, St Stephen's Hospital for Women, the Victoria School for Christian girls, and the Queen Mary School for (mostly non-Christian) girls of the 'best Delhi families'.[12] Chamar work was maintained. Reporting on the condition of the backsliding ex-Christian Chamars, Lefroy wrote in 1895 that 'We have been in touch with them as much as was possible and let them feel that we were only waiting for them to come forward again in one spirit and with deeper convictions, and we would be as ready as ever to welcome them.'[13] In 1906 the mission built for their Indian converts a new church on the model of a Greek basilica, a style thought to be more congruent with the oriental mind than was the Lombardo-Venetian style of the other, older Indian parish church in Delhi.

Pride of place, however, went to the work of influencing non-Christian students in the schools. The Cambridge Mission never abandoned in principle the ultimate goal of conversion, but in practice a more diffuse kind of 'influence' became the end of mission work. Influence came not so much through the logic of direct Christian teaching as through exposure to the ethos which surrounded men and women of good Christian character. In their view, St Stephen's College should serve the purposes which Westcott attributed to Oxford and Cambridge: '... the power of the Universities for good is nowhere exercised more largely than through the mass of graduates ... who would themselves find it hard to explain the subtle influences which have insensibly moulded their habits of thought and action.'[14] The mission's measure of success became the number of leading Indian gentlemen of Delhi who had passed through its schools.

Ethics rather than propositional doctrine lay at the heart of Imperial Anglicanism. Lefroy believed that 'an acute moral sense' lay 'at the very foundation of all truly practical religion'. He also believed that Hinduism and Islam 'lack it in an almost incredible degree',[15] a conviction which he explained in detail before hundreds of spectators in a series of public disputations with learned Muslims. Westcott's vision of a fruitful encounter between East and West was submerged in Lefroy's obsession with the moral weaknesses of Indian society. The Cambridge Brothers' uncritical faith in the benefits of British rule led logically, in a theological context, to the more controversial conviction that God had arranged this political system to facilitate the spread of Christian moral truth in St Stephen's College and Queen Mary's School.

Andrews entered the Cambridge Brotherhood in 1904 after a clerical apprenticeship which included service in the Pembroke College Mission to South London. In 1914 he left the mission for Rabindranath Tagore's retreat at Santineketan, having become convinced that, for a number of reasons, the Cambridge Mission and the entire missionary movement had failed. Although he had been an uncritical admirer of British rule in India when he arrived, Andrews always took seriously the Westcottian ideal of a sympathetic approach to the truths which might be found in Hinduism and Islam. Westcott had a direct personal influence on him, and his ideas are in some ways a twentieth-century extension of aspects of Westcott's vision. But within two years of his arrival Andrews had discovered Christian truth in an unexpected place: the newly assertive Indian national movement.

Through his St Stephen's colleague, S.K. Rudra, he met many leaders of the national movement. His missionary colleagues grew increasingly nervous as Andrews attended a National Congress meeting and began defending the national movement in the press. By 1908 Andrews discerned in the Indian national movement the '... seed of Christian ideas beginning to spring forth from the soil ... it is easy to take a superficial view and call the whole movement secular. Yet I cannot see how this can be maintained by anyone who holds intelligently the faith of the Incarnation, and who believes that Jesus is the Son of Man ... if the Christian nations are faithful to high principles, and the Christian messengers make clear their message, then it may come to pass that, amid the shaking of the nations of the East, we shall see the Son of Man coming in His glory, and, before this generation pass away shall welcome "one of the days of the Son of Man".'[16]

By 1914 Andrews's theology of the Indian national movement had evolved to the point where he could no longer accept the notion that Western Christians had anything to teach Indians. His missionary colleagues' contempt for Indian character appalled him. In early 1914 he wrote to Tagore: 'I know and recognize now how insolent and vain I was when I first came to India ten years ago, coming to teach instead of to learn and writing and speaking at first in the evil patronizing way.'[17] Early that same year he travelled to South Africa to participate in Gandhi's campaign of civil disobedience among the Indians of Natal. He discovered in Gandhi the fullest expression of the Christian ideal for India.

Andrews preached a farewell sermon to a crowded congregation of Anglican friends in Lahore Cathedral in early May 1914, summarizing with the concise elegance of the best kind of Anglo-Catholic sermon his reasons for leaving the Cambridge Mission:

> In South Africa I found Christ's presence more wonderfully near to me in all its beauty (moving me to adoring worship) among the patient, gentle Hindu ladies, just released from prison, speaking kindly to their gaolers, than in the churches of the wealthy in that land where doors were practically closed to coloured people ... And the question came upon me with a sad, a terrible insistence, as I travelled across many seas, past many shores, whether the modern, aggressive wealthy nations of the world, armed to the teeth against each other, trafficking in the souls of men for gain, can be for long the dwelling place of the meek and lowly Christ, whether the hour may not be near, when he will say unto them, as he said unto Bethsaida and Chorazin of old, 'Woe unto you', and will turn instead to the

poor and downtrodden people of the earth, and say unto them, 'Come Unto Me.' For in his Kingdom there are many that are last that shall be first and first that shall be last.[18]

Daniel O'Connor has written in detail about the evolution of Andrews' thought between 1904 and 1914, a period when he produced works of far greater interest than are the devotional and propaganda pieces he wrote in the twenties and thirties.[19] Many missionaries have written of the failure of earlier generations of missionaries to achieve the impossible, i.e. to foster the development of a truly indigenous Indian form of Christianity, something which the missionary presence itself prevented from happening. But no missionary has written with more poignancy than Andrews about the sense of failure which overwhelmed the missionary idealist forced into the role of 'Sahib' when he only wished to live on a basis of equality with Indians.[20] No missionary has written with greater insight into the anxiety with which many missionaries pondered the defects of the missionary enterprise such as careerism, excessive concern with professional privilege, uncritical deference to ecclesiastical hierarchy, and a confusion of Western culture with Christianity, and then saw those defects reproduced in the Indian Christian church. Most of Andrews' objections to the missionary presence can be found in writings produced while he was still a missionary, pleading with his colleagues and with Indian Christians to change their ways before it was too late.

Andrews identified several elements of the failure of the missionary movement to live up to Christ's standards. One was the British missionaries' identification with Imperial power at a time when the spirit of Christ was on the other side, in the national movement broadly defined. Another was the missionaries' failure to treat others with sympathy and love, and to look for truth in other religions and other cultures. The missionary tradition of emphasizing the aspects of Hinduism most offensive to Westerners – child marriage, caste, the mistreatment of women – especially distressed him.[21] He believed that such an emphasis pressed Christ's religion of love into the service of international misunderstanding. Finally, and as a consequence of the other failures, the missionary movement had failed to create an indigenous Indian church and had instead 'denationalized' Indian Christians, leaving them without influence in their own nation and isolated from the Christian spirit which he identified in the national movement.

It is also possible to see in Andrews' pre-1914 writings the elements of an alternative theory of missions, one which emphasized dialogue and service. Even after he rejected the missionary movement altogether as being Christian in nothing but name, Andrews never ceased to regard bearing witness to his own faith in Christ as his highest commitment, and never ceased to think seriously about how that might be done. In the 1930s his disagreements with Gandhi over conversion provided an opportunity to outline an explicit vision of a legitimate missionary role in India, one which was entirely consistent with his pre-1914 arguments.[22] Andrews drew a sharp line between bearing public witness to one's faith on the one hand and direct persuasion, or proselytism, on the other. He believed that Christians should bear witness to their faith through service to others, and look for opportunities to explain the Christian motivation for that service while engaging in respectful dialogue with men and women of other faiths. Implicit in much of nineteenth-century missionary practice, this concept of mission work was rarely put into theoretical form for fear of upsetting missionary supporters back home who thought their money went to convert the heathen as rapidly as possible. Andrews made the service and dialogue theory explicit.

But even though Andrews regarded conversion to Christianity as an uncertain consequence of service and dialogue, something which should not be aimed at directly, he always maintained that differences between the great world religions were important and that conversion should remain a legitimate option for the individual. Contrary to Gandhi's view that 'all religions are equal', and that 'a man should always remain in the faith in which he was born', Andrews argued in 1936 that 'there are clear cut distinctions between Christians, Hindus, and Muslims which cannot today be overpassed. But I do not think that we need to anathematize one another in consequence. We should rather always seek to see thc best in one another, for that is an essential feature of love.'[23]

There is one additional aspect of Andrews' thought which has received much less attention than his emphasis on dialogue and service, and that is his commitment to bringing influence to bear on those in positions of power. Throughout his life he shared with the founders and members of the Cambridge Mission to Delhi a geo-religious view of the world. They saw the great world religions and their non-religious rivals locked into a battle for influence with those in positions of power. It was a missionary theory which had changed little since the Jesuits had journeyed to Akbar's court in the late sixteenth century, hoping to convert him and thereby win India to Catholicism. For all of his genuine commitment to serving the poor and the marginal, Andrews believed in a Christian God whose fundamental concern was with the most important, central events guiding the course of history.

The Cambridge Brothers identified God at work in British rule in India. Their mission was to Indians, and they saw their proper Anglican role as chaplains to important Indians, or to the children of important Indians, even if they happened to be non-Christians. The Cambridge Mission to Delhi provided the sons of daughters of important people in Delhi with a sound Anglican education. Since these were the leaders of the India of the future, this was the best way to exert Christian influence at the centre of human events.

This partly explains their attitude toward the Indian Christian church. Indian Christians were not important. If not actually untouchables on the fringes of society (which a majority were), then they were 'denationalized' Indians imitating British ways and cutting themselves off from their fellow countrymen. Ignoring Westcott's warning that the English church would stifle the development of Indian Christianity unless 'we keep ourselves and our modes of thought studiously in the background',[24] the Cambridge Mission made no serious attempt in the 1880s and 1890s to give Indian Christians responsibility in the church.

The Anglican evangelical Church Missionary Society (CMS), which worked in central Punjab, had a much stronger interest in devising ways to foster the development of a self-governing

Indian Christian church. In 1900 the CMS Indian Secretary sent a circular to the major Indian missions inquiring about what steps had been taken to promote self-government in the Indian church. Allnutt replied for the Cambridge Mission that 'the ultimate formation of a purely Indian administration is not aimed at'.[25] In 1904 Allnutt wrote to a CMS official in London that the CMS's latest scheme to promote self-government in the Indian church 'is indeed radical, one might almost say revolutionary ... one is almost reminded of the ill effects of the too rapid emancipation of the slaves'.[26]

Andrews reacted strongly against that kind of attitude, and greatly admired some Indian Christians, especially his St Stephen's colleague S.K. Rudra, who he defended vigorously against what he regarded as racially discriminatory treatment by the SPG in London. But Andrews shared his missionary colleague's frustration with the lack of leadership among Indian Christians, leadership which could hardly emerge among people who were denied positions of responsibility and authority. His attitude is evident in his arguments about the proper relationship between the Indian church and the national movement.

Andrews and his missionary colleagues wished to exert Christian influence on the course of history. He parted ways with them, however, on the issue of what he often referred to as 'discerning the Signs of the Times', i.e. predicting the course of history. As Andrews came to discern God at work in the Indian national movement, and to identify the national movement as the crucial arena for Christian influence, he came to believe that the most important Christian task was bearing witness within the national movement.

The Indian church, however, was not fit to participate in this fundamental Christian task. In 1908 he told young Indian Christians that 'It is one of the tragedies of history that communities whose influence depends largely on being in touch with the new movements of humanity are often the least prepared for changes and developments when the awakenings come, and allow great epochs to arise without setting their house in order and preparing for a new advance.'[27] In 1910 he confessed that the Indian church had failed to produce 'men of spiritual genius ...

who have become "Indians to the Indians" and written theology from the Eastern point of view. If Bishop Westcott had only come out to India himself, we should have today been in a better case, but we have had no one like that.'[28]

Before 1914 he dealt with this problem by advising the Indian church to redeem itself by participation in the national movement, and especially in the work of uplifting the depressed classes. The Indian church could claim a leadership role in instructing the national movement on this issue, for Christians in the Punjab had been dealing with untouchables long before the national movement took an interest. During the time Andrews belonged to the Cambridge Brotherhood, the Punjab witnessed one of several waves of conversion to Christianity among the depressed classes, especially the sweepers of central Punjab, a movement which produced a very rapid growth rate. From a tiny handful of Christians in the 1840s the Punjabi Christian church grew to nearly half a million by 1947.[29]

These mass movements into Christianity caused problems of interpretation for Andrews very much like those facing his predecessors in the 1880s. 'Do not mistake my position,' he wrote. 'There is no one who rejoices more than I do in the welcome given to the Christian message by the depressed classes, and the uplifting change which it has brought into their sad lives.'[30] But Andrews position was internally contradictory. Although some untouchable conversions were spontaneous, others were the result of highly organized campaigns by the Anglican evangelical Church Missionary Society, the Salvation Army, and American Presbyterian and Methodist missions. He felt forced to celebrate a movement which depended on direct proselytism and de-emphasized the sort of indirect Christian influence on the educated classes which he continued to regard as crucial.

When the Bishop of Madras in 1907 suggested in a controversial article that missionaries should be redeployed from educational work to direct evangelism among outcastes, Andrews joined some of his most reactionary colleagues in defending the strategy of influencing the upper classes.[31] The Bishop pointed out that the twenty-eight missionaries and forty ladies stationed in

Calcutta, Cawnpore, Delhi, and Poona presided over a tiny Christian community 'which has been almost entirely unprogressive for the last thirty years', producing fewer than a thousand converts in the same period. Six Anglican missionaries bore responsibility for twelve thousand Telugu Christians and a community growing at the rate of two thousand a year. Furthermore, the Bishop reasoned, the liberation and subsequent elevation of pariah communities throughout India would do more to convert the educated classes 'than all the lectures and addresses in the world'.[32]

As early as 1907 Andrews shared the attitude of the national movement toward outcaste conversions to Christianity. Many nationalists regarded Christian conversions of outcastes as an exploitation of weaknesses in Hindu society for British Imperial purposes if not outright bribery by missionaries.[33] The work of uplifting should be done by Indians, not by foreigners, they believed, and Andrews urged Indian Christians to abandon independent Christian efforts to proselytize outcastes and instead join in a multi-religious nationalist effort.[34]

But Andrews had additional objections. To accept Bishop Whitehead's strategy would mean the abandonment of the geo-religious metaphor which portrayed Christianity as locked in a struggle for influence in the most important 'leading sectors' of world history. The Bishop had failed to discern the Signs of the Times, which indicated to Andrews that the years 1905–1907 were a crucial turning point for Christianity in India. The educated classes were only now abandoning Hinduism and Islam for science and nationalism, he argued. Christianity had yet to be presented to them in a truly national guise. Scientific nationalism by itself lacked the power to strike down barriers to national unity such as caste, superstition, and idolatry. The crucial time for dialogue had arrived. 'Each fresh position of reforming Hinduism and Islam must be met and answered, with patience and sympathy, and its inadequacy explained.'[35]

Soon after writing those words in 1907, Andrews found the true spirit of Christianity entirely inside the national movement itself, in the spiritual power of the Gandhian movement, rather than in the Western missionary movement or its colleges training 'subservient intellectuals cringing for government favor'.[36] The missionary movement, which he hoped to re-orient towards service to the Indian poor, dialogue with reforming movements in Indian culture, and influence upon the Indian national movement, he abandoned as a failure. He did not change his theory of missions so much as give up on the ability of the missionary movement to carry out the task. In an odd way, he shifted his allegiance to another establishment, abandoning the nineteenth-century Anglican establishment to become a chaplain in the twentieth-century Congress establishment.

Andrews had confidence in his ability to read the Signs of the Times and predict the course of history. He realized that the missionary movement was at a turning point in the years after 1905, and that a national movement in power in India would regard Christianity in its missionary form as either irrelevant or malevolent. This outcome could be avoided, he believed, only if missionaries and Indian Christians were to adopt his own approach of respectful dialogue, service, and nationalist commitment. With his great passion for personal friendship and influence, with Tagore, Gandhi, and many other lesser figures, Andrews struggled before and after leaving the Cambridge Mission for a new India in which Christianity would play at least some role in shaping the art, science, and literature of the new nation. By 1914 he was convinced that the Cambridge Brothers had failed to recognize in the national movement the crucial arena for the exercise of Christian influence.

Because of that failure, and despite Andrews' best efforts, the missionary movement has failed to have the kind of decisive impact in India that most missionaries hoped to see. The national movement has been hostile to missionaries and dismissive of Indian Christianity. Hinduism and Islam now face vigorous competition, but they are in some ways stronger now than they were in the nineteenth century. Hinduism has shown surprising powers of adaptation and renewal in India. Islam provides the governing ideology for both Pakistan and Bangladesh, and one of St Stephen's best known graduates, Zia-ul-Huq, pursued a vigorous Islamization campaign as President of Pakistan, before his death in an air crash in 1988.

The course of twentieth-century Indian history might have been different had more missionaries and Indian Christians heeded more of Andrew's advice. His missionary theory is certainly more appealing now than the nineteenth-century confrontational approach. Far better to look for the good in other religions than to shout at them in the bazaar. But it is important to keep in mind that Andrews' judgment on the missionary movement was a theological judgment, and the failure of the missionary movement a theological failure.

The nineteenth-century missionary movement not only failed by Andrews's standards; it failed by its own essentially theological standards as well, and not just in India. The goal of the modern missionary movement, which began in the late eighteenth century, was the conversion of the world to Christianity within a few generations. In India its goal was the moral and intellectual demolition of Hinduism and Islam, either directly through intellectual confrontation or indirectly through the educational strategy pursued in high schools and colleges. However, those goals were so unrealistic and unattainable that it tells us very little about the missionary movement to note its failure to meet them. It is more interesting and worthwhile to try to assess the importance of the missionary movement in the pursuit of those goals.

Andrews own hopes for the missionary movement were equally unrealistic. Indeed missionaries in India were doomed to failure in the eyes of someone who defined 'important' as 'important at the centre of things'. The national movement was bound to be anti-British, and the missionary movement so deeply entangled in the British presence in India that it is difficult to see how an adversary relationship could have been avoided altogether. Andrews showed very little interest in examining the unexpected ways in which the Christian presence might have been important in India, ways which did not fit into his theological definitions of importance.

For instance, the role of missionaries in shaping the Indian educational system in the late nineteenth century has yet to be examined in detail. Furthermore, missionaries and nationalists alike, including Andrews, have shown very little interest in the importance of Christianity to the hundreds of thousands of outcaste leatherworkers and sweepers who became Christians in the early twentieth-century Punjab. Indian historiography has recently been characterized by an interest in marginal groups formerly excluded from historical accounts, but even those historians have yet to examine the mass movements into Christianity.[37] We will know more about the importance of the missionary movement when these large-scale conversions have been examined by historians who are neither committed to the missionary movement nor hostile to it in principle.

Andrews himself had considerable influence on Gandhi, who was greatly interested in the questions posed by Christianity and in the missionary presence. In a limited way, Andrews achieved one of his goals by carrying his version of Christian witness to the heart of the national movement.[38] In a world in which religious rebels continue to play unexpected roles in unexpected places, C. F. Andrews' career reminds us of the importance of the global expansion of Christianity in shaping the course of nineteenth and twentieth-century history.

Notes

1. Hugh Tinker, *The Ordeal of Love. C. F. Andrews and India*, OUP 1979; Daniel O'Connor, *Gospel, Raj, and Swaraj. The Missionary Years of C. F. Andrews*, Frankfurt am Main 1990.
2. Hugh Tinker argues that '... the theological ideas and writings of Andrews are scarcely touched upon' in *The Ordeal of Love* which he wrote 'as much for the humanist as for those with religious faith' (p. xvi). It can hardly be true that readers 'for whom the spiritual has no special meaning' (p. xvi) are either incapable of understanding religion or unwilling to attempt such a task. In order to make Andrews intelligible, Tinker selectively ignores his own advice throughout his useful and interesting biography.
3. See John Kent's chapter on 'Failure of a Mission. Christianity Outside Europe' in his *The Unacceptable Face. The Modern Church in the Eyes of the Historian*, SCM Press 1987. This refreshing essay is the starting point for a reinterpretation of the missionary enterprise.
4. See Herbert Birks, *The Life and Correspondence of Thomas Valpy French, First Bishop of Lahore*, John Murray 1895, 2 vols; Arthur

Westcott, *The Life and Letters of Brooke Foss Westcott*, Macmillan 1903, 2 vols.

5. B.F. Westcott, *On Some Points in the Religious Office of the Universities*, Macmillan 1873, p.41; cf. C.F. Andrews, *What I Owe to Christ*, Abingdon Press, Nashville 1932, p.149.
6. *The Story of the Delhi Mission*, SPG 1908; F.J. Western, *The Early History of the Cambridge Mission to Delhi*, SPG 1950 (typescript); *One Hundred Years in Delhi: The Brotherhood of the Ascended Christ*, Delhi 1977.
7. Cecil H. Martin, *Allnutt of Delhi. A Memoir*, SPCK 1922; H.H. Montgomery, *The Life and Letters of George Alfred Lefroy*, Longmans 1920.
8. Society for the Propagation of the Gospel *Annual Report for the Year 1914*.
9. See Edward Bickersteth, *A Letter to the Rev. Canon Westcott, D.D.*, Cambridge Mission to Delhi Occasional Paper, Delhi 1881.
10. Montgomery, *Life*, p.32.
11. G.A. Lefroy, *The Leatherworkers of Daryaganj*, Cambridge Mission to Delhi Occasional Paper, Delhi 1884, n.p.
12. Martin, *Allnutt*, pp.115–6; F.F. Monk, *A History of St Stephen's College, Delhi*, Calcutta 1935; *Queen Mary's School, Delhi. Golden Jubilee 1912–1962*, Delhi 1962; on early work at St Stephen's Hospital see Marie Elizabeth Hayes, *At Work. Letters of Marie Elizabeth Hayes, M.B. Missionary Doctor, Delhi 1905–08*, Marshall Bros 1909.
13. Lefroy to SPG (London), January 1895, SPG Archives Series E (Mission Reports) 1895.
14. Westcott, *The Religious Office of the Universities*, pp.vii–viii.
15. Montgomery, *Life*, p.43
16. C.F. Andrews, *North India*, Mowbray 1908, p.190.
17. C.F. Andrews, *The Testimony of C.F. Andrews* ed. Daniel O'Connor, Christian Literature Society, Madras 1974, p.102.
18. *Tribune*, 6 May 1914. I am grateful to Daniel O'Connor for calling my attention to this sermon.
19. O'Connor, *Gospel, Raj, and Swaraj*; preface to Andrews, *Testimony* ed. O'Connor.
20. Andrews, *North India*. p.177.
21. See his response to Katherine Mayo's influential *Mother India*, Brace, New York 1927, in *The True India*, Allen & Unwin 1939, reprinted in New Delhi by Inter-India Publications 1985.
22. See 'Dialogue Between Mahatma Gandhi and C.F. Andrews on Conversion (1936)' from *Harijan*, 28 November 1936, reprinted in M.K. Kuriakose, *History of Christianity in India: Source Materials*, Christian

Literature Society, Madras 1982, pp.362–363; 'A Letter to Gandhi (1937)', reprinted in Andrews, *Testimony*, pp.118–122; also in Benarsidas Chaturvedi and Marjorie Sykes, *Charles Freer Andrews. A Narrative*, Allen & Unwin 1949; reprint by Government of India Publications Division 1971, p.310.

23. Andrews, *Testimony*, p.121.
24. Westcott, *The Religious Office of the Universities*, p.38.
25. CMS Archives c/ccb4/2c, *Abstract of Replies to the Circular Letter of the Conference Secretary*.
26. Allnutt to Eugene Stock. CMS Archives, Punjab Letter Book G2/I4/L8/1903–1907.
27. 'Indian Christians and the National Movement', *Young Men of India*, September 1908, reprinted in Andrews, *Testimony*, p.123.
28. *Ordination Study in India*, Cambridge Mission to Delhi Occasional Paper 33, SPG 1910, reprinted in Andrews, *Testimony*, p.190.
29. See Frederick and Margaret Stock, *People Movements in the Punjab*, William Carey Library, Los Angeles 1975; Jeffrey Cox, 'On Redefining Crisis: The Victorian Crisis of Faith in the Punjab, 1880–1900' in R. Helmstadter and B. Lightman (eds), *Victorian Faith in Crisis*, Macmillan 1990.
30. 'Christ and Educated India', a sermon preached at Agra in 1909 and reprinted in O'Connor, *Testimony*, p.138.
31. Henry Whitehead. 'The Progress of Christianity in India and Mission Strategy', *East and West*, January 1907, pp.21–28; editor's response, July 1907, pp.335–337 (probably from H.H. Montgomery, whose views on Hindu moral laxity were even more extreme than Lefroy's); Andrews' response, 'The Situation in the East', October 1907, pp.419–429. For the views of another Cambridge Brother who adopted Bishop Whitehead's views later see G. Hibbert Ware, *Christian Missions in the Telegu Country* SPG 1912.
32. Whitehead, 'The Progress of Christianity', p.27.
33. For Gandhi's attitude see M.M. Thomas, *The Acknowledged Christ of the Indian Renaissance*, SCM Press, London and Christian Literature Society, Madras 1970, p.217.
34. 'Christ and Educated India,' in Andrews, *Testimony*, pp.135–141.
35. Andrews, 'The Situation in the East', p.428
36. Andrews, 'The Situation in the East', p.428.
37. See for instance Sumit Sarkar, *Modern India 1884–1947*, Macmillan of India, Delhi 1983, ch. 3; Ranajit Guha (ed.), *Subaltern Studies. Writings on South Asian History and Society*, OUP, Delhi 1982–, vols 1–6. An exception to the general neglect of Christian popular movements is K.S. Singh, *Dust Storm and Hanging Mist: A Study of Birsa Munda and his Movement in Chota Nagpur, 1874–1911*,

Firma K.L. Mukhopadhyay, Calcutta 1966.

38. For the details on how he did this, see O'Connor, *Gospel, Raj, and Swaraj*, passim; and Thomas, *The Acknowledged Christ*, pp. 221–228.

13

John Collins, Gadfly of the Resurrection

HADDON WILLMER

Since my first year at Cambridge, reading history under John Kent's supervision, I have enjoyed his provocation and friendship. I should be ashamed at my ingratitude if I missed the chance to contribute to this book. But I am in difficulty. Amongst the people I have the interest and knowledge to write about, I cannot find an obvious and convincing modern religious rebel. Is that evidence that John Kent did not decisively shape my taste in subject matter or are religious rebels rare?

They are, I suggest, much rarer and often much less interesting than is commonly supposed. I think I can explain why, by testing the credentials as a rebel of John Collins, Canon of St Paul's Cathedral, founder and for many years leader of Christian Action with its Defence and Aid Fund and first chairman of the Campaign for Nuclear Disarmament.

In the staid ecclesiastical scene of the late 1950s, when I first met John Kent, not many senior Anglican clergymen had any public reputation as rebels. There was no rebellious bishop after Barnes of Birmingham retired and died in 1953 until Mervyn Stockwood in Southwark was made to look more of a rebel than he was by his suffragan, John Robinson, whose *Honest to God* was published in 1963. Archbishop Fisher was always efficient in tidying rebels away, as Victor Gollancz, friend and campaigning mentor of Collins had discovered when a young teacher at Repton in 1918.[1] To young people in the 1950s, represented by Jimmy Porter in John Osborne's *Look Back in Anger*, the church was part of the 'establishment', supplying 'spiritual varnish' and ducking every moral issue.[2]

Against this background, Collins attracted attention: some thought it his misfortune that the press found him useful as a source of sensational stories.[3] In that context, to get the label of rebel was not difficult for a person of commitment and flair. But what would it mean? If he was a rebel, he was no Jimmy Porter, however much he was touched by the temper of the times.

Collins wrote his autobiography, *Faith Under Fire*, partly to answer the accusation of not believing half the things the church stood for, and not daring to say so. He was asked and asked himself: 'Why don't I get out of the church?' His response was to present himself as a rebel. He had grown up in an inherited Anglicanism and 'did not rebel because on the whole I was happy and contented, and I loved and trusted my family; this religion was theirs and so it was mine'. His early wish to be like Mr Long, the vicar of his childhood, issued naturally in his own ordination. However, 'seeds of rebellion' had already been sown; they blossomed into 'discontent' when he was curate at Whitstable in 1928. It was discontent with 'the ordinary ecclesiastical set-up'. By the late 1940s he was 'an outsider of the Anglican Church and an insider of the Establishment; but a rebel against what I believe to be the pretensions of both'.[4]

He was therefore a religious rebel in the sense that he was rebelling against aspects of the religious organization to which he belonged. He was not a religious rebel in the sense that his religion inspired him to be a rebel in the world at large, even though from about 1935 he gave up his Toryism for Christian Socialism, along with Mervyn Stockwood.

As a chaplain in an Oxford college (1938–1940 and 1946–1949) and in the Royal Air Force he did not feel hemmed in by parochial restraints, though still working within disciplined structures. He was not a rebel in these contexts because he found the freedom to develop experimentally what he thought were the essential elements of a contemporarily relevant Christianity. His conflicts with commanding officers were not rebellions; just as Paul of Tarsus knew how to exploit the rights belonging to a Roman citizen, Collins was an awkward independent-minded chaplain, bringing the skills of a New Testament scholar to studying King's Regulations so that he could do what he thought right without giving his superiors the satisfaction of bringing him to a court-martial.[5]

When he became a canon of St Paul's Cathedral in 1949, he knew he was returning to the 'ecclesiastical set-up' which provoked him to rebel. Did his rebellion go any further than irritation with the institutional church? It is not obvious that it did, which is why the category of rebel may not help us to understand someone like Collins. We are alerted here to the negativity of the rebel. In some cases rebellion, a well-known adolescent affliction, may suggest a lack of positive creativity; since one has nothing to offer, one's action can only be a sustained *non placet*, a blocking disgruntlement. Thus, if personal qualities earn someone the title of rebel, and nothing more, it means he is not much of a person. But being a rebel may consist in more than personal characteristics. It may be a social location or historical destiny. If positive possibilities are frustrated and blocked, and people do not win support or power in struggles that are important to them, nothing may be left to them, except to make unavailing protest against whatever is in power. To be classed as a rebel is to be identified as defeated. We do not count Socrates a rebel but a gadfly because he lived and died as more than a defeated protester.

Those whom history remembers only as rebels are the defeated. Rebels who win are remembered under some other name. Some people and events are ambiguous; it makes a difference whether the history of England between 1640 and 1660 is seen as the 'Great Rebellion' (a past event now left behind as fortunately a failure) or as the 'Commonwealth' (an event of positive significance, for all its faults, with beneficial consequences and abiding symbolic value). When it is called the Commonwealth it is not treated as historically and deservedly defeated. Of course, it may have been neither.

How far do Christians make good rebels? Christians by nature tend to be as conservative as the run of humanity, as fearfully dependent on the stability of any status quo, when it is given them to find somewhere to lay their heads, which in this troublous world is not so freely available that one can blame them for being anxious about it. The question about Christians as rebels must go beyond assessing the human capacity for rebellion to considering the ethics of faith. Let us suppose Christians were humanly free from self-protectiveness and free for utopian visions of the kingdom of God; suppose they could live in a radically nonconformist way, risking the loss of all worldly supports, like Abraham leaving Ur by faith: there would still be a substantial obstacle to their being simply rebels (and therefore to our being able to interpret them adequately in that category). The obstacle arises from the fact that in Christianity the cross is not without the resurrection.

There has been much discussion whether, because of the resurrection, Christianity is compatible with tragic vision.[6] Implicit in that question may be the conviction that the rebel is the true human being. Humanity acting and knowing itself truly finds itself, at the deepest level of being, defeated. At that point, superficial and partial successes are no consolation and give no basis for denying the defeat. Human being is rounded off both by death, which means that life leads nowhere, and by sin, so that all we do is flawed. Even our good produces evil either because it is limited in itself or because it is thwarted by unhelpful circumstances. Denying these facts is no solution: to be blind to human reality, wilfully or out of pathetic weakness, is another twist in the defeat of humanity. Resignation may seem more honest, but often it is not honest enough, for it affects a sense of achievement, a triumph of power: it thinks it is able to master its victimhood and establish an enclave where it is safe from the enemy. Resignation is Petainist: it accepts the defeat and, because such acceptance is not easy, it comforts itself with a claim to great moral achievement. It makes a good out of evil. Resignation treats the pain of defeat as something which can be managed calmly, accepted as the indifferent backcloth of living. Thus resignation is less than honest. It does not consider the weight of sin. It collapses morally because of its self-contradiction: resignation cannot be a great achievement, overcoming the unacceptable, if all it does is to tolerate without agony the bitterness of utter defeat.

The rebel, by contrast, lives raw to the defeat. He will not pretend it is anything but bitter. There is no reconciling oneself to it, without saying that evil is good. To rebel may not alter the situation: it is the response to the situation by those who are defeated, and in the last resort at least, know themselves as defeated. They refuse, however, to accept as tolerable, or as righteous, what they cannot escape. They rebel.

Can the Christian live in unrelieved rebellion, as a true rebel? At the centre of Christianity is the cup Jesus was not spared: 'My God, My God, why hast thou forsaken me?' There is the pain and sign of defeat. But is it not so quickly followed by resurrection that the defeat is cancelled out? That is a theoretical danger. No one, however, who lived as Collins did, open to the suffering and evil of our century, can take resurrection glibly as the cancellation of the cross. The cross reminds us of the unacceptable contradiction of the hope of the gospel which comes upon us in historical pain and injustice. Such experience may leave us little to do but rebel: against evil, by appeal to God; against God, lest he disappears in, even colludes with, evil. Resurrection validates that rebellion; it does not cancel it or make it unnecessary. Without that moment of rebellion in the defeat of the cross there could not be a valid resurrection. So rebellion has its relative justification, even though it is not for Christianity an ultimate category. Resurrection sustains positive expectation and anyone who believes in it will rebel, but will not be content to be merely a rebel.

Many of Collins' colleagues in CND were not Christians. Years later, Mervyn Jones wished that 'once at least, he had talked about the resurrection over coffee after a CND executive committee meeting. He could have convinced the members that he believed in it, and that he was not merely a politician.'[7] Despite his reticence, there is plentiful evidence of the significance of resurrection for him not only in *Faith Under Fire*, but also in earlier work. In 1935 he had written a pamphlet for the Industrial Christian Fellowship on the resurrection. And in 1948 he developed a theology of Christian Action in which the resurrection played a key role.[8] Although in the 1960s, when the idea of rebellion had become fashionable, he chose to see himself in relation to the church as a rebel, the mainspring of the major intention of his life is to be discovered at the intersection of revolution and resurrection.

A Theology of Christian Action, written in the idiom of the Anglican biblical theology of the time, links incarnation, the apostolic church and contemporary civilization within a confident vision of the active purpose of God. The life of Jesus is the love of God incarnate; Jesus proclaimed the kingdom of God, giving an ethic in the Sermon on the Mount to be applied to actual situations. The kingdom is being established in the world in the likeness of Jesus' life, death and resurrection. The resurrection demonstrates that 'love which suffers will triumph'. God's victory is sure. 'His love is a refining fire to purge away sin, a revolutionary power against all justice and a healing medicine for all who suffer.' Therefore, 'the purpose of God and the Spirit of Man are indestructible'.[9]

This is 'the revolutionary gospel of love' which opens up 'a way of revolution against all that is contrary to God's will and in support of every moral imperative which is a hall-mark of the loving reign of God in the affairs of Man'.[10]

Christ laid on the churches 'the burden of continuing the revolution he began'. The revolutionary word of Jesus finds expression in living fellowships, from those in Acts 2.42 (the kingdom already established in Jerusalem) to recent developments like the Fellowship of the Transfiguration of our Lord which Collins led at RAF Yatesbury, which had convinced him that his ideas were 'not altogether off-beat'.[11]

God's revolution in Christ and church was sharply distinguished from rebellion. Jesus was revolutionary but he never incited the crowds to rebellion. The church is not committed to any action which would 'foment ugly discontent; it is not an instrument of bloody revolution for ushering in the reign of God's love in the world'.[12]

Talk of God's revolution in these terms raises questions about its historical reality and practicability. It involves a high expectation of the church. Collins in 1949 wrote in terms akin to George Bell's ecumenical vision of the kingship of Christ and to the WCC's reflection on God's order and the world's disorders at its first Assembly at Amsterdam in 1948. Within that way of thinking it was plausible to argue that, had the churches been more truly the church, they would have 'revolutionize(d) the heart of society, come into closer union, and they might even have saved Western civilization from its present impending doom'.[13] Where so much was expected, disappointment with, and even rebellion against, empirical churches was almost certain to follow.

Collins looked 'for a revolution in the secular and ecclesiastical world which would release mankind from those tyrannies which hinder the coming of the kingdom of God'. It was in this perspective that Collins appealed in 1946 for 'Christian Action', by which he meant Christians acting responsibly to realize the revolution of the gospel. It rapidly became the organization he led for the rest of his life. He saw the danger of mere organization, but was determined that Christian Action should not degenerate into groups for general discussion – a likely end, he feared, for a movement beginning in Oxford; that would be to concede that Christ's revolution was impractical idealism. Christian Action was to initiate 'particular actions', of which the first was helping to feed Germany.

Although the world needed revolutionizing, its order was sufficiently sound for such a revolution to be possible. Christian Action worked within a view of the political world as intelligible and manageable. Collins had a strong sense of the nation as a working unit. English people could still discern a moral world order, despite the war. The UK was in the Security Council of the new United Nations, which was born out of the struggle against international disorder. The British Empire, about to become the Commonwealth, gave people a too-British but not little-Englander view of the world. Within this framework, Collins would react to the development of apartheid in South Africa. There was confidence in the capacity of 'values' to mediate between God's kingdom and politics. Values were 'threatened' (the term used in the title of Gollancz's powerful tract of 1946, influential for early Christian Action) but not jettisoned beyond recovery. In the 1930s, Bishop Barnes had verged on the rebel's despair when he concluded that Christian civilization could not survive a war, but to most churchmen, certainly to Collins after 1945, Christian civilization remained a feasible historical project it was inspiring to struggle for.

Christian Action was initiated on a post-war wave of democratic hope. It seemed possible for ordinary people to participate in and to influence events. Social change and order depended on many complementary contributions, so that every individual was important. Hence, the founding meeting of Christian Action in 1946 called on all Christians

> to play a full part (according to opportunity and ability) as working members of one or more of the national and local organizations upon whose healthy operations our public life depends.

and:

> to do everything possible by example and by prayer to build up within the churches a fellowship of Christians actively engaged in trying to work out in everyday life the social, political and economical implications of the gospel.[14]

All this implied that there was such a thing as public life which depended on people as 'working members' not merely as docile observers or mere consumers.

The context of God's revolution as read by Collins was the promise of the Labour victory in 1945. It was not infrequently interpreted as revolution in a British style. It was to be the work of the people in peace, rebuilding and reforming Britain. Ushered in bloodlessly by a decently-conducted free election, its idealism was easily integrated with Christian love and respect for people. One side of the spirit of 1945 was represented by J.B. Priestley, later one of the founders of CND and a friend whom Collins loved and admired. In the war Priestley had been an inspiring broadcaster and writer partly because he expressed the plain person's refusal to fight the war simply to restore the unjust pre-war society: victory implied revolution. Through all his criticism, however, the note of a deep living love of the people's England was never missing. Thus the revolution of 1945 was felt to have deep roots; part of its strength and appeal as well as its weakness might without excessive simplification be found in its conservatism.

Collins the revolutionary always had this conservative ballast. To be a rebel in the church was, in his view, an irritation worth enduring, because the church was useful as a base for social reforming ministry. Even more deeply, he put up with the irritation because he believed in some aspects of the institutional church in its Anglican form. Collins fled parochial Anglicanism with its pettiness and mediocrity; he had more liking for Anglicanism as the vehicle of national symbolism and of national and international religio-political action. At St Paul's, he loved the choir and the building: he saw the aspiring dome surmounted by its golden cross calling us to a remembrance of the man of Galilee who said 'I, if I be lifted up, will draw all men unto me'.[15] No one who writes like that can be a simple rebel and any revolution he makes will have its conservative side.

Collins was not unlike the first generation supporters of CND in the 1950s, as they were described by Peggy Duff, who was more convincing than most in approximating to the rebellious revolutionary. She wrote: 'They thought banning the bomb was a fairly simple matter and they never recognized the revolution in British politics that it required. They wanted to get rid of the bomb, leave NATO and abandon the American alliance without upsetting the pattern of life in Sutton, Totnes or Greenwich SE9.' They wanted both 'to remain in the system and to destroy it'.[16]

It ought not to surprise us that such conservative traditionalists were in CND. One great objection to nuclear weapons has been that they are far too revolutionary: they would change the world – certainly the world as known to humans, if not the world known to cockroaches – beyond recognition. Maybe the willingness to risk being brought to the 'necessity' of using nuclear weapons is a sign of the 'ugly discontent' and the ultimate frustration of the rebel, rather than the constructive hopefulness of the revolutionary; a rejection of the world is implicit in nuclear calculations in so far as they imply a will to uphold and justify one's position regardless of global consequences. By virtue of his opposition to nuclear weapons, Collins and his friends belonged to the political left and were perceived by many to threaten society with upheaval. But the deepest intuition in CND and its like was conservative: to love the world, to keep it. This world with all its faults was preferable to a world with nuclear weapons, let alone after nuclear war.

It was an achievement of the nuclear age, born on 6 August 1945, that it reinforced the conservatism which had inspired much of the British opposition to Nazism. The humanity of the CND involved people in a Burkean defence of what had come into being through long growth. The rich fruits of slow maturing traditions could be instantaneously destroyed but not so speedily recovered. Unfortunately for British politics, it was not adequately appreciated that here a special challenge was directed to those who called themselves Conservatives, because the inspiration of opposition to nuclear arms was to so great a degree conservative, in patriotic, global and conservationist modes. In order to distinguish themselves at this point Conservatives became more radically ideological. They had to assert specific pessimistic theories about human nature and politics; they could not rely on their traditional appeal to ordinary human decency and deference. They were suspicious of any tendency to trust the 'Russians'. They had to prepare themselves to argue that it was permissible to kill on a large scale and to risk being killed, simply to prevent a Communist takeover. Although they took that line for the sake of peace (no one wanted nuclear war) it involved the promotion of massive non-peaceful thinking. A picture of the world in war terms, dominated by enemies or potential enemies, had to be maintained. Economic policy had to be geared to pay for escalating defence costs (which, as was often argued, would be much higher without nuclear weapons). As the argument polarized, it became one between hopeful humanists and tough realists. Those who defended nuclear policy found less spiritual or rhetorical leisure to elaborate the humane Burkean conservatism they once rejoiced in, let alone any Baldwinesque feeling for Britain. They were driven into a situation where they had to be hard, in opposition to what seemed to them to be dangerous and subversive sentimentality. They had to work with and appeal to cynical realism in politics. To do that, did they have to suppress their own humanity, to keep quiet about it in public and to privatize it, so that it did not disturb public policy-making and rhetoric? Having done this violence to themselves – or shall we say, having put themselves under this discipline? – it is not surprising that they feared those who still so naively articulated the humanity they suspected in themselves: nor that, over time, their fear escalated into contempt for those who disagreed with them and into the willingness to develop a more authoritarian state security against subversion. Is the reappearance of two-nation conservatism in British politics to be traced back to the argument about the nuclear deterrent, a decade or more before the consensus on the Welfare State and its economics showed signs of cracking?

Conservative elements in the presuppositions of Collins' work were apparent in the crises of CND in the early 1960s. At the very moment when the conversion of the Labour Party seemed possible – the party conference in 1960 adopted the policy of unilateral nuclear disarmament, with Gaitskell promising to 'fight' to reverse it – the Committee of 100 was organized under the leadership of Bertrand Russell, the President of CND, to advocate massive civil disobedience aimed at coercing the Conservative government through direct extra-parliamentary action. Collins, the chairman of CND, opposed them, insisting on 'legal and democratic methods of argument'. So, the rebel in the church defended a largely non-rebellious morality in politics. Minorities must respect the democratic rights of majorities lest the rule of law, which gave freedom to minorities, were undermined. Collins wanted the rule of law to be brought into international affairs, but thought a 'breakdown of the rule of law in Great Britain' unlikely to promote it. That rule operated in Britain through parliamentary democracy: 'the machinery for peaceful change exists'. He knew that in situations of 'unprecedented threat and unprecedented urgency', it required patience to sustain such a system, but he was committed to it.[17]

Despite this deep vein of conservatism, Collins continued to believe that 1945 had opened up revolutionary possibilities. In the 1960s, especially when the Labour government of 1964 maintained the nuclear policy, he was disappointed, even disillusioned. But still he thought the revolution of 1945 was not obliterated, merely 'muffled'.

The language of God's revolution in resurrection was losing its plausibility as the mood and movement of politics changed. It would be a gross error to suggest that all that was then left of

Collins was his conservatism. That idea would have brought out the rebel in him. In any case, I have not written in order to pass judgment on Collins by putting him in some category, rebel, revolutionary or conservative. My aim has been to see what these categories might mean in our culture and how in practice they interact. If, in the process, it has become evident that they are all very partial and unreliable in capturing what people are actually like and what their achievement adds up to, that is to the good.

There is one other category which might help us to assess Collins. Was he a (perhaps minor) prophet? And would his being a prophet bring us back to the rebel? In contemporary parlance, to qualify as a prophet one must be akin to a rebel, an uncompromising protestor, unassimilable in the institution or the large collective, where average mediocrity determines possibilities.[18]

The Old Testament prophets had their moments of rebellion, by temperament or by force of circumstance, but rebelling was not what made them prophets. In part what constituted them prophets was that they recalled the people to Yahweh and his ways, revealed in the law and in his actions. The recall was not simply backward-looking, because the prophetic ministry pointed to the reopening of the promise which was always attached to God's calling and law (to live long in the land, for example). The biblical prophet proclaims (often because he feels he stands within) God's revolution. In doing this he is both constructive and conservative; loving the people and looking to their future and trying to work for it without being very powerful or infallible. Collins' assessment of the usefulness of Christian Action suggests he fits rather more easily into this prophetic mould than into the rebel's:

> I think the church has gained, not lost, by the existence of this experimental organization that has acted as a kind of gadfly within churches, a body that has not been afraid of taking unpopular lines or of sticking its neck out ... Because the churches are bound to a greater or lesser degree by dogmas about the nature of the church, and are concerned to avoid causing any offence within their congregations, they are afraid of revealing themselves as fallible; whereas a body such as

Christian Action, which is tied to no doctrine of infallible authority, whether of Pope, or the church, or the scriptures, or the conscience, is able to take risks, and, if proved mistaken, can with good grace put on the white sheet of penitence and try again. We do not stand on our dignity; we have none to stand on. Of course, such a gadfly inevitably irritates the leaders of the churches, but is that necessarily a bad thing?[19]

Notes

1. Ruth Dudley Edwards, *Victor Gollancz*, Victor Gollancz 1987, pp. 103–124.
2. J.R. Taylor, *Anger and After*, Methuen 1969, pp. 41–44; Mervyn Stockwood, *Cambridge Sermons*, Faith Press 1959, pp. 80–85.
3. Ian Henderson (ed.), *Man of Christian Action*, Lutterworth 1976, p. 3.
4. L. John Collins, *Faith Under Fire*, Leslie Frewin 1966, pp. 11, 15, 34–35, 92, 144.
5. Ibid., pp. 82–84.
6. John Tinsley, *Tragedy, Irony and Faith*, Wyndham Hall Press 1985.
7. Henderson, op. cit., p. 80.
8. L. John Collins, *A Theology of Christian Action*, Hodder 1949.
9. Ibid., pp. 23, 32.
10. Ibid., p. 36.
11. Ibid. p. 74; *Faith Under Fire*, p. 78.
12. L. John Collins, *A Theology of Christian Action*, pp. 77, 82.
13. Ibid., pp. 64, 84–85.
14. L. John Collins, *Faith Under Fire*, p. 112; Diana Collins, *Christian Action*, Victor Gollancz 1949, p. 36.
15. L. John Collins, *Faith Under Fire*, p. 148.
16. Peggy Duff, *Left, Left, Left*, Allison and Busby 1971, p. 130.
17. L. John Collins, *Faith Under Fire*, pp. 332–336.
18. Robin Gill, *Prophecy and Praxis*, Marshall, Morgan and Scott 1981, pp. 20, 130.
19. L. John Collins, *Faith Under Fire*, pp. 119–120; cf. A.R. Vidler, *Prophecy and Papacy*, SCM Press 1954, pp. 275–280.

Main Publications of John Kent

1955 *Jabez Bunting, the Last Wesleyan*, Epworth Press

1960 'Protestantism since the Reformation' in *Encyclopaedia of World Religions* ed. R.C. Zaehner, Hutchinson

1961 'Bishops and Society' in *Anglican-Methodist Relations* ed. W. Pickering, Darton, Longman and Todd

1962 *Elizabeth Fry*, Batsford

1963 'The Historical Background of the Methodist Union of 1932' in *Institutionalism and Church Unity* ed. W. Muelder, Association Press, New York

1965 *The Age of Disunity, Essays in nineteenth-century Church History*, Epworth Press

1966 'Hugh Price Hughes and the Nonconformist Conscience' in *Essays in Modern English Church History* ed. G.V. Bennett & J.D. Walsh, A. & C. Black, pp. 181–205

1966 *From Darwin to Blatchford, on the Reception of Darwinism in the English Churches*, The Dr Williams's Library Lecture, London 1966

1969 'The Study of Ecclesiastical History since 1930' in *The Pelican Guide to Modern Theology*, vol. 2 *Historical Theology* ed. R.P.C. Hanson, Penguin

1970 'Models of the Nonconformist Ministry' in *The Christian Priesthood* ed. N. Lash, Darton, Longman and Todd

1973 'The Role of Religion in the Cultural Structure of the Later Victorian City' in *Transactions of the Royal Historical Society*, 5th series, vol. 23

1973 *Church Membership and Intercommunion*, ed. (with R. Murray), Darton, Longman and Todd. To this volume contributed 'Old-fashioned Diplomacy: a comment on some aspects of ecumenical negotiations in England', and two shorter articles

1973 'Feelings and Festivals, an essay in 19th-century working-class religion' in *Victorian City* ed. H.J. Dyos and H. Wolff, vol.2., Routledge Kegan Paul

1974 'Authority and Conscience: Newman and Tyrrell' in *Cardinal Newman Studien*, 9th vol., Glock und Lütz, Nürnberg

1974 *The Encyclopaedia of World Methodism*, 2 vols, The United Methodist Press, New York. Edited the large British contribution, and wrote a large number of entries on 19th-century Methodism

1975 'The Socinian Tradition' in *Theology* (1975), the text of a lecture given to the Society for the Study of Theology at its Cambridge Conference in April 1975

1976 'Wesleyan Membership in Bristol in 1783' in *An Ecclesiastical Miscellany* ed. P. McGrath, Bristol and Gloucestershire Archaeological Society Records Section, vol. 11

1977 'A Late Nineteenth-Century Nonconformist Renaissance' in *Renaissance and Renewal in Christian History* ed. D. Baker, Blackwell, Oxford

1977 'From Temple to Slant, Aspects of English Political Theology, 1945–70', *Epworth Review*, January 1977

1978 *Holding the Fort, Studies in Victorian Revivalism*, Epworth Press

1978 'The Church and the Trade Union Movement in Britain in the Nineteenth Century' in *Essays on the Relation Between the Church and the Poor* ed. J. de Santa Ana, World Council of Churches, Geneva

1978 'Wesleyan Methodism 1800–1850' in *A History of the Methodist Church in Great Britain* vol. 2 ed. E.G. Rupp, Epworth Press

1979 'A Christian Humanist replies to Edward Norman' in *Christian Faith and Political Hopes* ed. H. Willmer, Epworth Press

1979 'Christian Theology from the Eighteenth to the Twentieth Centuries' in *A History of Christian Doctrine* ed. H. Cunliffe-Jones, T. and T. Clark

1980 'From Temple to Slant, English Social Theology 1945–70' in *Agenda for Prophets* ed. Rex Ambler, Bowerdean Press

1980 'The Church and Education, a Radical Protestant View' in *Newman and Education* ed. Mervyn Davies, Spode House Press

1980 'The Secularization of Conscience' in *Cardinal Newman Studien*, vol. xi, Glock und Lütz, Nürnberg

1981 'Methodism and Social Change in Britain since the Eighteenth Century' in *Sanctification and Liberation* ed. Theodore Runyon, Abingdon Press, Nashville

1982 *The End of the Line?: The Development of Christian Theology in the Last Two Centuries*, SCM Press, London and Fortress Press, Philadelphia

1983 'Problems in Church History: Twenty Years On' in *Southern History*, vol. 5, 1983

1983 Entries on Freethinking; History; Oxford Movement; Positivism; Reductionism; Scepticism; Subjectivism and Unitarianism, in *A New Dictionary of Christian Theology*, ed. Alan Richardson and John Bowden, SCM Press

1984 'The Modern Masters and Religious Education' in *Theology at Sixteen Plus* ed. James Barnett, Epworth Press

1985 'John Henry Newman' in *Die Neueste Zeit, Gestalten der Kirchengeschichte*, vol. 9, ed. M. Greschat, Kohlhammer, Stuttgart

1985 'Religion and Science 1860–1914' in *Nineteenth Century Religious Thought in the West* ed. N. Smart, P. Sherry, S. Katz and J.P. Clayton, CUP

1987 *The Unacceptable Face: The Modern Historian and the Church*, SCM Press

1988 'The Case of the Lives of Jesus' in *The Critical Spirit and the Will to Believe* ed. D. Jasper and T. Wright, Macmillan, London and St Martin's Press, New York

1988 'Holiness and Heroism: Newman and Thérèse de Lisieux' in *Cardinal Newman Studien*, vol. 12, Glock und Lütz, Nürnberg

1988 'The Shadow of a Grove of Chestnut Trees: Thérèse de Lisieux' in *God's Truth*: Essays to celebrate the twenty-fifth anniversary of *Honest to God* ed. Eric James, SCM Press, pp. 124–138.

1989 'A Renovation of Images: 19th century Protestant and

Roman Catholic alleged appearances of the Virgin Mary' in *The Critical Spirit and the Will to Believe* ed. D. Jasper and T. Wright, Macmillan, pp. 37–53

1989 'Catholicism in England 1870–1914: Ultramontanism and Modernism' in *Vie ecclésiale: communauté et communautés*, University of Paris, Val de Marne and Didier érudition, Paris, pp. 156–166

1990 'Anglican Evangelicalism in the West of England 1858–1900' in *Protestant Evangelicalism in Britain, Ireland, Germany and America c.1750–c.1950* ed. Keith Robbins, Blackwell 1990, pp. 179–200

1990 'Newman and Lilley' in *J.H. Newman and Modernism* ed. A. Hilary Jenkins, Glock und Lütz, Sigmaringen, pp. 157–168

1990 'Newman and Science' in *John Henry Cardinal Newman 1801–1890* in *Louvain Studies*, Summer-Fall 1990, pp. 267–282

1991 'Women, Ministry and Apostolicity' in *Who Needs Feminism* ed. Richard Holloway, SPCK, pp. 117–125

1992 *William Temple*, CUP